CINEMATIC COMANCHES

INDIGENOUS FILMS

Series Editors

David Delgado Shorter
Randolph Lewis

Cinematic Comanches

The Lone Ranger in the Media Borderlands

DUSTIN TAHMAHKERA

UNIVERSITY OF NEBRASKA PRESS | LINCOLN

Portions of chapter 1 were previously published in
"Haaka tsa Kwitop Hahka? Seeking Representational
Jurisdiction in Comanchería Cinema," *Native American
and Indigenous Studies* 5, no. 1 (2018): 100–135.

An earlier version of chapter 2 was published as
" 'We're Gonna Capture Johnny Depp!': Making
Kin with Cinematic Comanches," *American Indian
Culture and Research Journal* 41, no. 2 (2017): 23–42.

Financial support was provided from the Office
of the Vice President for Research and the Office
of the Provost, University of Oklahoma.

Library of Congress Cataloging-in-Publication Data
Names: Tahmahkera, Dustin, author.
Title: Cinematic Comanches: the Lone Ranger in
the media borderlands / Dustin Tahmahkera.
Description: Lincoln: University of Nebraska
Press, [2022] | Series: Indigenous films | Includes
bibliographical references and index.
Identifiers: LCCN 2021017317
ISBN 9780803286887 (paperback)
ISBN 9781496230065 (epub)
ISBN 9781496230072 (pdf)
Subjects: LCSH: Comanche Indians in motion pictures. |
Comanche Indians in mass media. | BISAC: SOCIAL
SCIENCE / Ethnic Studies / American / Native
American Studies | SOCIAL SCIENCE / Media Studies
Classification: LCC PN1995.9.I48 T36 2022 |
DDC 791.43/6529974572—dc23
LC record available at https://lccn.loc.gov/2021017317

Set in Minion by Mikala R. Kolander.
Designed by N. Putens.

For Auntie Nita

Juanita Pahdopony-Mithlo (1947–2020)

CONTENTS

ILLUSTRATIONS

Maruawe in Medias Res

Maruawe.

In all the Nʉmʉ tekwapʉ, or the Comanche language, maruawe is the closest word we have to "hello." Maruawe signals beginnings—a start to conversation, a way of introduction, and a rhetorical mode of positioning oneself, and readers, into a Comanche-centric episteme.[1] The term has long been spoken from one Comanche to another in conversation, from our historical days of empire in our homelands of the Comanchería of the southern Great Plains and northern Mexico to today's talk of resurgence at our tribal complex in Lawton, Oklahoma. It's pronounced in our language classes across Comanche country. It's heard in personal introductions of who we are and where we come from. And maruawe is visible here to signal a greeting to you, dear reader, as we go forth into a critical-creative genealogy and geography of Comanches in film and media.

Upon closer translation maruawe is more direct and, perhaps, less amicable than simply saying, "hello." As my auntie and former president of Comanche Nation College Juanita Pahdopony explains, "The most common greeting in the Comanche language is *Maruawe*," but it means "report" or "tell it." It "goes back," she says, "to those times of warriors coming back from somewhere and reporting what they observed." It's also instructional, as it represents a Comanche value of "modesty" in letting another person report back on what one has done. "When warriors went into battle," Pahdopony says, "they went in pairs because one could return and report for one who may not. A warrior never 'bragged' on his or her own brave deeds."[2] "Like a buddy system in school," my daughter responded when she heard that.[3] Following years of conversations with Comanche relations, watching a curious mix of films and other media, and writing scores of drafts, I report back throughout on what Comanches and non-Comanches have done in producing "Comanche" significations in visual media through what I call *Comanchería cinema*.

As a catalyst into cultural production, maruawe is a method of accountability to one's relations and a dialogic invitation for entering into relationships and conversations on firsthand and subsequent-hand accounts and perceptions of past events. It represents both a momentary beginning and a point of entry in medias res (Latin for "in the middle of things"). Across temporalities each utterance of maruawe is an opportunity to speak back to (mis)perceptions, speak up on current politics, and speak forth into the futurity of Comanches. From within the borderlands of the Comanchería, I site maruawe as always-already a response in medias res of the annals of Comanche cultural history. Maruawe, or "tell it to me," initiates a call-and-response into a tribal history still very much in motion today. This book also follows a callout-and-critique of certain literature and media about Comanches or, more precisely, authors' and producers' ideas about Comanches.

Maruawe in medias res is to report in the midst of a Comanche and Comanchería history of mediated texts and borders. As a method extended herein, maruawe is a call to report on a media-centric borderlands of Comanche history *as* representation and of Comanche representation *as* history. For our history includes multitudes of media representations. Our representations in media constitute critical and creative areas of our tribe's history, not apart from it. In contrast to accounts of Comanches that marginalize media and our modernity in the past and today, this book is about real and reel Comanches in historical and contemporary mediascapes.[4]

Maruawe in medias res means to closely observe and read the stories long in motion of Comanches in fictional and nonfictional recorded media—film, television, news, and so on—and then to report the observations back to Comanche people and other readers. This is what I seek to do with my researched reports on centuries of cinematic Comanches in motion—as actors, filmmakers, producers, critics, viewers, and fictional characters and subjects—representing in what I call the *media borderlands*. Encompassing the intertextual and geopolitical space through which to articulate and maneuver maruawe, the media borderlands constitute sites of coexisting and contentious audiovisual semblances of Comanches in the midst of cinema and other media.

Mediated maruawe, though, existed long before cinema. You might say it is as old as the land we have traversed. For example, mediated performances of maruawe are in Comanches' scenic etchings and teachings on eighteenth-century Comanche rock art in New Mexico's Rio Grande Gorge near Taos.[5] Comanches enacted etched images of, say, a possible horse raid or early encounter with Spaniards in the Comanchería. The original Comanche artists enacted the aesthetics of maruawe for future onlookers. They reported on previous encounters and invited response to their telling of Comanche history in onlookers' future encounters with the rock art.

To move into the aesthetics of maruawe in rock art means an engagement indicative of critical media studies approaches to textual production, performance, and perception. It means observing the representation of visual scenes on rocks and its reception and also considering the production of audibly etching and performatively moving the hand in creating art. It is what archaeologist Severin Fowles and former Comanche Nation tribal administrator Jimmy Arterberry call "the gestural hand and body movements of the rock art as a performative movement" for reporting the scene. This, then, is more than drawn-on rock. This is rock art as an early communicative canvas of expressive culture for recapturing and reporting what happened through a Comanche lens. Maruawe. Report to the people and still tell about it three centuries later, like Comanches do up close at rock sites in "New World Rising," a 2018 Comanche-produced episode of the PBS documentary series *Native America*.[6]

Maruawe also is present in scenes of war. During World War II in 1944, thirteen Comanche code talkers landed on Utah Beach in France with scores of other U.S. soldiers. After forcing Native youth to speak only English in boarding schools and inflicting violence for speaking Indigenous languages, the United States asked the code talkers to use the Nʉmʉ tekwapʉ to send secret messages to the Allies against the Axis powers. The Germans never cracked the codes. "When the 4th Infantry Division landed on Utah Beach," the Comanche National Museum reports, "they were five miles off their designated target. The first message sent from the beach was sent in Comanche from Code Talker, Private First Class Larry Saupitty. His message was 'Tsaakʉ nʉnnuwee. Atahtu nʉnnuwee,' which translates to: 'We made a good landing. We landed in the wrong place.'"[7] The code talkers went on to creatively translate other terms, like calling a "tank" a *wakaree*, the Comanche word for a green turtle with its strong exterior shell. Or calling Adolf Hitler *posah thaivo*—"crazy white man!"

Marʉawe is in motion throughout the cultural history of Comanches in the media borderlands. Marʉawe is what I have asked of the performativity of Comanches and Comanche significations in media. As a Comanche writing about Comanches, I take notice of practically anything of mediated tribal representation and its performative possibilities, no matter how culturally recognizable or asinine it may be. With that interest also comes the politics of territoriality—of who and what constitutes "Comanche" and in what ways and according to whom—again questions of production, performance, and perception.

From Comanche artist Rance Hood's painting *Father Sky and Mother Earth* (1983), which depicts a Native man wearing an eagle headdress, to Gore Verbinski's *The Lone Ranger* (2013), starring Comanche-adopted actor Johnny Depp as a Comanche Tonto wearing a crow on his head, Comanche signifies self-representing and getting represented.[8] From real Navajos playing reel Comanches in John Ford's *The Searchers* (1956) to real Comanches playing reel Comanches in Rodrick Pocowatchit's zombie comedy *The Dead Can't Dance* (2010), Comanche signifies producers, actors, mediated subjects, and responses. From drum groups Wild Band of Comanches and Comanche Thunder representing on the powwow trail to Comanche artists Cynthia Clay's *Snake Medicine* and Eric Tippeconnic's *Comanche Woman* representing on canvas, Comanche means circulating through creative modalities. Or from, say, William Shatner, during a *Star Trek* hiatus, playing twin Comanche brothers in the film *White Comanche* (1968), also known as the title of my memoirs (aye!), to the romance novel cover of Fabio Lanzoni's *Comanche* (yes, *that* Fabio and, yes, the *cover* because I haven't read it—no, really!), Comanche also suggests noble savagery, wild fantasy, and *isa kwitapʉ,* the Comanche term for "bullshit."[9]

This book reflects some of my wide-ranging interests in cultural insider and outsider representation from my mixed-race insider-outsider positionalities as Anglo and Comanche. I have learned much from my relatives, and following the lead of my Comanche-Anglo great-great-great-grandfather and chief, Quanah Parker (ca. 1845–1911), I seek to learn more. This book was written as a tribute to the cultural convergence between two personal subjects relatively overlooked and underappreciated in media studies and Native studies: *tʉpuuni yʉ?yʉmuku* and Nʉmʉnʉ, or "cinema" and "Comanches." My relatives, as ancestors, aunties and uncles, cousins, and other Comanches, and their filmic relations, as directors, actors, consultants, viewers, and other roles, carry forth an expansive history of Comanche creativity, the discussion of which could easily fill another volume. The same goes for those Comanches who have inspired the narratives of non-Comanches' films and media, such as Quanah's white-captive-turned-Comanche mother, Cynthia Ann Parker, and her imprint on *The Searchers* and other Hollywood productions.

In the spirit of marʉawe, the chapters herein comprise essayistic reports on an eclectic and elastic series of Comanche significations circulating in the Indigenous and U.S. imaginaries of the media borderlands. Charting marʉawe in medias res in Comanchería cinema, I enter conversations on twentieth- and twenty-first-century filmic representational matters of jurisdiction (chapter 1), kinship (chapter 2), justice (chapter 3), and reception (chapter 4). In effect, I challenge the nauseating narrative of the so-called Comanche fall and its connoted cultural end that leaves representations of us stuck in the 1870s. Seeking significations of Comanches in both the historical and contemporary, I produce scenes of Comanche continuity that carry stories of us—sometimes by us, sometimes not—toward the vibrant now and into the future. I also seek to complicate the dichotomous story of good/bad representations pervading discourse of Natives in film by providing a more nuanced critique toward the shades of gray befitting the complicated politics of Comanche representation. Rather than reinforce notions of closed and unambiguous narratives, I opt for heightened ideas of openness and complexities that can often leave us with far more interpretive routes and engaging questions than predictable one-dimensional answers and dismissals.

This book is a call to continue reporting on the media borderlands as spatial and representational opportunities for dialogue, debate, knowledge, and kinship practices. The media borderlands also afford opportunities to continue the self-representing legacy of Comanche people. Cynthia Ann Parker, her son Quanah, and others never stopped being Nꭎmꭎnꭎ (Comanche) despite U.S. forces who did their damnedest to eliminate Comanche people and cultural lifeways. That this book on cinematic Comanches of the twentieth and early twenty-first centuries even exists is a testament and tribute to ancestral resolve.

Herein I work to reframe Comanches from uncredited marginal characters to credited co-stars, from the background and backstage to the foreground and center stage as off-screen social actors and on-screen subjects. In the process I question who's representing whom, who's telling whom, who's viewing whom, and, seriocomically, *hakarꭎ marꭎꭎmatꭎ kwitaka*, or who's shitting whom. There is far more to the story and its cinematic frames than this lone book can explicate, but this represents an attempt to assemble a Comanche-centric conversation on film and media that engages and transcends the "Comanch'" in *The Searchers* and the recent misguided spotlight on "Comanches" penned by Pulitzer nominee S. C. Gwynne and certain other non-Comanches whose research and texts have little to nothing to really do with us: ideas about us but without us. Hakaru maruumatu kwitaka, indeed.

In the rest of this book, I enact maruawe and report on a series of moments in the production, performance, and perception of my tribe's multimedia cultural history spanning the early 1900s to today. From Comanche silent films and other movies in Comanchería cinema to old songs, recent tweets, web TV, paintings, poems, photographs, and other media, maruawe is a charge to express and communicate Comanche culturality. Maruawe is in each telling of who we were, who we are, and who we may become in the borderland collisions and coexistences of competing jurisdictions over who represents whom. Such critical inquiry produces no easy response in the politics of representing Comanches, and Comanches representing, in the media borderlands that I map throughout this book. The "answers," like Comanche people, are not fixed or static. They are ambiguous, ambivalent, and open-ended in interpretation. They resist extremes in critique and celebration of representational matters in favor of polysemous possibilities, albeit ones still culturally accountable and creatively plausible.

With that said, may the ensuing explanatory reports of cinematic Comanches be a humanizing, nuanced, and lucid account of complex representational matters. May the accounts respond respectfully to those who came before us and began the legacy of the relational rhetoric of maruawe. And may the spirit of maruawe guide the ensuing responses into a living, not vanishing, history of cinematic Comanches representing in the media borderlands. Enjoy the show, but please watch your step: when it comes to Comanches in film and media, the isa kwitapu ain't never far away.

ACKNOWLEDGMENTS

I dedicate this book in memory of my auntie Juanita Pahdopony-Mithlo, who crossed over in 2020. She is one of my dearest teachers, supporters, and confidantes. Her loving and creative imprint and inspiration may be found throughout this project. I am so thankful and richer to have known her.

I am thankful for my uncle Don Lacefield, who crossed over in 2019, from his loving home in North Carolina. Despite our geographic distance after he moved from Temple, Oklahoma, we remained close. I cherish our visits and his love, support, and guidance.

I am thankful for my Muscogee Creek friend Durango Mendoza, who crossed over in 2020. A kind and wise human being, he embodied a model of masculinity. I hold close our heartfelt conversation over coffee in Urbana.

Urahkokị, special thanks, go to the many cinematic Comanches cited in these pages, for their generosity and support. To LaDonna Harris, Laura Harris, Julianna Brannum, Marc Hausman, Marti Chaatsmith, Paul Chaat Smith, William Voelker, Troy, Wallace Coffey, Nocona Burgess, Michael Burgess, Tim Nevaquaya, Calvert Nevaquaya, Jhane Myers, Terry Gomez, Sunrise Tippeconnie, Marthe Thorshaug, and Maree Cheatham: your work, words, and ways in relation to Comanchería cinema have helped to inspire, enrich, and shape this book.

Special thanks to my Chickasaw friend Towana Spivey for sharing his vast knowledge of Comanche history and pop culture and for providing the book cover image of my relative White Parker in the 1915 film *The Sign of the Smoke*. *Urahkokị* to Kathryn Pewenofkit Briner and the Comanche Nation Language Department for their leadership and assistance with the Comanche language.

To series editors David Delgado Shorter and Randy Lewis: thank you for inviting me on board and believing in this project from the start. From a brief email exchange with David, who planted the idea of this project, to its growth in twists and turns and eventually maturity into this book, I offer a heartfelt thanks for your invaluable feedback and guidance.

To editors Matt Bokovoy, Heather Stauffer, Sara Springsteen, and everyone at the University of Nebraska Press who played a role in seeing this book to publication: thank you for all your support, patience, and care. To copyeditor Susan Silver: thank you for your kind and close attention to the entire manuscript. It has been an honor and pleasure to work with you all.

To dear friends and colleagues who generously took time to review and discuss my work: I sincerely thank you for your friendship, collegiality, and support. A special shout-out goes to Joseph Bauerkemper, Marcel Brousseau, Kirby Brown, Rachel Buff, James Cox, Rachel González-Martin, Joanna Hearne, Matthew Sakiestewa Gilbert, and Erik Wade. Your enthusiasm and care for this project were contagious. To the two anonymous peer reviewers: thank you for your thoughtful comments and hard questions. Your attention and responses to a draft of the entire manuscript significantly strengthened this book.

To supportive colleagues and students at the University of Oklahoma, University of Illinois, University of Texas, and elsewhere: thank you for listening, discussing, and sharing your stories.

To Mom and Gran, I am here because of you and your love. To my Anglo and Comanche relatives from Temple, Lawton, Cache, and elsewhere, I offer my heartfelt thanks. May the words that follow honor you and your teachings. Following the lead of my ancestor the Anglo-Comanche statesman Quanah Parker, I hope this book further builds intercultural bridges over borders, peace over pain, and dialogue over diatribe.

To my favorite wife, Maria, and our children, Maya, Jonah, Ira, and Ezra: this book is made possible with your unwavering love, support, and encouragement. Day and night you represent beauty, laughter, and joy. U kuma kuta nu. Always.

First and foremost, this book is for my daughter and sons and other Comanche youth and for the next generations of Comanches representing in the Comanchería media borderlands. May you always use your medicine in a good way.

Finally, to my MacBook keyboard's possessed letter "I": I feared losing precious data and time if I had handed you over to tech support during the pandemic, so I grew accustomed to your random repetitiion of doublinig and triiplinig yourself inii words. To the delete button: I owe you for your overtime work.

Note: All errors, misreadings, and bad jokes are my own.

CINEMATIC COMANCHES

Introduction

The Comanche Empire Strikes Back

I come from a long line of people recognized nowadays as having constructed an empire, a historic superpower spanning northern Mexico, the southwestern United States, and the southern Great Plains. For centuries generations of Comanches have marked their presence as warriors and peacekeepers, traders and raiders, caretakers and captive takers, a proud and humble people who acquired horses from the Spanish and built a vast network that migrated through borderlands of unstable jurisdictions of Indigenous and colonial powers. Backed by our captive taking and captivating history on multitribal and multinational lands, Comanches strikingly prompt reconfiguration, if not marginalization, of the U.S.-Mexico borderlands binary. Before the lands were called the "United States" in 1776 or "Mexico" in 1810, Comanches and other Native nations already staked their jurisdiction and called them—as an old joke in Indian Country goes—*ours*.[1] No disrespect to our sometimes-relatives, sometimes-enemies Lipan Apaches, Tonkawas, Kickapoos, and other Tejas border-crossed Indigenes, but our Comanche ancestors were borderlands people before *the borderlands* was cool.

In the sixteenth century, Comanche oral tradition says, a group broke away from the Shoshones in the Great Basin region of present-day Wyoming. Explanations for what caused the split continue to circulate among Comanches and Shoshones. Some say the separation was over a dispute. Some say a disease or food shortage. "There is a story," one old source states, "that a dispute arose over division of the game killed."[2] A Comanche elder told me that, in anticipating the split, three runners went east in search of a new home for the group internally known as Nʉmʉnʉ, soon-to-be externally named "Comanche."[3] One runner made it all the way

1

to present-day southwestern Oklahoma, where the Comanche Nation Tribal Complex is now sited and from where we continue to host our Shoshone relatives when they visit.

Stories of who the Utes called Kumantsi or Komantcia (translated as "different" or "enemy"), subsequently Spanishized into Cumanche and Comanche, have spread from Durango, Mexico, to Durango, Colorado, the Yucatán to Kansas, across and beyond the 240,000 square miles of what Spaniards dubbed the Comanchería, a borderlands space apparently so dominated by us in the eighteenth and nineteenth centuries that others named it after us.[4] (Even those who traded with us then in New Mexico were called Comancheros.) A standard map of the Comanchería highlights parts of what became Texas, New Mexico, Colorado, Oklahoma, and Kansas, yet the traditional territory and travels of Comanches extend much farther.

A map by Jimmy Arterberry, former Comanche Nation tribal administrator and also Tribal Historic Preservation officer, outlines the eighteenth and nineteenth centuries' Greater Comanchería, "whose effective sphere of influence," Finnish scholar Pekka Hämäläinen concurs, "extended far to the south and west of its southern plains core area." In collaboration with Stephen Lee, the Comanche Nation director of realty, Arterberry's map highlights traditional territories of Comanches, including Wyoming, Montana, Alberta, Colorado, New Mexico, Nebraska, Kansas, Oklahoma, Texas, and northern Mexico.[5] Like Américo Paredes's conceptualization of Greater Mexico as "all the areas inhabited by people of Mexican culture," the Greater Comanchería covers the cultural inhabitations and influences of Comanches.[6] From days as a borderlands superpower extending in all directions to recent scholarship on Comanches shaping the historical formations of Chicana/o, mestizo/a, and genízaro identities to our resurgence in the cultural imaginaries of literature, cinema, and television, Comanches—and ideas of Comanches—carry generations of memories and association with territorial and representational might.[7]

However, the story in scholarship, literature, film, and elsewhere

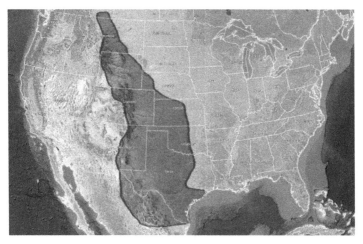

1. Traditional territory of the Comanche People. Comanche Nation Historic Preservation Office. Courtesy of Jimmy Arterberry and Stephen Lee.

in what I frame as the *media borderlands* often ends abruptly in the mid-1870s with the so-called fall of Comanches, marked by my relative (and *Cinematic Comanches* co-star) Quanah Parker, with his eventual decision in 1875 to lead the last Comanche hold-outs to the Indian outpost of Fort Sill in present-day Lawton, Oklahoma.[8] If generations up to then formed what Hämäläinen calls the "Comanche empire," then today's Comanches are descendants of an empire people.[9] But we go unrecognized as such by those who leave their representations of us in the distant past or, just as problematically, view us as remnants of a once powerful people, as if we are more *of* Comanche heritage than we *are* Comanches, or Numunu.[10]

In response I contend the narratives need to expand immensely to critically and creatively recognize Comanches as a much deeper storied people.[11] Contrary to popular opinion, the Comanche empire (and "real" Comanche people) did not end in 1875. The term "empire" descends from *imperare* (to command) in Old French from *imperium* (a command) in Latin. Mediated sites, historically and today, represent networked extensions of the Comanche empire. The media borderlands story that I share shows Comanches continuing to stake claims in representation and to command others to take notice of our rich cultural history in media. In the ever-expanding media borderlands of celluloid, digital, and other mediated territories, this story seeks narrative expansion by arguing for recognition of Comanche reality and fluidity.

To signify "Comanche" through vast borderlands, not restrictive borders, I call precisely for recognition of Comanches representing in the media borderlands an intertwined genealogy of our people: cinematic Comanches. "Cinematic" means "relating to motion pictures" and "having qualities characteristic of motion pictures."[12] As filmic visuality, cinematic comes from cinema (i.e., movies and movie production), which derives from the Greek word *kinema*, or movement. My use of "cinematic" similarly refers to real and reel Comanches' moves and relations in film and filmic characteristics, contexts, and conversations. Within a Comanche history of migrations and movements off-screen and on, cinematic Comanches are a performative people in motion (and motion pictures) in the media borderlands. Featuring an eclectic cast and crew, cinematic Comanches include filmmakers, actors (filmic and social), viewers, critics, consultants, Comanche characters (both the culturally grounded and culturally unfounded), and others representing off-screen and on-screen confluences. Like the media borderlands in and out of which they represent, interconnected real-to-reel Comanches are liminal subjects blurring lines between truth and fiction since the advent of filmmaking.

I engage cinematic Comanches by charting Comanche and non-Comanche productions of fictive and nonfictive representations of our people in texts set in and around the Comanchería. The representations thread together through what I call the three *p*'s of the media borderlands: production, performance, and perception. *Production* asks how the signifier "Comanche" is constructed; *performance* analyzes its performative and enacted motions on-screen and off; and *perception* responds to production and performance in cultural milieus of Comanche and non-Comanche critics. What binds them all together is their interdependence in the "circuit of culture" and the politics of power and history in representing Comanches.[13]

In contrast to other narratives *about* us but *without* us—more on that in a moment—my research engages Comanches representing Comanches. Enacting maruawe by reporting on and to one another in mediated scenes, real and reel "Comanches" take center stage, in effect asking readers to reorient approaches to so-called Native American representation in film.[14] What results in this projected history of cinematic Comanches is a production of tribal specificity told through both cultural close-ups and wide shots in expansive mediated layers of borderlands history.

Representing in the Media Borderlands

The late Gloria Anzaldúa sited the borderlands "wherever two or more cultures edge each other, where people of different races occupy the same territory."[15] Intertextuality also works in manifold through representations in borderlands to illustrate what media scholar Jonathan Gray calls the "inescapable interdependence" in relations between texts and their meanings.[16] Following Anzaldúan perceptions of borderlands as contested spaces inhabited with multiple Indigenous and non-Indigenous peoples and cultures, I map the media borderlands intertextually across symbolic territories, genres (e.g., western films, newspapers, blogs), and categories of cultural analysis (e.g., race, indigeneity, kinship) where media conglomerates, alternative media, textual producers, film advisers, performers, critics, fans, and others engage in the politics of representation, distribution, and reception. As producers involved in "constructing the filmic borderlands," to borrow from Dominique Brégent-Heald, these sites and actors coalesce around efforts to have a say in who represents whom, where, and for what purposes.[17]

Populated with symbolic taxonomies of texts and their intertextual relations with one another in film, television, literature, art, and other sites of pop culturality, the media borderlands are rugged terrain from which to consider historical and modern accounts of representing indigeneity and interculturality in media—rugged because the media borderlands, like Anzaldúan borderlands, can be unwieldy, as David Delgado Shorter says, with "contradictions, conflicting narratives, and opposing epistemic practices."[18] "Borderlands," Hämäläinen and Samuel Truett argue, "are places where stories take unpredictable turns" in "ambiguous and often-unstable realms."[19] Similarly, stories in the media borderlands circulate in contested spaces, on-screen and off, of intercultural and international crossings and collisions. The media borderlands represent mediated "contact zones," to cite Mary Louise Pratt, of "social spaces where disparate cultures meet, clash, and grapple with each other."[20]

As vast representational spaces of intertexts, the media borderlands include the mediated modes of representing and understanding Indigenous peoples and places, such as those outlined in Louise Erdrich's *Books and Islands in Ojibwe Country: Traveling through the Land of My Ancestors* (2003), Matt Cohen's *The Networked Wilderness: Communicating in Early New England* (2009), Steven Loft and Kerry Swanson's *Coded Territories: Tracing Indigenous Pathways in New Media Art* (2014), and the "network of relations" in Lisa Brooks's *Our Beloved Kin: A New History of King Philip's War* (2018). Such works take readers on creative, critical, and challenging journeys through networked intertextual sites populated by and filtered through Indigenous expressive ways of *kinema*, illustrative of what Anishinaabe writer Gerald Vizenor calls "transmotion, that sense of native motion and an active presence."[21]

The media borderlands, distinct herein to the Comanchería, also relate to Arjun Appadurai's concept "mediascape," or the production and circulation of media representations "as a complicated and interconnected repertoire of print, celluloid," digital, and other visual texts. Mediascapes include "image-centered, narrative-based accounts of strips of reality" with a "series of elements (such as characters, plots and textual forms) out of which scripts can be formed of imagined lives."[22] In their application of Appadurai's mediascape to Indigenous sites in the early United States, Matt Cohen and Jeffrey Glover associate it with the "distribution of the ability to create and spread information as well as the contents of that dissemination," including "images or stories about people—true or false."[23] Building on this work and siting it in the Greater Comanchería, the media borderlands in *Cinematic Comanches* engage historical and contemporary "true or false" scripts of power relations in creating and claiming what constitutes representational reality and reelity of the loaded, complicated signifier "Comanche." The possibilities of what signifies "Comanche" and "Comanchería" are practically endless.

Real Comanches (as human beings) and reel Comanches (as filmic representations) have long intervened into the visual regimes to construct and reconstruct narratives even as they were interpellated, directly or indirectly, into others' media archives. Multitudes of films are set in the Greater Comanchería, but not all explicitly include visual or discursive Comanche representations. When reframed to be read through a Comanche-centric lens, such texts, especially in the western genre, become opportunities for cinematic Comanches to guide the conversation and reroute the subject positions of who represents the familiar and at home (the Indigenous) or foreign and trespassing (the settler). For French theorist Gilles Deleuze, film is an "organ" for making and structuring a "new reality."[24] Following Deleuze, film and media scholar Kara Keeling utilizes "*the cinematic* to designate a condition of existence, or a reality, produced and reproduced by and within the regimes of the images." "Deleuze's theories of the cinematic," Keeling contends, encourage a "nuanced and critical understanding of film as part of reality, rather than as a reflection or representation of it."[25] This move into filmic reality encourages, in turn, a closer examination of the real and reel relations between the on-screen and off-screen in and around cinema, in this case, between cinematic Comanches— that is, I engage the real and reel as interrelated and interdependent subjects shaping popular perceptions of each other.

The familial lineage of cinematic Comanches in the media borderlands runs deep. From my nineteenth- and early twentieth-century ancestors inspiring, and occasionally starring in, a host of films and roles to twentieth- and twenty-first-century Comanches involved in cinematic productions, performance, and perception, they all configure and challenge on-screen how producers, casts and crews, and audiences and critics may interpret and represent our history, modernity, and futurity off-screen. In the Quahada band of Comanches alone, which includes Parkers, Tahmahkeras, and certain other families, cinematic Comanches have long been representing in the media borderlands.[26] Historical accounts of my great-great-great-great-grandmother Cynthia Ann Parker, a white-captive-turned-Comanche, inspired a co-starring role in the number-one ranked Hollywood western of all time: John Ford's *The Searchers* (1956).[27] Her son Quanah Parker, the last "chief" of the Comanches, co-starred in the silent film *The Bank Robbery* (1908) on his own homelands in Cache just as Oklahoma gained statehood and long before other movies attempted to represent him. Quanah's son White Parker starred in the silent short film *Sign of the Smoke* (1915). White and his sister Wanada Parker co-starred in the all–Comanche and Kiowa feature film *Daughter of Dawn* (1920).

More recently, Quanah's great-grandson, my late uncle Monroe Tahmahkera, guest starred in episodes of *Walker, Texas Ranger* (1993–2001) and other Fort Worth–area productions as well as the martial arts film *Once upon a Time in China IV* (1993). My cousin Benny (not to be confused with *My Cousin Vinny* [1992] — aye!) Tahmahkera portrays Quanah each summer in the musical *Texas* near Palo Duro Canyon, an area south of Amarillo, chockful of Comanche history. He also appeared as a Comanche in the movie *Too Many Crocketts* (2015). Juanita Pahdopony, daughter of Marjorie Pahdopony (née Tahmahkera), co-starred in Lummi filmmaker Steffany Suttle's documentary *Fry Bread Babes* (2008). She also was lead Comanche consultant on AMC's popular TV series *The Son* (2017–19), which included real-life Comanches playing Comanches in village scenes, and executive producer of Annalee Walton's Comanche short film *Thistle Creek* (2020). My auntie LaDonna Harris, founder of the nonprofit Americans for Indian Opportunity, starred in the PBS documentary *LaDonna*

Harris: Indian 101 (2014), which was directed by my cousin Julianna Brannum, granddaughter of Sophie Mahsetky (née Tahmahkera) and produced by Harris's adopted son Johnny Depp.

Cinematic Comanches also extend to our relations with non-Comanche actors' takes on fictional characters in symbolic semblances of imagined representations of Comanches. Will Sampson (Muscogee Creek), for example, played famous Comanche leader Ten Bears in *The Outlaw Josey Wales* (1976). Floyd Red Crow Westerman (Lakota) portrayed Ten Bears in *Dances with Wolves* (1990). In *The Lone Ranger* (2013) Saginaw Grant (Sac and Fox) played the made-up Comanche chief Big Bear, whose tribe, name, and monocles suggest a representational relation to the real eyeglass-wearing Ten Bears. Most Native actors pale in the popular imagination in comparison to the non-Native actors cast as Comanche characters. Serbian actor Gojko Mitic, "the most famous Indian in Eastern Europe" for his many Native roles, played Chief Tahmahkera in *In einem wilden Land/Striving for Freedom* (2013). Slovenian actor Sebastian Cavazza portrayed a sadistic Comanche chief in *Winnetou* (2016).[28] In *The Searchers* (1956) German American Henry Brandon, dubbed the "Kraut Comanche" by Navajo extras playing Comanches, was the Comanche character Chief Scar. Brandon then played the Anglo-Comanche leader Quanah Parker in *Two Rode Together* (1962). Anglo actor Kent Smith played "Quanah Parker" in *Comanche* (1956). *Star Trek* star Leonard Nimoy portrayed a Comanche leader in the TV western *Tate* episode "Comanche Scalps" (1960). One of his *Star Trek* co-stars doubled the fun in perhaps the most humorously egregious example. William Shatner, during a hiatus from *Star Trek*, played not one but two Comanche brothers warring against each other in the Razzie recipient *White Comanche* (1968). Yes, *that* William Shatner.

Representational Jurisdiction

Like other Native peoples invested in how they and others represent and speak on indigeneity, Comanches stake claims in *representational jurisdiction* and strike back at those who think Comanches are primarily pop cultural props frozen in the past, not the creators and shapers of U.S. culture that they were historically and are today. Through the media borderlands genres of film, social media, art, theater, television, music, photography, writing, advertising, and other communicative modes, Comanches have long taken it on themselves to express, educate, and engage. I am thinking here of Comanches like filmmakers Dan Bigbee, Sunrise Tippeconnie, and Rod Pocowatchit; artists Rance Hood, the late Leonard Black Moon Riddles, Cynthia Clay, J. Nicole Hatfield, and Ron Burgess and his sons, Nocona and Quanah; art curator and critic Paul Chaat Smith; playwright and educator Terry Gomez; language teachers Ron Red Elk and Kathryn Pewenofkit Briner; web and media designer Darrell Kosechequetah; film producer and artist Jhane Myers; film actors Gil Birmingham, the late Oscar Yellow Wolf, and the late White Parker; singers Marla Nauni and Apryl Allen; musicians Micki Free, the late Doc Tate Nevaquaya, and the late Ed Wapp; educators John Tippeconnic, Cornel Pewewardy, and Sunny Hegwood; printmaker John Hitchcock, photographer Walter Bigbee; and poets Sy Hoahwah and Joe Dale Tate Nevaquaya, among many, many others.

Comanches struck back, for example, in 2005 when artist, educator, and film/TV consultant Juanita Pahdopony, the Comanche Nation Elder Council, and other Comanches convinced city officials in Lawton, the home area of the Comanche Nation, to change the offensive and dated "Squaw Creek" to "Numu Creek." Numu is our word for one Comanche.[29] In nearby Cyril, Oklahoma, ethno-ornithologists and film/TV consultants William Voelker and Troy changed their street name from "Texas" to "'Looking Glass Way' to honor the Looking Glass Family," who originally inhabited the town site, named after the Comanche Louise "Cyril" Looking Glass.[30] In late 2019 the Comanche Nation unveiled a stretch of Highway 277 near Walters, Oklahoma, as the newly named Comanche Code Talker Trailway to honor the code talkers of World Wars I and II.[31] In each of these topographic instances, media-savvy Comanches utilized their cultural power to recognize and actualize Comanche ways of knowing, to rename territorial sites of creeks and streets, and to representationally reclaim spaces in Comanche country.

The "power of naming and claiming," to borrow from environmental activist Winona LaDuke (White Earth Anishinabe), also extends to material goods, where "Comanche" is removed or repurposed. For example, in the early 2010s Comanches and other Natives spearheaded a swift and decisive social media campaign on Facebook. A California-based company was making and selling T-shirts emblazoned with a headdress-wearing skeleton on a bike. The image was captioned "Comanche." After Comanche filmmaker Jason Asenap and other Natives socially called for the company to cease and desist with appropriation, the company pulled the shirt from its online store within twenty-four hours. Comanches also demonstrate today the power to negotiate and co-opt others' constructions. In the 1950s two Anglo historians called Comanches the "Lords of the Plains." Now the moniker appears on license plates, coffee mugs, and official tribal T-shirts, sold by the Comanche Nation gift shop and artisans.

This book enacts maruawe by reporting on contested moments co-starring the signifier "Comanche" and seeks to reclaim and resituate a jurisdictional share of the significations into a Comanche tribal archive of narratives from film and other sites in the media borderlands. Comprising a tribalography, or the stories that "author tribes," the competing narratives that follow from the media borderlands meet at overlapping symbolic jurisdictions.[32] I move through the textual boundaries of representational jurisdiction to prompt questions of who represents whom and, in effect, who lays claim to Comanche significations. For centuries Comanches and non-Comanches have imprinted their articulations and visualities of Comanche representations through media, via mediated texts of inscriptions and indentions into the landscapes and mediascapes we travel through, but whose story is predominantly seen and heard—that is, whose version of the story?

In the borderlands of the Comanchería, as elsewhere in Indian Country, the politics of jurisdiction over representation questions who controls Indigenous representations and how they are claimed. From narrations of Comanche captivity and media culturality to historiography and literature, coupled with the next chapter's focus on Comanches in old and new cinema, the textual circulation of Comanche significations *chronicles*, in all of the verb's fictive and nonfictive connotations, how the Indigenous is (mis)represented and (mis)understood through the *longue durée* of history. Such is the politics of representational jurisdiction, a conceptual frame for addressing cinematic proxy, or acts of assuming the power to represent.

Representational jurisdiction is at the core of internal and external productions, policings, and perceptions of Indigenous epistemologies, frames, and identity formations and claims. Its conceptualization entails Pierre Bourdieu's "symbolic power" struggles sited in the media borderlands, where contests and claims transpire over the power of persuasion and control of media communications, including how one should and should not produce, portray, and perceive sonic and visual indigeneity in media, such as the much-discussed and controversial speech and look of Johnny Depp's Comanche Tonto in *The Lone Ranger*.[33] Politically related to the legalese of *territorial jurisdiction* on the competing claims and differential sovereign rights over (border)lands and resources, representational jurisdiction is a symbolic cousin concerned with the storied geopolitics of how Indigenous representations impact the perceptions of Indian Country and the United States and how nationalistic narrations of lands and territories impact the development of representing and understanding indigeneity.

As the Dakota scholar Elizabeth Cook-Lynn observes, "The role of Indians, themselves, in the storytelling of Indian America is as much a matter of 'jurisdiction' as is anything else in Indian Country." For this project jurisdiction similarly means addressing the politics of the territorial assertions over the representational parameters of constructing and reconstructing Indigenous roles in Hollywood and independent filmmaking. In larger terms it means analyzing the jurisdictional formations of how the fictional Indigenous is storied and represented in the pop cultural imaginary of the media borderlands. "How the Indian narrative is told," Cook-Lynn continues, "how it is nourished, who tells it, who nourishes it, and the consequences of its telling are among the most fascinating— and, at the same time, chilling—stories of our time." Translated into the media borderlands of the Comanchería, the narratives of Comanche performativity in cinema may qualify as the most ambivalently captivating "storytelling of Indian America" in recent Indigenous cultural accounts.[34] At stake is the critical consideration of how "popular culture as a vehicle for social change has worked for and against us" in Indian Country. But it also is more than that. It means to engage how rugged Natives have constructed and managed their own pop cultural discourse and performance to effect change.

Comanche Citations inside the U.S. Imaginary

Illuminating the politics of representational jurisdiction in the media borderlands is the vast number of published and produced accounts about Comanches. As Anglo historian William Hagan observed back in the late 1970s, Comanches are the "subjects of a volume of paperwork that is positively staggering."[35] Hagan's revelation challenges popular perceptions of a people too often written off as monolithic warriors standing in the way of another's progress. I recall, as an undergraduate in the mid-1990s, searching the term "Comanche" in the index of my U.S. history textbook. Despite the staggering Comanche citations, the result was brief, as it led me to a lone page that cast us as an obstacle. Obstacle is code for a barbarous barrier to be eliminated in the name of manifest destiny of westward expansion in the late 1800s. That textbook memory and others like it from my younger days mark a momentary presence of Comanches discursively locked in a permanent pastness and disregarded in the absence of Comanche movement, fluidity, and futurity.

The term "Comanche" today can still draw similar "barbarian" associations with fierce, captive-taking, horse-riding male warriors of the past.[36] This dominant image of a dominant people that disavows alternative or more expansive representations comes from primary and subsequent secondary historical accounts that feed into pop cultural productions that have rarely recognized Comanches and other Native peoples as fully human beings. "During the eighteenth century," as Lindsay Montgomery and Severin Fowles observe in cinematic and theatrical terms, "a rotating cast of equestrian nomads, including the Comanche, Ute, Apache, and Navajo, played the role of the barbarian in New Mexico."[37] To replay a familiar colonial citation, "Comanche" appears in a document from July 15, 1706, when Spanish explorer and soldier Juan de Ulibarrí noted that the Taos Pueblos in New Mexico reported that "the Ute and Comanche tribe were about to come to make an attack upon" them. On July 28 an "Apache Indian," Ulibarrí wrote, was preparing to ally with others "to defend themselves together from the Utes and Comanches."[38] Similar warlike rhetoric continued in a 1723 report by New Mexico's Spanish governor Juan Domingo de Bustamente, who wrote that Comanches "had attacked" Jicarilla Apache and "killed many men, carrying off their women and children as captives."[39] Such entries of violence set an early tone for how Comanches would come to be represented elsewhere in mediated borderlands for centuries to come. In his 1986 musical comedy *True Stories*, for example, David Byrne offers a somewhat honest and humorous view of Texas history: "The Spaniards were fighting the Mexicans, Mexicans fought the Americans, Americans were fighting the Wichitas, the Wichitas were fighting the Tonkawas, the Tonkawas fought the Comanches, the Comanches fought everyone."

Recent rhetorical moves in scholarship suggest that ideas of the Comanche empire strike back at the highly fragmented and Anglo-biased accounts of Comanches as just warriors and barriers. In the historiography of Comanches, Thomas Kavanagh has long-standing relations with and extensive research publications on Comanches. Additional recent ethnohistories by James Brooks, Brian Delay, Julianna Barr, and Ned Blackhawk have reframed and resituated Comanches of the eighteenth and nineteenth centuries as a greater and more diverse and complicated force than previous Anglocentric accounts suggested. Building onto Kavanagh's and others' work, historian Pekka Hämäläinen conceptualizes the "Comanche Empire" in his 2008 Bancroft Prize–winning book of the same title. The Finnish historian contends Comanches "built an imperial organization that subdued, exploited, marginalized, co-opted, and profoundly transformed near and distant colonial outposts, thereby reversing the conventional imperial trajectory in vast segments of North and Central America."[40]

Hämäläinen's conceptualization of a "Comanche empire" indicates an "imperial power" whose "aim was not to conquer and colonize, but to coexist, control, and exploit." Adapting to film his characterization of our ancestors' agency in the Comanchería, cinematic Comanches sought and seek, both on-screen and off, to *coexist* in shared media borderlands, *control* Comanche representations, and astutely (and sometimes humorously) *exploit* the politics of technology, namely the medium of film and the power dynamics of cinema. Such cinematic tactics frame this book's discussion of Comanches striking back at, and being struck by, popular one-sided narratives of Hollywood dominance, marginalization, and erasure of the Indigenous.

Hämäläinen's Comanche empire strikes back at the old guard of Texas historians' scholarship on Comanches that represents us as a predominantly reactive and defensive savage barrier and resistor to European settlement, not as a "fluid and malleable" empire.[41] Texas historians Walter Prescott Webb and Rupert Norval Richardson may have inspired scholarly interest in studying Comanches in the 1930s, but they "portrayed them simply as warriors," not "diplomats, raiders, allies, foes, traders, spouses, and kinspeople." "Webb, Richardson, and the scores of historians and nonhistorians influenced by them," Hämäläinen continues, "created a caricature of Comanches' culture and their place in history." They "promoted," Barr similarly adds, "a caricature of cardboard 'warriors' reveling in raw mindless violence."[42]

Yet the old guard continues to admit new heirs in the ongoing popular and scholarly formations of competing Comanche citationalities, in which the same dated literature serves as an unmatched model and inspiration for "new" work that rehashes old anti-Indigenous ideology. The latest prominent initiate is Texas-based journalist and author S. C. Gwynne. His 2010 *Empire of the Summer Moon: Quanah Parker and the Rise and Fall of the Comanches, the Most Powerful Indian Tribe in American History* quickly became a *New York Times* best seller and even a Pulitzer Prize finalist. A skilled storyteller and colorful writer of narratives ripe for hyperbolic Hollywood fare (*Empire of the Summer Moon*, incidentally, is in cinematic preproduction as of this writing), Gwynne follows a genealogy of Comanche citationality in which he threads the old guard's white-dominated accounts of Comanche warriors and Anglo settlers through an extremely violent and graphic narrative of Texas history.

Unabashedly promoting racist discourse and narrow Anglo views on Comanches, Gwynne calls Webb's discussion of Comanches in the 1931 book *The Great Plains* a "masterpiece" that "got me interested in the subject in the first place." Webb's "work on the Texas Rangers," he continues, "remains definitive."[43] At one point Webb names us "the never-to-be-misunderstood Comanches," as if a one-dimensional menace.[44] The Hollywood translation is that Comanches are the villains and terrorists, and Texas Rangers the heroes and protectors. Gwynne also calls Ernest Wallace and Adamson Hoebel's 1952 book *Comanches: Lords of the South Plains* a "magisterial ethnography" that no other "secondary sources . . . can quite match," and T. R. Fehrenbach's 1974 *The Comanches: Destruction of a People* "remains the modern classic in the field."[45] Gwynne's celebratory bibliography sounds like something out of the *Onion*, if only it was satire.

Nowhere to be found in Gwynne's pop history is a reference to the updated and robust new history by Delay, Barr, and others. And, of course, none of Hämäläinen's *Comanche Empire* is included, even as the terms "Empire" and "Comanches" show up in Gwynne's lengthy title. In an otherwise glowing review of Gwynne's book, the *New York Times Book Review* is among the very few popular publications to note that Hämäläinen's book is "oddly not cited" by Gwynne.[46] One might attribute it, generously, to publication dates: Gwynne's book came out in 2010, Hämäläinen's in 2008. It becomes, however, more than odd that Gwynne did manage to cite fellow Texas writer Mike Cox's book *The Texas Rangers*, published in March 2008, just two months before Hämäläinen's book. Conspicuously absent, too, from Gwynne's bibliography is Gary Clayton Anderson's 2005 *The Conquest of Texas: Ethnic Cleansing in the Promised Land, 1820–1875*, which derides the Texas Ranger as the epitome of real savagery against the Indigenous and Mexicans. As Gwynne recognizes a Comanche empire as "vast, primitive, and equally lethal" to the "American empire," he ideologically and politically *cannot* cite the Hämäläinens and Andersons, whose sharp scholarship too often runs counter and far more expansive than his own research cares to recognize and replicate.[47]

Nor did he visit with contemporary Comanches. It's not that he had to consult with Comanches—most scholars and writers don't—but he became outspoken on why he didn't, and he missed possibilities to learn from deeply knowledgeable Nʉmʉnʉ. Gwynne claimed to western writer and reporter Johnny Boggs that Comanches would not have anything to "add to something that happened 200 years ago" in reference to events involving Quanah Parker and his family.[48] One journalist later paraphrased Gwynne saying that "gathering interviews with living descendants would [have amounted] to collecting family lore, not facts."[49] Nearly a decade later, in 2019, Gwynne still defended his choice not to consult contemporary Comanches "for things that happened two or 300 years ago" because "that's sort of a non-starter for a historian."[50]

Imagine the journalist (and self-identifying "historian") Gwynne saying that to Anna Tahmahkera, going strong at age 103 in 2021. Glenn Frankel was thankful to visit with her for his book *The Searchers*. Grandma Anna was raised by Topay, a widow of Quanah

Parker's. He is featured in the title and, unsettlingly, on the cover of Gwynne's book, which I first saw in a bookstore display in Austin while holding my son who, get this, carries the name of Parker's father, Nocona. Grandma Anna, a "Comanche treasure" of deep cultural knowledge, tells firsthand accounts and shares stories told directly to her by those who were there in Comanche history.[51] But as the old Floyd Westerman song goes, "They didn't listen."

Nocona Burgess, great-great-grandson of Parker, struck back at Gwynne's arrogance by publicly challenging his work at a 2011 book signing in Fort Worth. As a direct descendant of Quanah Parker, named after Quanah's father, Peta Nocona, Burgess drove in from Santa Fe and questioned Gwynne's decision not to talk to us and his refusal to believe Comanche oral history and written records that say Peta Nocona did not die in a surprise attack by Texas Rangers. One reporter called Burgess's approach an "ambush," reminiscent of dated rhetoric about marauding Comanches and Apaches in Texas, despite Gwynne knowing Burgess would be in attendance.[52] On writers' decisions not to visit with Comanches when writing about Comanches, Burgess later told me, "This isn't Greeks and Romans. . . . It's not ancient history. We [Comanches] are right here." Later that evening at the book signing, some folks asked Burgess to sign their copies of Gwynne's book. Burgess humorously wrote, "Eshop! Eshop!" In Comanche, *eshop* means lies.[53]

Who Was That Masked [Co]Man[che]?

From Webb to Richardson, Wallace and Hoebel, Fehrenbach, and Gwynne, the old guard of Comanche citationality runs deep, even as its Anglocentric framework stays shallow and largely silences Comanche, Spanish, Mexican, French, and Indigenous accounts of Comanche power. Similarly, white settler characters are repeatedly the stars in the history of Hollywood films with Comanche representation, which are frequently set in the 1860s and 1870s, during the fall of the Comanche empire. The on-screen result skews a reel history, which is largely void of Comanche scenes with nonwhite Indigenous (e.g., Lipan Apache) and Mexican characters.

To begin to represent Natives "as fully human," Paul Chaat Smith argues, is to address Indigenous history between Native peoples and without white settlers always securing the leading or even supporting roles.[54]

I intervene in a distorted Comanchería cinema by rerouting old citations and reimagining new ones through an intertextual Comanche lens that challenges the silencing acts of Comanches in the media borderlands. I peer into centuries of Comanche representation on-screen and off, but my lengthiest look is into the Comanchería mediascape of Disney's recent feature film *The Lone Ranger* (2013). It represents the latest take on the duo of the "masked man" Texas Ranger and the Indian Tonto fighting outlaws, con artists, and other criminal elements in an imagined U.S. Old West. The most popular version, and the one most related to Disney's take, was the televised *Lone Ranger*, starring Clayton Moore and Jay Silverheels (Mohawk) on ABC in the mid-twentieth century. Disney makes Tonto a Comanche who partners with the title character, a strange pairing given that the real Texas Rangers were created to exterminate Comanches.

Let me be clear, though. This is not a book on *The Lone Ranger*, whether Disney's 2013 version or previous mediated iterations from the past ten decades, most of which starred the Lone Ranger and marginalized his Indian sidekick, Tonto. In *Cinematic Comanches* I do not situate Comanches into a study of the film; rather, I position the film inside a larger eclectic genealogy of cinematic Comanche history. Here *The Lone Ranger* (as film and title character) is the sidekick. The Comanches are the stars.

A case in point comes from centering, as I do in chapter 2, what off-screen Comanches did when they heard of an on-screen Comanche version of Tonto during film production. On May 16, 2012, something happened that really set this book into motion: my Comanche auntie LaDonna Harris captured actor Johnny Depp. In alternative parlance she adopted him into her family in a traditional ceremony, but I like (and laugh) when she seriocomically says "capture." It plays off a Comanche history of taking captives and points toward a future with, not without, Comanches and captives/adoptees. Her articulation also shows a Comanche woman coauthoring a contemporary captivity narrative, in which the Comanches have a say in representation. At the confluences of the real and reel, she says with a grin, "We made him a Comanche, so he'd learn to act like one." If not for Harris's behind-the-scenes agency in creatively making kin with a Hollywood celebrity playing a Comanche, then this book would not be what it is, if it would even be at all.

Harris herself has been likened to *The Lone Ranger* through a common line that settler characters asked at the end of the show after witnessing the title character's heroism: "Who was that masked man?" In the 2014 documentary *LaDonna Harris: Indian 101*, a chorus of activists, celebrities, and politicians rightly applaud Harris's long-standing political work for tribal justice and women's rights in Washington DC and across Indian Country. Reflecting on the incredible impact she has on others, one Osage interviewee says she was "like the old Lone Ranger" and left folks asking, "Who was that woman?"[55]

I too revise the question "Who was that masked man?" to ask instead, "Who was that masked Comanche?" Like Comanches saying maruawe to command a response, to ask of masked Comanches is to expect a culturally grounded reply. "Masked" suggests cultural complexity and creativity over the simplistic and superficial "never-to-be-misunderstood" accounts plaguing popular perceptions of Comanches. A reputation as savage, Morris Foster once wrote, "masked the integral redistributive role that Comanches played in the political economy" of the Comanchería.[56] Masked, too, has been our roles as cinematic Comanches. Comanches "beautifully" represent, Harris says, being both "individual" and "collective," but such Comanche diversity and multidimensionality are often absent in Hollywood films and other mainstream sites in the Comanchería media borderlands. Relatedly in film, the compositional technique of masking sets up borders for what the camera both reveals and cuts out. To ask about masked Comanches is to acknowledge and open up possibilities of analytic layers and creative dimensions in Comanche representation in filmic and mediated contexts. It means to put a more humanizing approach to the production of Comanche signifiers and to seek more interpretations of performances of cinematic Comanches. It also is a question to which there may be, and perhaps should be, no clear-cut answers if one truly recognizes the complexity and creativity and the autonomy and ambiguity of tribally and individually sovereign Comanche people.

Whereas Hämäläinen focuses most of his hefty book *Comanche Empire* on seventeenth- and eighteenth-century Comanches before concluding with brief nods to twentieth-century U.S. pop cultural productions of Comanches, *Cinematic Comanches* moves into narrations of masked modern descendants of the empire maneuvering through the media borderlands of the twentieth and twenty-first centuries. This book picks up where Hämäläinen and others leave off in the late nineteenth century to report a modern media borderlands story engrossed in more cultural continuity than stories of historical finality allow. Productions and recordings of cinematic Comanches continue to represent in the media borderlands of new texts and reruns and replays, but too often the texts are isolated and individualized, not intertextually situated to deliver a richer and fuller story befitting of the Nᵾmᵾnᵾ, a people inspiring media makers to produce both the regressive representations of simplistic savagery and the endless possibilities of progressive humanizing representational justice.

In the rest of this book, I advocate for humanizing by the maruawe method of narrative reports on the politics of representational jurisdiction in cinematic production, performance, and perception unfolding at the confluences of Hollywood, Comanche, and Indigenous imaginaries. In conversation with Hämäläinen's *Comanche Empire*, I seek "to recover Comanches as full-fledged humans and undiminished historical actors underneath the distorting layers of historical memory."[57] I navigate through recent cultural history to recognize and explicate cinematic Comanches as on-screen performers and characters and off-screen social actors and critics maneuvering through thorny layers of enactments and expectations of representing the Indigenous. By positioning the significations of "Comanche" at the intersections of production, performance, and perception, I center jurisdictional struggles over cinematic Comanche representations in chapter 1, making kin in cinematic Comanche captivity narratives in chapter 2, performing justice and injustice with and without cinematic Comanches in chapter 3, and producing Comanche reception of cinematic Comanches in chapter 4. My approach throughout is tribal-centric in coordinating and contextualizing a genealogy of cinematic Comanches and their intertextual connections in the media borderlands.

Each chapter constructs Comanche-centric conversations over popular Native American discourse. Chapter 1, "Jurisdiction: Reclaiming Comanchería Cinema," reads a cultural history of Comanches in mainstream and independent film. It addresses competing visions on how the recurring complicated signifier of "Comanche," performed in and around fictional and nonfictional film by real-life Comanches and fictional Comanche characters, has long captivated, or taken captive, the imaginations of media producers and audiences during the history of Comanchería cinema. Including features, documentaries, and other films made by or about Comanches and set in the Comanchería borderlands, Comanchería cinema is built through a tribalography of the stories, films, performances, migrations, and other histories that "author tribes."[58] The borderlands of Comanchería cinema can not only help and hinder comprehension of Comanches but also represent the spaces from which to create and critique texts.

Chapter 1 charts a media archive of producers' efforts to stake claims of representational jurisdiction over who represents whom in the visualization of cinematic Comanches. From Comanche leader Quanah Parker's co-starring role in the 1908 silent film *The Bank Robbery* to his mother, Cynthia Ann Parker, and her captivity narrative inspiring the 1956 western *The Searchers* to Norwegian filmmaker Marthe Thorshaug's 2007 short film, *Comancheria,*

Comanchería cinema signifies scores of narratives and genres in motion long before Disney's *The Lone Ranger*. Similar to Randolph Lewis's approach to cinematic tribal specificity in his chapter "A Brief History of Celluloid Navajos" to intertextually preface his multifaceted analysis of Arlene Bowman's documentary *Navajo Talking Picture*, I provide a brief history of fictional Comanche characters and real-life Comanche filmmakers, actors, and consultants in Hollywood and independent productions to provide a Comanche-centric cinematic backdrop for comparative points of consideration in subsequent chapters.

Chapter 2, "Kinship: A Captivity Narrative," analyzes the cultural politics of Comanche elder LaDonna Harris's adoption, or captivity, of Johnny Depp after hearing of the actor's role as a co-starring Comanche character in *The Lone Ranger*. Through interviews and textual analysis, I contend that the adoption's telling from Comanche perspectives inverts the classic genre of the Indian captivity narrative, which is typically told, if not embellished, by the white captives of the Indigenous. Harris's self-determination and historically informed moves to capture Depp rekindles a Comanche legacy of agency, not erasure, across generations of how Comanches make kin. The adoption-captivity expanded Comanche relationships and ensured space for Comanches to be heard in the cacophonous conversations about Depp and the current state of Native representation in Hollywood.

Harris's modern-day captivity is foundational for facilitating and continuing the rest of this book's organization as a cinematic case study. By adopting Depp, Harris set into motion a series of pre–film release Comanche interactions with Depp and other Comanche-centric collaborations and controversies (which I address in chapter 2); contributed to Comanche efforts to make "him a Comanche, so he'd act like one" for his on-screen role (which I analyze in chapter 3); and preceded dueling imprints of intrigue and puzzlement, rejection and support, in Comanche and non-Comanche film reviews and responses (which I discuss in chapter 4).[59]

After chapter 1 asks who is representing whom in the production and claims of representational jurisdiction and chapter 2 asks who is capturing and captivating whom, chapter 3, "Performance: Seeking Representational Justice," questions who is deciding what is just and for whom through representation and its performance. For most critics of *The Lone Ranger*, the answer may be simple. Jerry Bruckheimer, Gore Verbinski, Johnny Depp, Justin Haythe, and Disney executives possess and control the financial, technological, and creative resources to make the film. That response recognizes part of the power dynamics, but it also excludes the collaborative efforts and individual agency of the film's Comanche consultants, actors, and researched borderlands history, not to mention the implications of Harris's captivity of Depp, the tribe's film premiere, and other Comanche interventions.

Following the quadrangular relations between Comanches, Depp, Disney, and Indian Country amid the hype and protest of *The Lone Ranger*, chapter 3 analyzes another quadrangular relationship, this time between the on-screen performances of who I call the four bands of Comanches in *The Lone Ranger*: the "band apart" outcast Tonto, Chief Big Bear and his band of ousted Comanche men, the band of silenced and slaughtered Comanche women, and villain Butch Cavendish and his pseudo-Comanche band of outlaws who raid white settlements in Comanche clothing to mount opposition against Comanches. As a borderlands text set in the overlapping "Colby, Texas" and "Comanche Territory," *The Lone Ranger* is populated not only with Comanches but also white settlers, Spaniards, Chinese, African Americans, and—as evident from an Indian scout (actor David Midthunder) for the U.S. Cavalry and a reference to another tribe ("Apache")—other Native peoples. What, I ask, are the film's narrative elements of justice and injustice toward Comanches when viewed through a media borderlands intertextual web involving the representational development and underdevelopment of Comanches? To further this analysis I also engage producers' preproduction rhetoric of intent to bring justice and honor on-screen to Comanches and other

Natives by reshaping Hollywood's notoriously dehumanizing Native roles. The performative intent toward the bands of Comanches provides a window into the representational implications—namely, the ambivalently progressive and regressive politics of on-screen "Comanche" performances. Rather than echo the dichotomous discourse in Indian Country by opting for a one-sided perspective of how just or unjust Comanches are produced and performed in *The Lone Ranger*, I offer a nuanced Comanche-centric reading of a highly charged film and its representational endeavors to reshape perceptions of the masked Comanche Tonto and other Native characters.[60]

Chapter 4, "Audience: Comanches Viewing Comanches," picks up on competing camps' expressed perceptions of the film's Comanche performativity discussed in the previous chapter. In the complex arena of audience reception and attempts by producers to reshape reception, I begin with a Comanche-excluded collision between the film's producers and non-Indigenous film critics in news reports and media interviews. Non-Native film reviewers on news sites and social media largely lambasted the movie with (Comanche-less) critiques that drew the ire of the movie's producers and principal actors. Bruckheimer and company publicly and problematically tried to counter the negative reviews by blaming reviewers for causing the movie to fail and at the same time by constructing and praising an ideologically homogenous "Native American community" that adored the film. To complicate and counter critics' written Indigenous erasure and producers' selective listening to an overly generalizing "Native American" and singular "Comanche" perspective, I focus at length on Comanches' diverse ways of responding to a single film and its portrayals of Comanches.

To center competing and coexisting Comanche perspectives, I concentrate on two overlooked and underheard examples of responses in the media borderlands sites of independent online television and radio. In addition to citing other Comanches in news reports, I listen closely to Comanche guests on Al Jazeera's *The Stream* episode "Hollywood's Native American Narrative" (July 16,

2013), with *Lone Ranger* consultant William Voelker and filmmaker Jason Asenap finding common ground; and the call-in program *Native America Calling* episode "Tonto Rides Again, Love Him or Lasso Him?" (July 3, 2013), with educator and playwright Terry Gomez and film producer and artist Jhane Myers, who strongly disagree about *The Lone Ranger* and its Comanche portrayals.[61] Together cinematic Comanche critics and other Natives provide discursive doses of cultural close-ups into twenty-first-century Indigenous film criticism. The reviews and subsequent reactions—like the contours of representational jurisdiction over Comanche film, captivity, and justice in earlier chapters—vie for receptive territory over how to interpret representational indigeneity and illustrate timely conversations on the state of (mis)perceptions of Comanches and Native peoples in cinema.

Throughout this book cinematic Comanches are the primary people maneuvering in the media borderlands of populated sites, where I engage the politics of Comanche filmic visuality, kinship, justice, and reception. In all, by deploying the maruawe method of reporting back on the production, performance, and perception of Comanches in the media borderlands, *Cinematic Comanches* seeks to advance ongoing conversations on the state of Indigenous representation. Navigating the complicated contours of representational jurisdiction, the cinematic Comanches herein represent and get represented in on-screen and off-screen scenes of the Comanchería, a highly contested space not only in territorial borderlands history but also in the media borderlands of cinematic imaginaries.

CHAPTER 1

Jurisdiction

Reclaiming Comanchería Cinema

> Comancheria is the historical territory of the Comanche
> Indians. It was the largest area of land claimed and
> defended by any Indian tribe in North America. Right
> now, the Comanches are again expanding in the American
> Heartland. There is something in the wind on the prairie.
> —*Comancheria*, directed by Marthe Thorshaug (2007)

On May 3, 2006, four Comanches playing Comanches appeared
on PBS television stations across the media borderlands in the
new reality series *Texas Ranch House*. A year earlier producers
invited fifteen people, among the pool of applicants, to come live
together back in time in 1867 Texas on a ranch near the border
town of Alpine. Their objective was to run a successful ranch and
a cattle drive in their roles as ranch hands, cooks, vaqueros, and
wranglers. Following other PBS time-traveling House series such as
1900 House (2000), *1940s House* (2000), and, set in 1628, *Colonial
House* (2003), *Texas Ranch House* asked actors and viewers to step
back into imagined times over the course of eight highly edited
episodes.[1] In episode 6, "Lords of the Plains," named after a popular moniker for Comanches, then tribal administrator Michael
Burgess, artist Calvert Nevaquaya, and married couple Glen and
Mary Heminokeky played themselves, ironically, as guest stars in
the traditional homelands of the southern band of Comanches called
Penatekas.[2] Throughout the show the Comanches-as-Comanches
enacted maruawe by narratively reporting back to Comanche viewers and others.

Ten years to the day after the episode aired, Burgess told me
they arrived in Texas for filming from the Indian Fair in Anadarko,
Oklahoma, in his truck "loaded with all our gear," including "tipis

and poles and our 'authentic' Comanche clothing."[3] The four Comanches set up their camp with two traditional tipis near the ranch along what Burgess calls on-screen the "Comanche war trail," an old term for raiding routes.[4] One series producer likens the vast filming location to a "John Ford–esque palette," invoking Ford's 1956 film *The Searchers* (filmed in Monument Valley on the Navajo Nation) and its problematic "Comanch'" characters (played mostly by Navajos). The Comanches, who joined *Texas Ranch House* with "a desire to give their version of history," challenge the comparison to Hollywood's take on Navajoland.[5] Wearing traditional clothing, including leggings from his late father, Doc Tate Nevaquaya, guest star Calvert Nevaquaya tells the cast and crew, "1867 was a tough time for our people. You can feel our people once here. . . . You can feel their presence." Burgess tells the ranchers, "It's not that we don't own this land. This land is still ours even though there's a government and other people who live here."[6] The Comanches' sovereign, unscripted statements are spoken in 2005 in an imagined 1867 that is not far removed for the Comanche actors.

The year 1867 marks the address of real-life Yamparika Comanche leader Ten Bears at the Medicine Lodge Treaty Conference in Kansas, where he reluctantly agreed to a reservation and houses in Oklahoma. "I do not want them," he told the U.S. federal agents. "I was born on the prairie where the wind blew free and there was nothing to break the light of the sun. I was born where there were no enclosures and where everything drew a free breath." He later said, "When I was at Washington [in 1863] the Great Father [Abraham Lincoln] told me that all the Comanche land was ours and that no one should hinder us in living upon it. So, why do you ask us to leave the rivers and the sun and the wind and live in houses?"[7] Just two decades earlier, in 1844, Old Owl (Comanche) had told Republic of Texas president Sam Houston that west-central Texas is "Comanche land and ever has been." Coahuiltecans, Tonkawas, and Lipan Apaches may disagree, but "Old Owl was displaying his rhetorical skill" and letting the newcomer settler Texans know what's up.[8] Two centuries later, on *Texas Ranch House*, Nevaquaya similarly said what's up in practicing maruawe, telling the ranchers, film crew, and viewers, "This is our country." Is—not was—and ever has been.

In each of these recorded scenes, stretching across the Comanchería, Comanches represent and stake rhetorical claims in territorial jurisdiction. They also claim, whether as historical leaders off-screen or contemporary Comanches on-screen, shares of representational jurisdiction. As explained in the introduction, representational jurisdiction concerns articulated and performed claims of "Comanche" significations. In *Texas Ranch House*, for example, Comanches and non-Comanches collide and coexist to add another mediated story to the ever-expanding archive of Comanche representations in the media borderlands. From the Latin *jur-* and *dictio*, meaning "saying law" or, as Émile Benveniste translates, "the speaking of the sovereign law of the community," jurisdiction involves "the power to decide, the power to act, and the power to govern."[9] Preceded by Randolph Lewis's "representational sovereignty" in a media context to indicate similarly "the right, as well as the ability, for a group of people to depict themselves with their own ambitions at heart" inside Michelle Raheja's "virtual reservation where Indigenous people can creatively reterritorialize physical and imagined sites," representational jurisdiction questions the politics of power over the depictions and reterritorialization. It asks who is representing whom and who shapes and controls the production, performance, and perception of Indigenous representations.[10]

As illustrated by *Texas Ranch House* and other works in this chapter on Comanche representational history in film and television, Comanches in the media borderlands have long engaged in efforts to reclaim self-representation on our homelands of the Comanchería. The Palestinian writer Edward Said argues that "the struggle over geography . . . is not only" militaristic with "soldiers and cannons but also" representational concerning "images and imaginings."[11] As scholar Annita Hetoevėhotohke'e Lucchesi concurs, the "struggles over geography are also struggles over representation and imaginations of the land and the people that belong to it."[12] By turning in this chapter to visually mediated scenes with real and reel Comanches, I engage a history of not only hotly contested territory but also its visually recorded depictions and inhabitants in what I call *Comanchería cinema*. The real and reel conjoin in the liminal media borderlands of the "Comancheria," which, as Norwegian director Marthe Thorshaug explains at the outset of her 2007 short film *Comancheria*, "is the historical territory of the Comanche Indians." The words in *Comancheria*, shot on location in the Wichita Mountains near the Comanche Nation tribal complex, greet viewers from within the territorial borderlands of the Comanchería and the media borderlands of Comanchería cinema, which includes films made by or about Comanches, often set in Comanche homelands.

In Comanchería cinema Native and non-Native filmmakers, actors, and critics have long staked claims in assuming representational jurisdiction over cinematic Comanches. Following Western Shoshone historian Ned Blackhawk's assertion that "the spread of the horse in the seventeenth century accelerated [Comanches'] territorial expansion" in highly contested borderlands, I contend that the movie camera of the twentieth and twenty-first centuries has accelerated our representational expansion, albeit ambivalently, in Comanchería cinema.[13] Rather than sit idly by, however, as others seek to capture reel Comanches on camera, the real Comanches of empire have always been in transmotion on horseback and otherwise, moving too quickly, too slyly, and too spiritedly to ever be fully captured in motion pictures. Sure, some symbolic semblances of Comanches may get snared in the Hollywood system, but this chapter also shares storied scenes of how cinematic simulations of the Comanche empire strike back through the performativity of on-screen characterizations and off-screen social actors.

This chapter addresses the politics of performance involving numerous cinematic Comanches, particularly characterizations in films featuring Comanche and non-Comanche actors. In assembling an intertextual and fragmented bricolage of cinematic Comanches informed by Comanches' transnational relations across the Comanchería borderlands, I chart on-screen fictional reel and off-screen real-life representational routes to underscore the politics of performance in the ongoing relations between representations of Comanche people and Comanche territory in cinema. Rather than treat the on-screen and off-screen as separate performative entities, representational jurisdiction recognizes the hybridity of each impacting how the other is represented and perceived. Through competing narrations in film of how Comanches represent and get represented at the on-screen and off-screen confluences of representational jurisdiction, I discuss how recurring fictional and nonfictional significations of "Comanche" are performed and demarcated by casts, crews, and critics.

To map the politics of representational jurisdiction and the contours of Comanche subjectivity and spatiality in film, I offer a history spanning over a hundred years of mediated representation. While this history details a large number of films, actors, and themes, such a history is important to Comanche readers. I aim to be comprehensive to show the breadth of Comanche representations in cinema to demonstrate our omnipresence in Indigenous film and popular culture more broadly. Rather than treat the representations as a monolith of stereotypes on the big screen, I choreograph creative movements by real and reel Comanches on- and off-screen. The result reveals an expansive look, through a Comanche lens, into a tribal-specific filmography. To illustrate where the fictional and nonfictional come together, I discuss a co-starring role by Comanche chief and U.S. celebrity Quanah Parker capturing the public's attention off-screen and capturing thieves on-screen in *The Bank Robbery* (1908) and his children's subsequent silent-film performances in southwestern Oklahoma; his mother, Cynthia Ann Parker, and cinematic Comanche characters in *The Searchers* (1956); and the nearly all-Comanche cast of Comanches playing Comanches in *Comancheria* (2007) in Oklahoma. Interspersed in the discussion of these extended examples are gestures to other films with Comanche representation, such as the westerns *Comanche* (1956), *The Outlaw Josey Wales* (1976), and *Comanche Moon* (2008). In all the overview of Comanches in film represents a wide and strange range of symbolic claims to constructing Comanchería cinema in the twentieth and twenty-first centuries.

Hakarʉ Marʉʉmatʉ Kwitaka

To further frame my focus on representational jurisdiction in Comanchería cinema, I turn to a rhetorical reminder of an age-old seriocomical question spoken by Thorshaug. During a 2009 Q&A, after screening *Comancheria* at the Quai Branly Museum in Paris to an audience of anthropologists, Thorshaug was criticized for not being in the film.[14] "As a matter of fact," she replies, "I am acting in the film, as a character, as everybody else [is]." She and her entire crew—that is, her sound engineer and animator (and husband) Christian Falch—play the "Seeking Visitors," whose faces are never shown up close and who never speak in the film but who are presumably paying the tribe to visit Comanche enterprises and thus contributing to Comanche capital. Thorshaug added the visitors, she explains, "maybe to underline their impossibility to get into the Comanche culture" to emphasize what "they [Comanches] have and we [non-Comanches] don't have." Like her film's seeking visitors, "we can," she continues, "swim in the sauna and go to the casino instead, and give our money to the Comanche Nation. And who is shitting who becomes an open question."[15]

Thorshaug's inquiry—"hakarʉ marʉʉmatʉ kwitaka?" in Comanche—opens up possibilities to critically and creatively rethink how one responds to who has, or who thinks they have, representational jurisdiction.[16] Emerging from the slippery and ambiguous realm of trickster aesthetics, her question may be built on dichotomous conceptualizations of insider/outsider (they have/ we don't) and deceiver/deceived or trickster/tricked. But her setup for the incisive inquiry suggests a rich recognition of contemporary irony in Indian Country. Across centuries of colonization, militarization, forced removals, boarding schools, intrusive scholars, and settler-colonial settlements, many non-Natives also frequent Native enterprises and give their money to Indigenous-run efforts for economic prosperity and sustainability. Applied more broadly to the medium of film, Thorshaug's "open question" cuts to a core, yet often overlooked, interpretive mode of analyzing the history of Indigenous subjectivity in media, Comanchería cinema included, through the Comanche conceptual lens of isa kwitapʉ, or "bullshit."

From George Catlin's paintings and Edward S. Curtis's photographs to William Cody's Wild West shows, James Mooney's ethnographies, and Thomas Edison's films, Natives have long been the subjects of non-Indigenous captivation. For just as long Native subjects and audiences have called isa kwitapʉ on the production, representation, and reception of—to borrow the title of Hopi filmmaker Victor Masayesva Jr.'s 1992 documentary—"imagining Indians." In Masayesva's film, Marvin Clifford, an Oglala Lakota and *Dances with Wolves* (1990) extra, literally calls "bullshit" on his perceived ill-treatment by Kevin Costner's crew. Hopi elders call it on Robert Redford and his crew's planned filming of *The Dark Wind* (1991) on sacred sites. Masayesva calls it throughout his film on non-Native appropriation and commercialization of Indigenous representations and cultural practices, or "all of the lame bullshit," to quote Paul Chaat Smith (Comanche), "the mascots, the pickup truck commercials, the New Age know-nothings."[17]

That's calling isa kwitapʉ on the isa kwitapʉ, as my late uncle Monroe Tahmahkera—great-grandson of Quanah Parker, "consummate horseman," and recurring invited extra on Chuck Norris's *Walker, Texas Ranger*—humorously did when he said of the star's equestrian skills, "Chuck Norris couldn't ride worth a damn!"[18] Or, in the martial arts film series *Once upon a Time in China*, my uncle—according to adopted Comanche and film extra Paul Davis—refused the director's charge to retrieve firewood in the plot because Comanche men traditionally would not have done that.[19] In such moments Comanche relatives enact agency onscreen and off in performing and telling more of the story of how we represent in the media borderlands.

Horses also factor in contests of hakaru maruumatu kwitaka, or who is shitting whom, in *Texas Ranch House*, where the Comanches repeatedly outsmart the ranchers on-screen. They steal four horses and seriocomically take Jared, a white male ranch hand, captive along with a fifth horse, the one Jared rode into the Comanche camp. Later in negotiations with the white ranch owner Bill Cooke, the Comanche leader Michael Burgess speaks to his tribe's power in 1867 and tells him, Jedi-like, "You want to trade with us." Burgess trades Jared and presumably the four initial stolen horses for twenty-five cattle. However, one of the horses, the ranchers learn after the trade, is Jared's. "Deceptive and pretty underhanded," says Cooke. "They considered they owned the horse that Jared rode in on." The ranch hands laughed and appreciated the Comanche cunning. "I never heard him ask the question" of which horses, Jared notes. "When you leave the grocery store," he quips, "you check your bags and make sure you have everything." The camera cuts to one of the horses who humorously nods in agreement.

In her analysis of white filmmaker Robert Flaherty's 1922 documentary *Nanook of the North*, Michelle Raheja deploys "visual sovereignty" by reading Inuit star Nanook's amusement with Flaherty, what Fatimah Rony calls an Inuit way of "laughing at the camera," as a "tactic . . . to confront the spectator with the often absurd assumptions that circulate around visual representations of Native Americans."[20] That Indigenous legacy of agency of not only laughing back but also speaking back continues in Cree filmmaker Neil Diamond's documentary *Reel Injun*. He visits Navajo couple Effie and James Atene, who worked as Hollywood extras decades earlier. Watching together the Hollywood western *A Distant Trumpet* (1964), the Navajos translate for Diamond what an on-screen Navajo leader says in a tense exchange with a white lieutenant, all without any on-screen captions:

SOLDIER: [in English] If I do not return, then General Quaint will find you, and you will be dead and all your people.

CHIEF: [in Navajo] Just like a snake, you'll be crawling in your own shit.

SOLDIER: No, he is not a fool! You are!

CHIEF: Obviously you can't do anything to me. You're a snake crawling in your own shit.[21]

Presumably having no clue that the Native actor went off-script, the film's white cast and crew experience translational failure. Diamond calls the moment "sweet revenge" for outsmarting what Raheja calls "the often disempowering structures of cinematic dominance and stereotype." The scene and others like it illustrate Homi Bhabha's notion of "sly civility" when Indigenous actors perform both professionally and slyly for the camera by playing to and playing with expectations of Indianness in Hollywood.[22]

In asking "Hakaru maruumatu kwitaka?" we have to remember that movies are movies—reels of data captured on camera, never to be trusted—producing multitudes of incommensurable interpretive possibilities. We also have to remember that movies are far more than that, something far-reaching, endless, and rooted in ancient traditions of storytelling and storied tales. Isa kwitapu is both a framework and a response to teasing out the politics of those who hold, or think they hold, representational jurisdiction over screening and viewing Indigenous peoples and geographies in heavily populated, transnational media borderlands.

To theorize about cinematic isa kwitapu is not to dismiss or diminish critical conversations on Comanchería cinema but, rather, to participate in those conversations by considering the very politics and parameters of representational sway and performative play. It is to ask who's capturing and captivating whom—performatively, ideologically, discursively, and ontologically—on- and off-screen. To ask "Hakaru maruumatu kwitaka?" through film and mediated performance generates a critical position from which to better engage how off-screen social actors and on-screen fictional characters collide and capture, trap, and tease one another in the narratives that Americans and residents of Indian Country, not to mention Scandinavians, tell themselves and screen for viewers around the world.

Take One: Listening to the Silent Era

According to Paul Chaat Smith, a Comanche writer, art curator, and even part-time actor in Mohawk filmmaker Shelley Niro's film *Honey Moccasin* (1998), there's the good and there's the bad with "being Comanche" in the twenty-first century. For the good, Smith says, first, "we're quite famous . . . in the Indian all-time top five"; second, "we're not whiners"; and, third, we've "made no extravagant claims other than once being rich and powerful and really, really good with horses." As for the bad, it includes "the widespread idea that we were vicious and cruel," which "is tough to refute because it's true. . . . [While] not cruel and vicious all the time . . . the glory days of the Comanche were [undeniably] built on raiding and economies built on the taking of captives." "Also bad," he adds, "is that we had no super famous leaders," no "central casting superstar." Instead, "just scenes of Indians on horseback committing murder and mayhem."[23] I like to think, though, that Smith might agree with me, Comanche to Comanche, that based on representations of Comanches in oral and written histories, nonfiction and fiction literatures, and in popular discourse, Quanah Parker is arguably the most captivating cinematic Comanche in media borderlands history, our closest relation to a "central casting superstar." Quanah is our Crazy Horse and Geronimo, our Sitting Bull and Chief Joseph.

Born into his father's Nokoni band around 1845, Parker grew up to become a fierce *paraibo*, or leader, of the Quahada band of Comanches. Contrary to reductive narrations of Parker as predominantly a warrior, he also was a husband (at least seven wives), father (twenty-five children), homeowner (of the eight-bedroom Star House), farmer, judge, stockholder (he co-owned the Quanah, Acme and Pacific Railway), entrepreneur (he founded a school in Cache, Oklahoma, and became its first board president), religious leader (he significantly furthered the Native American Church), and much more. As an early practitioner of the tactic to which Thorshaug alludes in her question, Parker also required payment from white ranchers who wanted to graze their cattle on Comanche lands.[24] As Quanah's great-grandsons Vincent Parker and Ron Parker narrated in their short film *Quanah Parker: The Last Comanche Chief* (2012), he was not only an "intrepid warrior" but also a "vigorous and enlightened protector of Comanche interests," "courageous and strong-willed," and a "natural diplomat."[25] The late Vincent Parker even moved to Hollywood in the mid-1980s to try to commission a feature film about Quanah. While there he also worked on projects for Walt Disney Studios but grew "tired of playing the social circuit, putting up with the Hollywood bullshit. At any given moment I question it."[26] If he had managed to commission a feature film about Quanah, Vincent Parker would have further contributed to a remarkably robust tradition of movies about his great-grandfather.

With a formidable stature and strong résumé, Quanah Parker soon inspired Hollywood roles after his passing in 1911. Fictional roles named after Parker range from the late 1910s to today. For example, in *The Heart of Wetona* (1919), white British actor Fred Huntley played "Chief Quannah," albeit a Blackfoot character with a Comanche name, alongside a white character named Comanche Jack (possibly named after the real-life Permansu, or Comanche Jack, who, like Quanah, also profited from cattlemen). In George Sherman's *Comanche* (1956), white actor Kent Smith received second billing for his portrayal of Parker, indicative of how prominent a role the filmmakers considered the Parker character. In John Ford's *Two Rode Together* (1961), German American Henry Brandon (born Heinrich Kleinbach) assumed the Quanah Parker role. The 1993 A&E series *The Real West*, hosted by actor and singer Kenny Rogers, devoted an entire episode to Parker's biography and included interviews with Wallace Coffey (Comanche), Jim Cox (Comanche), and Towana Spivey (Chickasaw).[27] In *Comanche Moon* (2008) and *The Legend of Hell's Gate* (2011), Lakota actors

Eddie Spears and Zahn McClarnon, respectively, assume the Parker persona. The Oglala Lakota actor Moses Brings Plenty portrays Parker in the History Channel documentary *Comanche Warriors* (2005). Portraits of Parker grace its DVD cover as well as the book covers of S. C. Gwynne's Pulitzer Prize–finalist book *Empire of the Summer Moon* (2010) and R. David Edmunds's edited collection *American Indian Leaders* (1980).

Aligned with settler-colonial parameters of representational jurisdiction, producers tend to remain selective by playing up Parker's U.S. acculturation, coded distortedly as "assimilation" in the building of the U.S. nation-state. Producers also focus on the liberal multicultural marker of his mixed-blood identity to suggest that his whiteness facilitated his becoming an acceptable American and that being both white and Indigenous represents the union of bridging cultures. As thinly veiled commentaries on federal Indian policy of the 1950s and 1960s, westerns like *Comanche* and *Two Rode Together* suggest that Indigenous termination and assimilation are best. Characters named Quanah Parker are the "good," reformed (white) Comanches who wish to be American, the representational antithesis of the concocted "bad," unregenerate cinematic Comanches named Black Cloud and Stone Calf who ultimately meet their demise in their relentless acts of defiance. In *Comanche* the Parker character even has a hand in the killing of Black Cloud in an iteration of the classic Hollywood binary of barbaric savage versus noble savage. Apparently, Hollywood suffered a name shortage as another character named Black Cloud represents the title character in the 1953 western *Last of the Comanches*. That film begins with the title card "The Indian tribes of the southwest were at peace, except for the notorious renegade Comanche chieftain, Black Cloud, and his savage followers."[28] Incidentally, their cinematic cousin Chief Dark Cloud showed up in the first *Lone Ranger* film in 1938, determined to kill Tonto and the title character before realizing the duo had not attacked Comanches.

For *Comanche*, a film that showed sympathy toward its imagined American-accommodationist Comanches, the marketing hyped its cinematic Comanches in movie posters as the killers of "more white men than any other tribe in history."[29] The film is set in 1875 on both sides of the Kwana Kuhtsu Paa, or Rio Grande, where the Parker character finds himself at a crossroads. He could continue fighting on the highly contested southern plains or surrender to the Oklahoma reservation and, as the character says, "learn from [the Americans] so that our children will not hunger, so they will be warm in the winter, so they will be strong as the Americans are strong." The film reeks of U.S. paternalism just thirty years after the invasion of Mexico and paints a troubling picture of harmonious alliance between the United States and Mexico joining forces against Comanches. Still, *Comanche* acknowledges Comanches' raids in Mexico and efforts to keep the ever-expansive U.S. territory and white U.S. population from taking over the Comanchería. When the on-screen Parker learns that Mexico and the United States have made a treaty without Comanche consent, he is outraged and declares, "A line has been changed in the Earth. The Americans and Mexicans agree [with] no Comanches [present]. We were here [already] . . . but no one thought to agree with us. Yet we are not a conquered people, no one has defeated us." Here is a Comanche character in the mid-1950s who questions the disregard and disrespect for the unconquered sovereign Comanches amid other countries' treaties and, in effect, asks, "What about us?" (or, in PG-rated parlance, "Are you shitting me?").[30]

Decades earlier, however, the real Quanah Parker had already answered his future Hollywood simulation's question of "what about us?" off-screen and on, as he worked to ensure a prosperous future not dependent on the eradication of Comanche culture but in ensuring that others *did* and *will* ask Comanches. Before any of these fictional roles in which others play Parker, the man himself co-starred in the 1908 short silent film *The Bank Robbery*.[31] Parker's own appearance in this relatively obscure half-hour film shows a Comanche speaking for himself with more volume than most cinematic Comanches in subsequent talkies. *The Bank Robbery* is not rare during its time for featuring a Native actor—hundreds

2. Quanah Parker in the foreground, in *The Bank Robbery*. Courtesy of the Library of Congress.

of silent films include Indian roles, albeit often played by non-Natives—but what is unique here is to see a credited Comanche celebrity on-screen in modern everyday clothes on his horse, not in buckskin and feathers like, say, D. W. Griffith's savage Indians in *The Battle at Elderbush Gulch* (1913).[32]

As perhaps the earliest film to show a Comanche presumably playing a Comanche, *The Bank Robbery* was filmed by the Oklahoma Natural Mutoscene Company in 1907 in Cache, Oklahoma, and the neighboring Wichita Mountains. That same year Indian Territory and Oklahoma Territory merged into the forty-sixth U.S. state, Oklahoma; President Theodore Roosevelt officially dubbed the mountains the Wichita National Forest and Game Preserve; a herd of buffalo was reintroduced from the Bronx Zoo; and Parker continued to be recognized by the U.S. government as the supreme leader of Comanches.[33] Parker also played a role in inspiring another film shot in 1907. After riding his horse in Roosevelt's inauguration parade in March 1905 and inviting him to Comanche country, Parker accompanied Roosevelt, John "Catch 'Em Alive Jack" Abernathy, and others on a wolf hunt in April in the Big Pasture area near Cache. When Roosevelt arrived to Oklahoma by train, he "gave a brief speech and then invited Quanah to talk." Parker biographer Bill Neeley says Quanah claimed to have received "more applause than Teddy," a humorous invocation of hakaru maruumatu kwi-taka.[34] The Oklahoma Natural Mutoscene Company later made the short film *The Wolf Hunt* (1908), starring Abernathy and directed by U.S. marshal–turned–movie director Bill Tilghman.[35]

In *The Bank Robbery* director and co-star Tilghman films Parker, law-enforcement friends Frank Canton and Heck Thomas, and former-outlaw-turned-lawyer-and-actor Al Jennings, who essentially play versions of their previous and current selves.[36] Tilghman uses local townspeople to play background extras, including Quanah's daughter Neda Birdsong, who is seen briefly in a medium shot stepping inside a building. In the film's narrative Jennings and his gang rob the Cache Bank; then Tilghman, Parker, and others engage them in a shoot-out and capture them in the Wichita Mountains before they return to the bank at the end.

In 1908, when the film was released, during the state of Oklahoma's first birthday party and exactly one hundred years before Johnny Depp officially announced his (Comanche) Tonto role for Disney's *The Lone Ranger*, audiences saw Parker perform his own lawman-for-justice role in an effort to claim his own representational jurisdiction.[37] Unlike the Tonto popularized in 1930s cinema by Chief Thundercloud and 1950s television by Jay Silverheels, Parker in the role of *tuutamu taibo*—Comanche for "policeman"—does not serve as subservient sidekick. Parker's role is a Native semblance of himself as protector of the people, both Comanches and all other locals, including when Comanches elected Quanah as deputy sheriff in Lawton in 1902.[38] In this light Parker representationally defends his people's shared homelands from theft in Cache, a town that, as several old Comanche stories go, he may have named.[39] Rather than potentially question if this lone Comanche is an accommodationist Uncle Tomahawk who does the bidding of the white lawmen, I see a relative who performatively protects the people and captures the wrongdoers.

Few published sources make any mention of the film. Those who do tend to downplay Parker's portrayal. Stanley Noyes and Daniel Gelo call Parker's role a "bit part." Hadley Jerman calls it a "cameo appearance." John Wooley deems Parker a "tracker assisting Tilghman and the rest of the posse." Critic Jerry Holt recognizes Parker on-screen but calls his off-screen self the "pacified but unregenerate Comanche chief."[40] Trite, misguided name-calling aside, I argue that Parker deserves more credit. To borrow from Joanna Hearne's book *Native Recognition: Indigenous Cinema and the Western*, I want to "recredit" Parker by recognizing his role as far more than a bit role.[41] As *Lone Ranger* Comanche consultant Troy puts it, "Quanah don't do bit!"[42] Rather than position him as a marginal assistant tracking at another's bidding, the Quanah Parker I see on-screen and report on here *co-stars* in *The Bank Robbery*.

Parker attempted to maintain representational jurisdiction over his own image and perception in the U.S. public imaginary. On her Carlisle Indian Industrial School record, his daughter Laura Parker says her father requested she write a book about his life "so people might see in a true light as newspapers get so many things out [of] shape."[43] As Glenn Frankel says of Parker after he went to Fort Sill in 1875, Parker "decided to recast his own narrative" from a "proud, independent warrior, beholden to no one, who had held out as long as he could," to a "man who was half-white and half-Comanche, and who longed to bring those two worlds together, explaining each to the other and linking the two." If, as Frankel contends, "this was the role he had decided to play," then to imagine that Parker brought such narrative self-determination to his on-screen role in *The Bank Robbery* sounds more than plausible.[44]

Frankel, too, calls Parker "one of its stars," but his reading of Parker in the film positions him and "his Comanche ethnicity" as "undifferentiated from the rest of the volunteer lawmen—just a good citizen doing his duty."[45] While Parker wears no headdress or other noticeable markers of difference and does not represent the savagery that plagues Indigenous portrayals in film, Frankel's sentiment leaves unchecked the specification of which citizenry at a time when U.S. citizenship was not extended to Comanches and when a white male polity, presumably possessed by the other leading actors in the film, dominated the U.S. cultural imaginary.[46] As a leading "citizen" of the Comanches and a Comanche celebrity in the United States just three decades removed from war with the United States, Parker's very presence and embodiment of his role on-screen suggest that his affective ancestral and cultural ties to the area in the Comanchería do not fully resonate with his settler co-stars and other relative newcomers to the Wichita Mountains.

Appearing to be as much, if not more, of a leader of the "good guys" as Tilghman, Parker and his white horse ride in front and lead the way toward justice in multiple close-up shots, including one in which Parker communicates through Comanche sign language with fellow rider and Lawton's first elected police chief, Heck Thomas. In her 1938 book on Quanah, Tilghman's wife, Zoe Tilghman, says the sign language communicated if Quanah "had seen the bandits."[47] In another shot of numerous actors on their horses taking the bad guys and stolen money back to the bank, narrator Henry "Hank" Elling on a YouTube version of *The Bank Robbery* says, "Quanah Parker's kinda riding in the lead" beside another rider.[48] In the very next shot, Parker is seen in front, leading everyone else to the bank, where, according to Zoe Tilghman, "Quanah had several Indians, in costume, about the place."[49] Quanah dismounts from his horse and shakes hands, presumably with the banker. After milling around the bank for a few moments, "Quanah Parker," the narrator notes, "comes riding out of the group" first and turns his head back to the others, motioning several times with his left hand for them to join him, as the director may have wanted or, as I am more inclined to think due to his off-screen legacy of agency, as Parker decided when and where to ride his horse in front of the camera. As this concluding scene unfolds, narrator Elling confidently adds, "Riding in the lead is Quanah Parker" as the film is paused for approximately a full minute on a close-up of Parker, during which time Elling offers a brief bio of "the warrior chief among the Quahada band of Comanche." Interestingly, this is the narrated version's only paused moment on one of the film's principal actors, an on-screen recognition of Parker's off-screen prominence. Tilghman and the others receive no such treatment.

Then, in an ambiguously rich moment invoking the uncertainty of "hakarʉ marʉʉmatʉ kwitaka?" Parker's facial expression appears to change slightly as he exits the film's closing scene.[50] In contrast with his earlier stern look en route to the bank, his face now suggests a smirk toward the camera. The grainy footage in this one moment of the 1908 film prompts not a dismissal of analysis but a critical speculation of the visual from which to see the potential (formation of) amusement at the camera, an imaginable look in the historical context of Indigenous sly civility and Parker's renowned ability to navigate through multitudes of relationships. Finally, in the film's closing seconds, Parker even reenters the frame from the left and exits to the right, the only rider to reappear and go his own way, possibly back toward his own nearby two-story, eight-bedroom home called the Star House. The reappearance may seem inexplicable and unnecessary, but the movement means the Comanches' central casting superstar gets in more screen time and further presides over his representational jurisdiction. Parker also is the only co-star who uses two modes of transportation in the film. Early on Parker rides into town on his personally owned stagecoach in a cinematic shot of a chauffeured Comanche at its finest. He then walks into the Cache Bank.

The cinematic imprint and motions of the Parker family continue in the silent-era films *Sign of the Smoke* (1915) and *The Daughter of Dawn* (1920), both of which star Quanah's children. His son White Parker, born in 1887, co-starred in both. As former Fort Sill Museum director Towana Spivey told me, White toured and performed Comanche songs and dances in Fort Worth and other

3. & 4. Quanah Parker's changing expressions toward the camera, in *The Bank Robbery*. Courtesy of the Library of Congress.

cities in his late teens and early twenties. Then he filmed *Sign of the Smoke* in late 1914 in the Wichita Mountains with Frank V. Wright's Geronimo Film Company. According to Spivey, the film premiered at the Murray Theatre in Lawton on April 2, 1915, before screening elsewhere in Oklahoma and Missouri, Wright's home state.[51] Billed as representing "The Real Comanche Indian Pictured in His Native Haunts," *The Sign of the Smoke* boasted that it featured "more than 100 full-blood Comanche Indians" in "a scenario written about an actual life incident of a famed Comanche Chief that had much to do with his final submission to the white man's laws and his later profession of Christianity."[52] An ad in the April 10, 1915, Saturday edition of an El Reno, Oklahoma, newspaper calls *The Sign of the Smoke* "a five reel Western picture out of the ordinary, featuring White Parker, son of Quanah Parker, late Chief of the Comanches."[53] The ad references additional actors, including Comanches, as a "Full Cast of Competents" in "the Biggest Western Feature Ever Produced." Promoting the film's screening in El Reno Theatre two days later with tickets ranging from a nickel to a dime, a second

5. White Parker in the Wichita Mountains, in *The Sign of the Smoke* (1915). From the collection of Towana Spivey.

ad calls the film "An Indian Picture Out of the Ordinary!"[54] The Lawton-based *News Republican* read the fictional film as factual: "A picture showing the Indian as he really was in the past and he really is today." After screening it in April 1915, a theater manager in Hennessey, Oklahoma, echoed the real-to-reel conflation: "So true to nature—its many thrilling scenes—its real portrayal of Indian life and characteristics, along with the roaming buffalo on the plains and the hunt by the old-time Indians, makes the show that catches everybody."[55] Like his father's symbolic captivity in the U.S. imaginary, White Parker, the film's Comanche star, represents critics' really real Indian.

No reels of *The Sign of the Smoke* are known to exist, but White Parker reemerges on-screen five years later in *The Daughter of Dawn* (1920). It was considered gone too, until a private investigator in North Carolina claimed to have received the film's only copy as payment for his services on a case. He contacted Spivey, who had incredibly pieced together film slides and a script for *The Daughter of Dawn* based on photographs and news fragments he collected over the years. In the late 1970s and the 1980s, Spivey also delivered public educational lectures and slideshows on several silent films from Oklahoma, including the films that co-starred Comanches from the Parker family. Spivey twice referred the investigator to the Oklahoma Historical Society, which eventually purchased *The Daughter of Dawn* in 2007 for $5,000.[56] The nitrate copy was converted to safety film and kept intact for public viewing in 2012, making for more modern-day news headlines of captivating Comanches.[57] The Historical Society commissioned the late Comanche composer David Yeagley to score the film. In 2013 the *Washington Post* and others reported that the Library of Congress added *The Daughter of Dawn* to its National Film Registry. It has streamed on Netflix, and distributor Milestone Film and Video began selling DVD versions in July 2016.[58]

Heralded as the first feature-length silent movie with an all-Native cast, *The Daughter of Dawn* includes off-screen Kiowas playing on-screen Comanches and off-screen Comanches playing on-screen Kiowas, an early cinematic Indigenous instance of playful *isa kwitapu*. Richard Banks's Texas Film Company produced the movie, and Anglo writer and first-time director Norbert Myles, a former vaudeville and short-film actor and future film-makeup artist, shot the movie with one camera in the Wichita Mountains, where hundreds of Comanche and Kiowa actors provided their own clothing and tipis in a story of love, captivity, war, and death. Its co-stars include Quanah's children Wanada Parker and, again, White Parker as on-screen Kiowa siblings Red Wing and White Eagle.[59] Comanches Esther LeBarre and Jack Sankey-doty play Dawn and Black Wolf.

The film screened on October 17, 1920, in Los Angeles and the following three years in such cities as Topeka, Kansas; Joplin, Missouri; Janesville, Wisconsin; and Altoona, Pennsylvania.[60] The film's narrative is reportedly similar to a real-life experience involving Quanah and his temporary early marriage to Ta-ho-yea (Mescalero Apache), who later returned to her Apache relatives.[61]

White Eagle and Dawn love each other, but White Eagle thinks Dawn and Black Wolf are together; Black Wolf loves Dawn, and Red Wing loves Black Wolf. To determine who will marry Dawn, her father, "The Chief" (Hunting Horse, Kiowa), challenges the two young men who claim to love Dawn to jump off Medicine Bluff. White Eagle jumps, but Black Wolf is too afraid. A disgraced but vengeful Black Wolf goes to Comanches and leads them to attack his Kiowa people. Black Wolf then captures Dawn. White Eagle and other Kiowas find them and attack. White Eagle kills Black Wolf, Red Wing kills herself, and White Eagle and Dawn are reunited to live happily ever after.

Myles called the Kiowa and Comanche cast "very shrewd," an unsurprising descriptor for peoples following performative legacies of agency that now translate onto the big screen. Wild West show performer Pawnee Bill described the film as "the best Indian picture I think was ever made." He said the "acting" showed "wonderful talent."[62] Not all were fans. In her July 31, 1920, weekly report to the Bureau of Indian Affairs, the assistant field matron and Mennonite missionary Magdalena Becker complained of the production as distracting the Natives from work like cooking and sewing: "Went to a camp close to headquarters where their [sic] are about 300 Kiowas and Comanches gathered dancing and having pictures taken to be used in the movies. . . . I talked to the manager to have the camp broken up and dances stopped. These dances and large gatherings week after week are ruining our Indian boys and girls as they have been going on for about three months at different places. No work done during these days."[63] The killjoy Becker's amusing attempt to claim jurisdiction over "our" Natives' labor and assembly joins centuries of colonizing tactics against the Indigenous, this time in the arena of Comanchería cinema. Even though Quanah Parker, father of two of the film's stars, allowed Becker and her husband, Abraham, to set up the Mennonite-based Post Oak Mission in Comanche country years earlier, she still tried to intervene in Comanches' representational jurisdiction in a media site that, for her, apparently did not constitute legitimate labor.

Becker failed, of course, as the Comanche and Kiowa actors suggestively called isa kwitapʉ by completing a film that their descendants and others continue to view and learn from today. For example, contemporary Kiowa critic and filmmaker Deron Twohatchet calls *The Daughter of Dawn* "technically superb. I know films from that era . . . and it's technically terrific, the photography, even the acting and the editing. . . . The filmmakers were experienced." As a Kiowa with relatives in *The Daughter of Dawn*, Twohatchet speaks to the significant confluence of the real and reel, saying that "this film was part of our family history."[64] As a Comanche with relatives on-screen too, I wholeheartedly agree. From *The Bank Robbery* to *The Daughter of Dawn*, cinematic Comanches represent strongly and proudly in the silent-film era, leaving a lasting impact for generations to come.

Take Two: Searching for Comanches and the Comanchería

By the 1930s and 1940s, Oklahoma- and Texas-based filmmakers employing Comanche actors had long stopped making movies, and Hollywood studios like RKO and Warner Bros. churned out cowboy-and-Indian westerns such as Wesley Ruggles's *Cimarron* (1931), Cecil B. DeMille's *The Plainsman* (1936), and John Ford's *Stagecoach* (1939) and *Fort Apache* (1948). Howard Hawks's *Red River* (1948), starring John Wayne, shows white settlers shooting at and attacking nameless Comanche men on horseback. For cinematic Comanches the shift from silent films to talkies marks a new chapter of distorting who and what constitute Comanches and the Comanchería in a medium seeking representational jurisdiction over Indigenous characterization. "From the first days of still photography," Smith observes of Comanche visuality, "anthropologists and artists found us a subject of endless fascination. When the pictures began to move, and then talk, they liked us even more."[65] As evident from films like *The Bank Robbery*, *The Sign of the Smoke*, and *The Daughter of Dawn*, the silent era portrayed Comanches playing Comanches and other Indigenous subjects, and southwestern Oklahoma represented the Comanchería. By the mid-twentieth century, during the heyday of the western genre, whites, Mexicans, Navajos, and others routinely played Comanches on-screen. The geography changed too, as Hollywood film and television represented the Comanchería, particularly in story lines set in West Texas and on studio sound stages and in filming locations of Monument Valley, Arizona; the Black Hills of South Dakota; New Mexico; and other sites exuding popular expectations of Indianness.

The changes in representational and territorial characterizations are illustrated in the most critically acclaimed Hollywood flick ever to feature Comanches: the 1956 western *The Searchers*, directed by Ford and starring John Wayne. The film cinematically imprints "us" into the new mid-twentieth-century U.S. imaginary of representational isa kwitapʉ. Arguably Wayne's most popular role of all the westerns "encoded in our [U.S.] cultural DNA," *The Searchers* gained international fame in part through its infamous representation of Comanches.[66] Whereas numerous scholars have convincingly read the epistemological and psychological complexity of the film's narrative and settler stars' performance, I suggest *The Searchers* contributed far more than its fair share of framing the parameters of representational jurisdiction over Comanche portrayals in 1860s and 1870s Texas on the eve of defeat and forced reservation life.[67] As in other westerns that freeze cinematic Comanches in their historical downfall, representation of a Comanche empire is disavowed in another U.S. narration of settler colonialism and brutal Indigenous destruction. Over the course of 119 minutes, Comanches are instead visually and sonically marginalized as "above all," for historian Arthur Eckstein, "grim killers" and, for Frankel, mostly "rapists and killers."[68] Meanwhile, the Comanchería is transformed on location into the scenic wonder of Monument Valley in Navajoland, Hollywood's dream site of "authentic" Indianness.

Arrogantly abbreviated as "The Comanch'" throughout the film by Wayne, Hollywood's archetypal cowboy, in the role of Civil War veteran and Indian killer Ethan Edwards, the discursive dehumanization of "Comanches" aligns with the pronounced on-screen savagery of Comanches. They are the villains and, in Smith's words, "simply a plot device" to show Ethan's blatant hatred of the Indigenous.[69] By, say, shooting out the eyes of a Comanche corpse so he "can't enter the spirit land" and later sadistically killing buffalo so, he snarls, "they won't feed any Comanche this winter," Ethan's acts do not make him the role-model cowboy in the white hat popularly associated with old westerns. But he is still, as he had been since his starring role in Ford's *Stagecoach*, the hero. He is in pursuit of his settler niece Debbie, who, along with her older sister, is captured as a child early in the film by the Comanche lead villain, Chief Cicatriz (Scar), portrayed by Henry Brandon, and nonspeaking Comanche extras played mostly by local Navajos, who reportedly teased Brandon as the "Kraut Comanche" off camera.[70] Although Comanches strike first on-screen against the Edwards ranch and kill or capture everyone there, Tom Grayson Colonnese (Santee Sioux) says, "Scar's attack is in fact a *counterattack*" against a previous and unscreened settler-colonial attempted takeover of Comanche homelands. Near the movie's conclusion, viewers learn that "whites had murdered [Scar's] sons," but those murders are only referenced, not seen, unlike how audiences "see the results of the atrocity at the Edwards ranch committed by Scar."[71]

After years of searching for Debbie, Edwards and his Anglo-Cherokee nephew, Martin Pauley, locate her in Scar's camp, now possibly one of his wives or an adopted daughter.[72] Later, fearing she has gone Comanche, Ethan draws his gun to shoot Debbie, but Martin shields her. "She's been living with a buck!" Ethan snaps, referring to sex. Scar and his band are obliterated, save for Debbie, by Ethan and Martin, Texas Rangers, and the U.S. Cavalry. *The Searchers* climaxes in a chase scene in which Ethan captures Debbie, hoists her in the air, contemplates what to do, and finally cradles her in his arms. "Let's go home, Debbie," he says exhaustedly in the film's last line of dialogue. Against Comanche oral history and scholarly accounts, the line exudes representational isa kwitapɨ. Debbie concedes as she rests her head on

Ethan's shoulder and returns to her extended settler family, who welcome her into their home and presumably reassimilate the last Comanche into white society.

The Searchers, an adaptation of Alan LeMay's 1954 novel of the same name, is a twisted configuration of my extended Comanche family's history. The "Debbie" in our family stories had no interest in leaving her Comanche captors-turned-relatives. Narrations of Cynthia Ann Parker, Quanah's mother, likely inspired the formation of Debbie more than anyone else. As Frankel explains, LeMay researched "sixty-four Indian abductions, including Cynthia Ann's," and left behind notes with references to both Parkers. Just before writing *The Searchers*, LeMay also visited family patriarch Ben Parker in Elkhart, Texas, where he inquired about Cynthia Ann's anti-Comanche uncle, James Parker. When a fan wrote to LeMay to ask him to write a book on Cynthia Ann, he replied, "[*The Searchers*] represents about all I have to contribute on this particular subject."[73]

Like Debbie in the novel and film, Cynthia Ann was captured by Comanches at the age of nine. On May 19, 1836, Comanches attacked Fort Parker east of present-day Waco, Texas, and took her captive.[74] Her uncle James, like Debbie's uncle Ethan (John Wayne), spent years searching for her. She remained with Comanches until 1854, when, after she married Comanche leader Peta Nocona and had three children, Texas Rangers "rescued" and returned her to settler relatives. Unlike Debbie, who has no Comanches to return to after Wayne's character and other settlers and soldiers kill them, Cynthia Ann reportedly tried to escape to be with her Comanche family before she died, some say of a broken heart, in 1871. Cynthia Ann's story of a loving Comanche family is drastically different from the movie's depiction in one scene featuring Comanches' former female captives. When searching for Debbie, Ethan and Martin survey a group of Comanche captives at a U.S. Army post. Several act insane, constantly weeping and shaking or grinning hysterically "just from *being* with Comanches."[75] "It's hard to believe they're white," says one soldier who keeps them quarantined. "They ain't," snaps Ethan. "They're Comanch'."

In the end *The Searchers* largely represents Comanches as unremorseful and violent savages. One exception is actor Beulah Archuletta's character, Look, a subservient recipient of abuse, ridicule, and death. In thirty-one of her thirty-three listed career roles, Archuletta went uncredited by producers (*The Searchers* was an exception), including a 1960 performance as a nameless "Comanche Woman" in the TV series *Rawhide*.[76] Portrayed in *The Searchers* as a grinning and offensive "comic squaw figure," she represents antimiscegenation and a direct connection to Comanche men, who settlers fear will sexually assault and taint settler women.[77] Look is enamored with Martin and thinks they have married in a fictive Comanche way. Martin thought he was just buying a blanket from her Comanche father, but Ethan tells him, "You bought yourself a wife!" Similar representational isa kwitapʉ occurs elsewhere in the media borderlands, such as episodes with hokey cross-cultural unions in situation comedies *The Munsters* and *Here's Lucy*.[78]

Not comedic is when Look snuggles next to Martin that night, and he viciously kicks her down a hill. The moment of "racially pathological" rage prompts Wayne's character to laugh sadistically in a scene that Indigenous viewers have long called isa kwitapʉ on.[79] Then, upon realizing she knows Scar, Ethan and Martin aggressively grab her arms and demand to know the whereabouts of his camp with Debbie. Later, after she leaves them, Ethan and Martin find her and other Comanches killed by white soldiers in a cinematic gesture to the Washita Creek Massacre of 1868, when George Custer's Seventh Cavalry massacred Southern Cheyennes. In contrast to his earlier rage, Martin momentarily feels remorse for Look. Coupled with another sympathetic moment in which Scar tells Ethan that white men had killed his sons (which prompted Scar's vengeance against settlers like Debbie's family), the film's brief acknowledgments of injustice toward the Indigenous are darkly overshadowed by the final climactic battle, in which Ethan, Martin, Texas Rangers, and the U.S. Cavalry join forces to ambush and destroy Scar's sizable camp, all to seek revenge and one captive, Debbie.

In *The Searchers* John Ford and John Wayne establish the blueprint for violent "Comanches" in the pop cultural imaginary. It overshadows relatively nonviolent cinematic Comanche portrayals in 1956, such as the co-starring Quanah Parker character in *Comanche* and real-life Comanches, including actor Oscar Yellowfish, and Kiowas round dancing (symbolic of unity and peace) in the Wichita Mountains in *Around the World in 80 Days* (1956). The latter suggests a silent-era throwback to *The Daughter of Dawn* cast, also with Yellowfish. In 1961 Ford represented Comanches again, as noted earlier, in *Two Rode Together,* oscillating between violent and nonviolent Comanche camps.

Wayne shares the screen again with Comanches in *McClintock* (1963) and *Cahill U.S. Marshal* (1973), but both times in alliance, not opposition. In the comedic western *McClintock,* Comanches speak Navajo again as in *The Searchers.* They ask Wayne's white title character to read their testimony at a hearing where they refuse to go to a reservation at Fort Sill. Although one of the chiefs knows English, McClintock agrees and says, "I speak for the Comanche." It doesn't work. Sentenced to prison for their refusal, the Comanches plead with McClintock to intervene further. He doesn't. So they gather some guns to fight one last battle. They ride through town shooting haphazardly, but the scene plays for laughs, with settler characters performing slapstick bits in taking cover. The Comanches then exit the town, pursued by the U.S. Cavalry and presumably to their demise to echo their vanishing act in *The Searchers.* A few years after *McClintock,* violence and death mixes with comedy again in the comedic western *Shakiest Gun in the West* (1968), when Don Knotts's bumbling lead character shoots at Comanches. *Cahill U.S. Marshal* comes after Wayne's infamous 1971 interview, where he expressed no "wrong" was committed in "our so-called stealing of this country from" Natives "selfishly trying to keep [the land] for themselves."[80] Wayne's comments reflect his Hollywood western persona known for bringing justice to white settlers at any cost, even by killing the Comanch' and other Indians. In *Cahill* Wayne is still the star. He hires Lightfoot (non-Native actor Neville Brand), an old Comanche and Anglo acquaintance, as sidekick and tracker to find white bank robbers. Lightfoot gets derogatorily called "half-breed," and he comedically identifies as a "bonafide war chief of the Comanche Nation." Cahill eventually kills the robbers in a shootout, but not before Lightfoot gets killed and vanishes like cinematic Comanches before him. The film reportedly met Native protest for unjust Indian portrayals at the June 1973 premiere in Seattle, just a few months after Sacheen Littlefeather famously declined the Best Actor Oscar on behalf of Marlon Brando and after the Indigenous occupation of Wounded Knee, South Dakota, concluded. Unlike *Cahill*, which cast a non-Native as a Comanche character, a September 1973 episode of the TV western *Gunsmoke* cast a Comanche, Edgar Monetathchi, as a Comanche chief who speaks the Nɨmɨ tekwapɨ on-screen.

Cahill continues the trademark western swagger of Wayne in a rather simplistic story line, all increasingly out of place in changing political as well as cinematic landscapes with the arrival of revisionist westerns like Arthur Penn's 1970 *Little Big Man*, co-starring Dustin Hoffman and Tsleil-Waututh First Nation actor Chief Dan George, and Sergio Leone's mid-1960s *Dollars* trilogy. The trilogy stars Clint Eastwood before he directed and starred in another revisionist western, *The Outlaw Josey Wales* (1976), also with Chief Dan George. Set around the Civil War, the film shows Eastwood's Wales seeking vengeance against Union soldiers who killed his family. The outlaw eventually forms a tense truce with the Comanche leader Ten Bears, played by Will Sampson (Muscogee Creek). Rather than get vanquished or vanish on-screen, the Comanches have as much of a say as Wales in agreeing to share the land. The film was based on a novel by pseudo-Cherokee and former KKK member Forrest Carter. In the mid-1970s, when the film was in production, Carter visited with the Comanche artist and flute player Doc Tate Nevaquaya in Anadarko, Oklahoma. Nevaquaya shared Comanche history of traditional sites, regalia, and warriors' looks, but as his sons Calvert and Tim Nevaquaya told me, Carter and Eastwood did not credit him.[81] Ten Bears and other Comanches also figure prominently in Michael Blake's revisionist western novel *Dances with Wolves* (1988). However, when producers of Kevin Costner's 1990 movie version "couldn't find enough buffalo in Oklahoma," Paul Chaat Smith writes, they "changed" the Comanches to Lakotas and filmed in South Dakota. Certain characters' names did not change, including Ten Bears, performed by Lakota actor Floyd Red Crow Westerman. "Saying Ten Bears is Sioux," Smith rebuts, "is like saying Winston Churchill is Albanian."[82] In another character twist, the Comanche captivity story of Cynthia Ann Parker inspired a novel and screen adaptation again, this time for Blake's white female captive character, Stands with a Fist, who later marries Costner's white lead character.[83]

The year before Costner went Native, *The Searchers* may have inspired the Comanche characters in the low-budget monster movie *The Cellar* (1989). "From my recollection," *The Cellar* co-screenwriter Daryl Emberly told me, "the Native American dimension was in response to John Wayne's *The Searchers*."[84] After a white family moves into a home, an ancient Comanche spirit monster appears, looming ominously in, well, the cellar. Like the Comanches in *The Searchers*, the monster seeks death and destruction. *The Cellar* follows other horror films associated with underground Indian evil, namely the Indian burial ground trope in Stuart Rosenberg's *The Amityville Horror* (1979), Stanley Kubrick's *The Shining* (1980), and Brian Gibson's *Poltergeist II* (1986). "Years ago," begins the film's eerie voice-over, "the Comanche war council met on this land to decide the fate of many nations and the promise of annihilation to the white man. Those days are past, perhaps. The Indian war council is gone. Unfortunately, the hate created by that time is not." The omniscient narrator says the house "is guarded by the Comanche spirit who rides the wind to keep the evil here alone, away from all else. The white man did not understand. Treaties between men were dishonored. The word broken in the name of progress." A Comanche medicine man named Sam John (Michael Wren) oddly hangs out on the property in efforts to keep the relatively unknown monster at bay. John claims his "great grandfather was a very powerful medicine man," who was forced by "the war council . . . to create a creature that would destroy the white man." When asked why he doesn't just let the monster destroy, John (humorously) complains and foreshadows his on-screen fate: "because the son of a bitch kills Indians, too!" Spoiler: the white newcomers—a boy and his parents—eventually blow up the Comanche monster and the house in a movie that begs to be remade through a Comanche lens by a Comanche filmmaker like Rodrick Pocowatchit and his penchant for comedic horror in his 2010 movie *The Dead Can't Dance.*

Comanche spirits continue to haunt white settlers in the TV series *Walker Texas Ranger* episode "Evil in the Night" (1995).[85] Boldly ranked by one critic as the "Most Ridiculous" episode in the highly ridiculed series, "Evil" includes ambiguously ethnic actor Billy Drago as shape-shifter Running Wolf who morphs into, what else, a flying eagle![86] Identified by one character as a "Comanche medicine man known for practicing evil magic," Running Wolf summons Comanche spirits from a new business construction site, which viewers learn doubles as a burial ground where local authorities uncovered remains of "Indian men, women, and children." The spirits go on a rampage of killing anyone near the site. Norris's title character researches and associates them with "Comanches [who] were defeated at Bandera Pass in 1841," or what historians call the Battle of Bandera Pass, near San Antonio. "The ones [Comanches] that escaped," he adds, "were tracked down and killed." Holding a copy of historian Carl Coke Rister's book *Comanche Bondage*, Walker says to his white girlfriend, "It's all here in the book if you want to read it." He neglects to mention, however, that the killers were from his professional lineage of Texas Rangers who used Colt revolvers against Comanches. Norris's Walker eventually kills Running Wolf after the Ranger "gets a crash course in Native American ghost busting from" the Cherokee elder White Eagle (Frank "Grey Wolf" Salsedo, Wappo). In sum a Cherokee teaches a Cherokee-Anglo Texas Ranger to do as nineteenth-century white Rangers had done: kill a Comanche.

Disturbing ironies notwithstanding, I like the episode for a personal reason: my uncle Monroe Tahmahkera appears twice on-screen. He transforms into a headdress wearing "Cherokee" ceremonial elder. Although Cherokees are not known for headdresses, Comanches like Monroe do wear them on occasion. He raises a feather and "ceremonially" prepares Walker for his showdown with Running Wolf. (He also smudges Walker in another episode.) At the conclusion of "Evil in the Night," my uncle's unnamed character reappears to bless the "Comanche" burial ground to give peace to the avenging spirits. His appearances are brief, without lines, and uncredited, but his transformation shows—like his great-grandfather Quanah Parker before him in the silent film *The Bank Robbery* and Parker's children in *Daughter of Dawn*—a Quahada Comanche in transmotion, even if as a stereotypical Cherokee elder who fictively frees hurt Comanche spirits.

Take Three: Returning to the Reel Comanchería

The Searchers, often heralded as a tour de force, was ranked number ninety-six on the American Film Institute's top hundred U.S. movies of all time in 1997. It rose to number twelve and the top western on the 2007 list.[87] The 2007 ranking of *The Searchers'* popularity temporally coincided with a renewed prominence of Comanche representations marked by borderlands tension, violence, and death in U.S. pop cultural currency. For example, the History Channel original documentary *Comanche Warriors* (2005) emphasizes Comanche-Anglo conflicts and bloodshed and reduces Comanche "culture" to, as the narrator says, "the cult of the warrior." On-screen interviewees include Comanche elders Ava Doty and Patricia Morrow, the self-proclaimed "Conservative Comanche" David Yeagley, and historian T. R. Fehrenbach. "War was not a situation with [Comanches]. It was a continuous state of mind," faux mind reader Fehrenbach asserts on camera. The one-track mentality of violence continues in the Spike TV series *Deadliest Warrior* episode "Comanche versus Mongol" (2010), which brings in weapons "experts" and hypothetically stages a battle to the death between a nineteenth-century Comanche, played by Moses Brings Plenty following his Quanah Parker role in a 2010 documentary, and a thirteenth-century Mongol. Spoiler alert: the Comanche "wins." Unfortunately, the Comanche lost in a scripted Toughman competition in the 1983 film *Tough Enough*, starring Dennis Quaid. Symbolically framed by the Comanche and Kiowa artist John Hitchcock as "a giant Comanche man versus the white man," Darryl Poafpybitty (Comanche) portrayed Mad Dog Redfeather, who lands a couple of solid punches before being knocked out.[88]

In the six-hour CBS miniseries *Comanche Moon* (2008), part of the *Lonesome Dove* trilogy, Indigenous actors Wes Studi and Adam Beach play the most prominent Comanches, Buffalo Hump and Blue Duck. Real Comanches from the Hitchcock, Sovo, and other families also play Comanches. Based on the novel by Larry McMurtry, who co-wrote the screen adaptation with Diana Ossana, *Comanche Moon* stars a group of Texas Rangers chasing the Comanche horse thief Kicking Wolf (Jonathan Joss) and battling Comanches in the 1870s Comanchería-Texas-Mexico borderlands. Zahn McClarnon, David Midthunder, and other Native actors appear as well. Producers also hired Comanches William Voelker and Troy to serve as consultants, who instructed actors on speaking the Comanche language and provided intricate cultural details for how Comanche characters and camps should appear. The miniseries also represents rare efforts in non-Native filmmaking to include exchanges between Comanches and nonwhite characters, which reflects the broader historical Comanchería.

Despite producers' commendable moves in casting, consulting, and expanding the borderlands story, *Comanche Moon* is riddled with violence and death, which reflects parts of Comanche history, but their representational dominance disavows other dimensions of portraying Comanches on-screen as full-fledged human beings. Like the real Rinches, a group founded to exterminate Comanches, Apaches, and Mexicanos, the Rangers in *Comanche Moon* seek to annihilate the Comanches, yet producers dramatically downplay the Rangers' acts of violence.[89] Gus and Call, the leading two Rangers throughout the trilogy, are clearly the courageous heroes, replete with backstories of love interests with female settler characters. In the biased borders of representational jurisdiction in *Comanche Moon*, Comanche men receive no love interest stories, and Comanche women never speak. Instead, following *The Searchers*, Comanches are mainly shown killing or getting killed. In one brutal scene Comanches raid a settlement, burn down businesses, and rape settler women in broad daylight. Beach's Blue Duck becomes one of the vilest cinematic Comanches of all time. Leading a ragtag renegade party against anyone in their way, Native or non-Native, and (another spoiler alert) even killing his Comanche father, Buffalo Hump, Blue Duck harks back to the sinister ultraviolent Comanches Black Cloud (Henry Brandon) in *Comanche* and Stone Calf (Woody Strode) in Ford's *Two Rode Together*, both of whom kill at will. "The Indians of *Comanche Moon*," the *New York Times* concludes, "are either spiritualists who speak in methodical cadences and stroke feathers to the sound of wind instruments, or patricidal maniacs bent on racial vengeance."[90] The critique, harsh in its dichotomy of noble savagery and violent savagery, picks up on dominant themes that overshadow other more humanizing and culturally nuanced moments in the series.

Less humanizing is the *Comanche Moon* prequel, *Dead Man's Walk* (1996). Set in the early 1840s Comanchería/Republic of Texas, a young Gus and Call pursue, and get pursued by, the Comanche leader Buffalo Hump, portrayed by Inuit actor Eric Schweig after his prominent role in *Last of the Mohicans* (1992). Named after the real-life Buffalo Hump, who led a series of raids in 1840 after Texans killed thirty-five Comanches during peace talks, Schweig's character is, like his nameless Comanche comrades, mostly off-screen and a muted threat, always near and striking fear among their Mexican captives and the starring white Rangers. In sum, for one critic the representations of Comanches "may be the most retro depiction of Native Americans in years. At its worst, it harkens back to the western movies in which indigenous peoples appeared to have no interests beyond torturing, burning and killing—of which there is plenty in this often harrowing picture."[91]

Following the violent clashes between Texas Rangers and Comanches in *Comanche Moon* and *Dead Man's Walk*, the dismally reviewed miniseries *Texas Rising* (2015) on the History Channel stars Bill Paxton as Sam Houston, with Brendan Fraser as a settler captive raised by Kiowas before fighting against them as a Texas Ranger. *Texas Rising* fictively narrates the Texas Revolution and the creation of the Texas Rangers. The trailer features Kris Kristofferson covering a slowed version of Tom Petty's "I Won't Back Down," including the lines, "You can stand me up at the gates of hell, but I won't back down." On the word "hell," a Comanche appears on-screen, serving as foil to the settler "I." The sonic-visual overlay echoes a plethora of Comanche references, from Rangers fighting off Comanches in *Comanche Territory* (1950)—its promotional tagline: "The Wild, Wanton Fury of 1,000 Howling Savages!"—to novelist Cormac McCarthy's fierce, and reportedly Fehrenbach-influenced, one-sentence, page-long description of Comanches in *Blood Meridian* (1985), likened to "a horde from a hell more horrible yet than the brimstone land of Christian reckoning."[92]

In Marthe Thorshaug's *Comancheria* (2007) an alternative portrait to representations of Comanche violence emerges. The representational politics at play in *Comancheria* feature real off-screen Comanches playing reel on-screen Comanches, both of whom project a cultural continuity and survivance that adhere to a principled responsibility to past, current, and future generations and teachings of Comanches, but without setting fixed parameters on the representational jurisdiction of how to be Comanche.[93] Like the Comanches as Comanches in *Texas Ranch House*, the cinematic Comanches in *Comancheria* return to the agency, self-representation, and traditional homelands seen in the silent-film era. The depictions of Comanches also suggest increased control in how to represent on-screen. In all they are culturally informed and, like Pekka Hämäläinen's argument about historical Comanches, "fluid and malleable" in recognizing how culture continues and changes.[94] Throughout, however, one constant remains: Comanches never stop being Comanches.

In Thorshaug's *Comancheria* cinematic Comanches and Comanche homelands (not Hollywood studios and Navajoland) practically fill the screen. In Hollywood's contributions to Comanchería cinema, Comanche representation is practically always about the fall, not the rise, of Comanches through narrations of brutality and tragedy. As for Comanche futurity, forget about it. Rather than show Comanches as ultraviolent savages and "warriors" before freezing them in a postempire past of the late 1870s, *Comancheria* recognizes both Comanche history and contemporary presence at the confluences of fluidity and motion. In contrast to the plethora of films set in Indian Country with no representational evidence of extant Indigeneity—and unlike most filmmakers who mark "Comanche" characters as vanquished former occupiers and, ironically, as savage invaders of their own homelands against courageous newly arrived settlers—Thorshaug features a reemergent cinematic Comanchería not relegated to history alone but populated first and foremost by contemporary Comanches in support of the filmmaker's thesis of tribal permanence, expansion, and futurity.

Calling her film a "travelogue in a Comancheria, in a mental Comancheria that might come, some day," Thorshaug filmed on location in the Wichita Mountains, "the heart of Comanche Country," as Comanche co-star Wallace Coffey says, to construct a realistic but fictive road trip.[95] Over the course of one day, the camera critically and humorously follows young Comanche characters, "The Scouts," gathering materials for a sweat lodge ceremony, and a couple of non-Native "Seeking Visitors" at local Comanche businesses. Collaborations with the cast become, Thorshaug says, the process that facilitates blurring the lines between reality and fiction. Like the aesthetics of a trickster with a movie camera, the slippery questions of what is "real," what is scripted, who is speaking, who is in charge, and, yes, who is shitting whom all relate to the politics of representing Comanchería through the portrayals of peoples and places in Comanchería cinema. "By blurring the boundaries between fact and fiction," Thorshaug contends, "the appearance of a new Comancheria comes forth."[96] The non-Native filmmaker and predominantly Comanche cast stake claims in representational jurisdiction, but the politics of power in the representations prompt rethinking the real-life and fictional roles of Indigeneity in cinematic histories.

Thorshaug was initially inspired to visit with Comanches after reading Fehrenbach's 1974 book, *The Comanches: The Destruction of a People* (or *The History of a People* in its republished 2003 format). She had been temporarily working in Texas, where she borrowed the book from a friend. Equipped with knowledge of Anglo perceptions about Comanches, Thorshaug traveled to the Comanche Nation headquarters outside of Lawton, Oklahoma, to do what most directors never really did or do: she talked to us, modern-day Comanches, even if it meant stepping out of her cultural comfort zone. "In the chairman's office," she recalls, "I was introduced as a documentarist from Norway who was overwhelmingly interested in making a film about the Comanche. At that point I felt like a social anthropologist from hell."[97] Thorshaug's discomfort and recognition of anthropological objectification of Indians reflect a humorous, if not humbling, awareness of her self-perceived positionality among the tribe, reinforced later by her on-screen performance as one of the seeking visitors.

After visiting with four-time Comanche Nation chair Wallace Coffey, Thorshaug attended the annual Comanche Elder Day and met soon-to-be co-stars for her film. After Fehrenbach's literary introduction to us, we real modern-day Comanches took it from there as Thorshaug learned in person that we were never destroyed, as the literature says, and that we are back, even though we never really left. Thorshaug recognizes Comanches as different from her Norwegian self and experiences, without necessarily exoticizing us, as marginalized Others on the brink of, to borrow from Fehrenbach's ideological extreme, "destruction."

Comancheria features cinematic continuances of Comanche

6. Wallace Coffey on top of Mount Scott with his Lincoln Town Car, in *Comancheria*. Courtesy of Marthe Thorshaug.

citationality across generations. It stars numerous Comanches, including Coffey, great-great-great-grandson of Comanche *para-ibo* (leader) Ten Bears. Martin Flores, another Comanche co-star, drives through the Wichita Mountains, where he suddenly begins reciting Ten Bears's famous 1867 anticolonization speech: "I was born upon the prairie, where the wind blew free, where there is nothing to break the light of the sun, where everything drew a free breath."[98] Coffey plays "The Chief," who begins the film describing Comanche country's geography across four directions of rivers, hills, canyons, and mountains in a voice-over with aerial stock footage of the Wichita Mountains.[99] Sounding scripted, he starts, "Up north is the Arkansas River. A number of rivers cut through southeast across Comanche country. The Arkansas, the Canadian, the Washita, Red River, the Brazos, Colorado, the Pecos, and the Trinity Rivers. They are all low-banked, sand-filled and sinuous." For viewers versed in dated and low-budget Indian history fare, the film's first one hundred seconds may feel like yet another dry documentary about Indians, until Coffey alters the history lesson, and possibly audience expectations, at the end of his monologue:

"One day in the Wichita Mountains, a gang of Comanches were roaming around, preparing for a sweat lodge."

On the word "lodge," guitar legend Link Wray's 1959 track "Comanche" thumps hard in one of the coolest moments and tonal shifts in the history of Comanchería cinema. Wray's signature amplified guitar sonically marks *Comancheria* as no typical "documentary" of Native history, as three young Comanches in the roles of "The Scouts" (Flores, Patrick Attocknie, and Mame-Neta Attocknie) slowly come into focus in their red Pontiac Grand Prix, a modern-day pony, on a long stretch of asphalt road. Like a director's call to *action*, the song's lone but elongated lyric of "Comaaanche" bellows ambiguously. From the aural perspective of a historical Texas settler, "Comaaanche" could represent a cry of fear of dreadful Comanches like those in *The Searchers* who attack, kill, and kidnap settlers. But Link Wray, purportedly a Shawnee and Eastern Cherokee descendant, and his backing band, the Ray Men, also sound playful, as if teasing listeners and offering an audible reminder of Comanche presence, phantasmal or real, or both.[100] Sonically situated in the film and territory known as Comanchería, the song signals Comanche movement, literally, of the Comanche-driven car and then fades as the car eventually stops in front of the camera for a close-up shot of the front Comanche Nation license plate, grinning the printed moniker "Lords of the Plains," a reference to Comanches, who ran the plains on horseback and whose descendants now claim the discursive space from inside a four-wheeled pony. By appropriating the moniker coined by white historians Ernest Wallace and Adamson Hoebel in their book *Comanches: Lords of the South Plains*, Comanches capture it for their own ponies, not to mention event flyers, T-shirts, and other tribal marketing and merchandise.

Over the course of the next thirty minutes, Thorshaug's lens privileges Comanches playing Comanches who gather in the film's short chapters, aptly named "Rock," "Water," "Cedar," "Wood," "Fire," and "The Sweat." In the last chapter they meet for a traditional sweat lodge ceremony. Despite the ritualistic framing in

7. Comanche scouts (*left to right*) Mame-Neta Attocknie, Patrick Attocknie, and Martin Flores in the Wichita Mountains, in *Comancheria*. Courtesy of Marthe Thorshaug.

the chapter titles, Thorshaug's film never oversteps the Comanche characters' culturally implied jurisdiction on what to represent and not represent in film. As Thorshaug recalls a "medicine man of the Comanche Nation" telling her about the sweat lodge, "I am just giving the ingredients, not the recipe."[101]

The film is representational jurisdiction in action, a cinematic Comanche reclamation of narrative, territorial, ceremonial, and peopled spaces. "We got ways; yes, sir, we got ways," extols the scout Patrick Attocknie. Like in *Texas Ranch House*, in which contemporary Comanche play historical Comanches as practically themselves with ancestral affect and accountability, the Comanche scouts in *Comancheria* play liminal fictive-nonfictive selves who also cite and continue ancestral ways.

Along the way Thorshaug also runs into quite the cast of

characters, including "The Buffalo Wrangler" (Mike Mithlo Jr.) and "The [Comanche Nation] Sheriff" (Ray Anderson), who matter-of-factly explain their work; "Medicine Man" (Lans Saupitty), who gathers wood and sings peyote songs; and "Smokeshop Saleswoman" (Sandra Yellowfish Gallegos), who sells a pack of Marlboro Lights to the scouts. In another scene the scouts drive behind characters identified as "two Kiowas in car" (Jasper Michael Mithlo and Cody Christopher Tonips). Thorshaug also features "The Cowboy" (Ronnie Brewer), an older Anglo rancher who anxiously surmises that competing land claims over old "Indian land," including the land he rents, is "gonna be a major issue" in the United States, as if foreshadowing an increase in Comanches' territorial power as an outcome of Thorshaug's representation of a "mental Comancheria that might come."

As noted earlier, Thorshaug and her partner are also in the film, playing the outsider characters, "Seeking Visitors." Significantly, in the film's closing shot, the visitors become ambiguous captives. With all ceremonial materials gathered, the scouts and medicine man are running the sweat lodge at the end of the film in an undisclosed wooded area of the Comanchería. Meanwhile, Thorshaug and the other seeking visitor arrive to the nearby Comanche Nation Casino off of Interstate 44. As we hear the distant off-screen ceremony's rapid drumbeat and singing, the seeking visitors enter the casino underneath a Comanche moon, a full moon historically associated with Comanche raids. Moments later, amid flashes of blackened screens, Thorshaug and Falch can suddenly be glimpsed in a spot-lighted flash, tethered to a tree, in another undisclosed wooded site. Closing credits immediately ensue, as the seeking visitors presumably become symbolic captives in a modern-day fictive but realistic Comanchería, where they support a tribal enterprise, as they are possibly captivated by expectations of Indianness and the colorful entertainment owned and operated by the Comanche Nation *and* captured in conversation with the historic power of Comanches who took captives to reconstruct the tribe, the effects of which are still felt and lived. As Coffey tells the camera earlier in

8. Comanche Nation Casino and Comanche Moon, in *Comancheria*. Courtesy of Marthe Thorshaug.

Comancheria from atop Mount Scott, a sacred site, "A long time ago, it was a consensus of the people to take captives for the purpose of repopulating the tribe. But when we took captives, we raised them as Comanches. Today, we have captives all over the place." Long ago *and* today rhetorical moves toward the then *and* now![102]

Thorshaug's decision for her and the other seeking visitor to be captured is a self-penned trap that signals the film's end but continues to raise more questions than answers. As she told me, "The filmmaker is also a character . . . who gets trapped. But trapped by who? By one's own expectation?" She stops short of clarifying whose "expectation" of whom or what: Comanches? Indigenous enterprise? Comanchería? When she asked her similarly unanswered and complicated "open question" of "who is shitting who," she added right afterward that "maybe I made my own trap," which suggests the filmmaker may have set herself up for captivity.[103] As director, she carries some agency over the speculative snare of that captivity, but it could be that the trap, in the *longue durée* of history, was centuries in the (film)making by both Comanches and non-Comanches.

In all *Comancheria* calls isa kwitapʉ on the nominal and

9. "Seeking Visitors" Marthe Thorshaug and Christian Falch tied to tree, in *Comancheria*. Courtesy of Marthe Thorshaug.

territorial foreclosures of the Comanchería and questions who is really running the show off-screen and on-screen between culturally and geographically grounded Comanches and newly arrived non-Comanche filmmakers, between cinematic Comanches and seeking visitors, between the Indigenous and non-Indigenous. To offer an alternative to Hollywood's isa kwitapʉ archives of Indians, *Comancheria* complicates dated public and anthropological expectations of performing "authentic" Indianness by privileging the real (the actors are really preparing for traditional ceremony) and the fictive (the actors are really playing roles for the camera). For Thorshaug both fact and fiction need each other for what she calls the "unpredictable mood" and "uncertainty" that she seeks against a U.S. nation-state founded "on the borderline between facts, fiction, propaganda, and myth."[104]

As Thorshaug traverses and complicates the borderlines, she says her making of *Comancheria* "is all about catching a certain spirit."[105] To capture that "spirit" of what it means to work with Comanche people and geographies sounds more open and complex than Hollywood's dated and rigid definitions of "Comanche." "Many viewers in Norway have told me," she explains, "they really got the feeling that the Comanches are back. That they are reemerging. It was this positive forward looking spirit I was after. Because this was the spirit I myself had glimpsed after all my visits in Oklahoma. And it was new to me, since I've mostly been confronted with a stigmatized negative image of contemporary Native Americans."[106]

Conclusion

That "Comanches are again expanding in the American Heartland," to recite an opening line from Thorshaug's film, extends to the ongoing representational expansion in Comanchería cinema. In 2016 my auntie, film consultant and producer Juanita Pahdopony, summed up the expansion: "We're trending right now!"[107] The expansion includes a growing number of dramatic and comedic films by Comanche filmmakers such as Dan Bigbee, Julianna Brannum, Rodrick Pocowatchit, Jason Asenap, Sunrise Tippeconnie, and Peshawn Bread. Significantly, like Thorshaug's *Comancheria*, Numunu films are filmed across Comanchería sites like Oklahoma, Kansas, and New Mexico. They are also grounded in history but depict contemporary Comanches doing contemporary, often funny things, however realistic and fantastic. For example, Dan Bigbee and Mohawk artist Shelley Niro's *Overweight with Crooked Teeth* (1998) humorously and directly challenges the isa kwitapu of stereotypes and misperceptions against Natives through the film's star, Mohawk poet Michael Doxtater. Rodrick Pocowatchit's *The Dead Can't Dance* (2010) follows Comanches playing Comanches in a zombie apocalypse where Natives are immune. Pocowatchit calls it the "first Native American zombie film! That we know of." Pocowatchit stars as a comedic Native superhero in *The Incredible Brown NDN* series (2019 and 2020), whose superhero power is, as he says, "representing." Jason Asenap's *Rugged Guy* (2012) and *Captivity Narrative* (2017) provide comical and engaging close-up looks at modern Natives. They include lead characters played by Asenap, moving about in search of self and, when Asenap's doppelgänger hilariously appears in *Captivity Narrative*, selves. Sunrise Tippeconnie's films also turn toward Comanche modernity and futurity, such as *Leave Durov to the Dogs: A Comanche Parable* (2011), which features siblings debating traditional and new ways of technology, and *Anticipation of Land in 2089* (2008), which reimagines the 1889 Oklahoma land run through Indigenous sovereignty over who takes what in a 2089 land run, where possibilities for hakaru maruumatu kwitaka abound. Tippeconnie also is the cinematographer for Peshawn Bread's *The Daily Life of Mistress Red* (currently in postproduction). *Daily Life* is a "mockumentary short film about a Native dominatrix for hire finding healing in whipping apologies out of her white supremacist clients."[108]

Recent representational expansion also comes from Comanche actor Gil Birmingham. In director David Mackenzie's *Hell or High Water* (2016), Birmingham co-stars as Alberto Parker (yes, Parker), a contemporary Comanche and Mexican Texas Ranger (yes, a Comanche/Mexican Ranger) instead of the usual nineteenth-century Comanche. He is a strong, multidimensional character with deep borderlands history, but unlike the Parker who caught the bank robbers on-screen in 1908, Birmingham's Parker eventually gets killed by the white bank robber. Originally titled "Comancheria" in its Comanche homelands setting of western Texas, *Hell or High Water* includes Comanche casino scenes with several paintings by my cousin Nocona Burgess, a direct descendant of Quanah Parker. Comanches star elsewhere in humorous independent short films, such as Daniel Pewewardy as a lonely man in search of love in Patrick Clement's dark comedy *Must Love Pie* (2020) and Eddie Morales gourd dancing in his kitchen with a pill bottle and oven mitt in the 1491s's *Represent: Gourd Dance* (2012).[109]

Mainstream representations still tend to focus on nineteenth-century Comanche history, but they come with increasing possibilities for added historical context and character development, especially with hired Comanche consultants and actors on set. *Magnificent Seven* (2016), set in the late 1870s, includes Martin Sensmeier (Tlingit) as Red Harvest, a Comanche and one of the seven title characters. In his first appearance Red Harvest exchanges Comanche words at length with star Denzel Washington's character—both of whom were taught their lines by Jhane Myers, the film's Comanche adviser—before proceeding with a number of violent on-screen encounters. Myers also served as cultural adviser and dialect coach for the period drama TV pilot *Monsters of God* (2017). The series, set in 1867, featured a U.S. colonel bent on killing all Comanches. The pilot was produced for TNT but did not air after the network dropped the project. Scott Cooper's *Hostiles* (2017), set in the early 1890, opens similarly to the early raid scene in *The Searchers*, with Comanches again attacking and killing white settlers. Comanches return later as a violent threat to the safety of co-stars Christian Bale, Rosamund Pike, and Wes Studi (Cherokee) in their group's travels to Studi's character's Cheyenne homelands in Montana. Positioning the violent portrayals in historical context, the film's Comanche consultant William Voelker applauded "everyone's willingness and openness to make every effort to get things accurate" but was a bit amused with how Cooper was initially "apologetic about the Comanche being perceived as ruthless." Voelker replied, "We don't try to candy-coat our history. The people were bloodthirsty. We lost everything, and we were very angry at losing our freedom."[110]

Comanche determination and survivance continue in the AMC television series *The Son* (2017–19), based on Philipp Meyer's Pulitzer finalist novel. *The Son* features well-developed Comanche characters, such as Lakota actor Zahn McClarnon's Toshaway, in a mid-nineteenth-century Comanche camp filmed near Austin, Texas, on what may have been an actual Comanche campsite long ago.[111] Also playing Comanches are at least twenty real Comanches from the Nauni, Weryackwe, Heminokeky, Nevaquaya, Cox, Kosechequetah, Komahcheet, and other Comanche families.[112] Most had attended casting calls at the Comanche Nation Tribal Complex in Oklahoma, which resulted from the dedication of Juanita Pahdopony, who served as technical adviser. That her presence also was prominent on the set of *The Son* is an understatement, as heartfelt tributes from her colleagues poured in after her passing in 2020.

From the Parker family silent films to modern-day productions like *Comancheria* and *The Son*, generations of cinematic Comanches, including actors, filmmakers, consultants, and critics, have long strived to self-represent even as others try to represent Comanches. The seemingly infinite possibilities in the media borderlands for telling the histories of centuries ago, today, and those still awaiting continue to expand and trend to challenge fixed, bordered scenes of a heterogenous people. The cinematic efforts of Comanches on-screen and off also continue to make marks in representational jurisdiction and challenge who is running the show in the ever-contested, ever-expanding sites of cultural production in the media borderlands.

During the silent-film era, the Parker family and Comanche homelands represented and refused to vanish. Even as U.S. westerns, led by their white heroes, increasingly filled the big screen and killed off the Indigenous, Comanches persevered and pervaded (colonizers might say "invaded") film narratives, from *The Plainsman* and *The Searchers* to *McClintock* and *Dead Man's Walk*. As one western wrapped up, another started, and ideas of Comanches, however distorted or doomed, were reproduced and rerun. Comanches were not to be forgotten in films where their presence loomed and frightened others with the possibility of a settler-colonial downfall. In recent decades real Comanches have increasingly returned on-screen to the Comanchería in productions sited in Oklahoma (e.g., *Comancheria*), Texas (e.g., *Texas Ranch House*), and elsewhere in expanded views of how Comanche people and places represent. Comanchería cinema is trending not only with non-Native filmmakers starting to listen again to Comanches but also with the creative input and output of self-determined Comanches creating, consulting, and critiquing media.

In the formations of Comanchería cinema, the casts, crews, and critics continue to portray, produce, and perceive the Indigenous; of course, not all directors, actors, and other cinematic agents share the same jurisdictional politics in how Comanches or any other people, for that matter, should be represented. The representational jurisdiction they and we seek may be, as noted at the start of *Comancheria*, the "something in the wind," yet the something can and does differ in the on-screen enactments of, and off-screen stances on, representation from film to film featuring the Indigenous. In effect, films in Comanchería cinema produce something in the wind, but beware: sometimes the something empowers and enlightens, sometimes it entertains, and, well, sometimes it reeks.

The mysterious something in the wind continues in the next chapter, where I report the story of a Comanche elder capturing/ adopting and making kin with an actor who happened to be playing an on-screen Comanche. The story moves not only into the production of a contemporary film co-starring a Comanche but also the production of a modern-day Comanche captivity narrative, in which the elder makes kin in the spirit and jest of traditional kinship practices. Note: Like in the making of Thorshaug's captivity narrative, chapter 2 may be best read by the light of a Comanche moon.

Kinship

A Captivity Narrative

We're gonna capture Johnny Depp.
—LaDonna Harris, 2013

On June 7, 2013, I called the Comanche elder Ladonna Vita Tabbytite Harris. We visited that afternoon across the airwaves of the Comanchería from Austin to Albuquerque. Harris, a champion for transnational Indigenous rights and star of Comanche filmmaker Julianna Brannum's PBS documentary *LaDonna Harris: Indian 101* (2014), reflected on recent deeply politicized events.[1] In early 2012 she had been reading about the controversial casting of Johnny Depp in the role of a Comanche Tonto in the forthcoming blockbuster reboot of the classic film and TV series. We spoke two weeks to the day before the Comanche Nation hosted an advance screening of Disney's and Gore Verbinski's western *The Lone Ranger* (2013). She heard of critics' suspicion and rejection of his longtime claims to Cherokee or possibly Creek ancestry, which were now amplified in response to Depp's playing Tonto. Even some self-identifying Cherokees in Depp's Kentucky birthplace did not support him. The skepticism of this Kentucky community is ironic, since some citizens of the federally recognized Cherokee Nation based in Tahlequah, Oklahoma, doubt the legitimacy of this group's claims to Cherokee identity.[2]

In addition to these already-vexed Cherokee contexts, Harris expressed concern about the Cherokee freedmen. They had recently been disenrolled from Cherokee Nation of Oklahoma citizenship by a referendum of Cherokee voters, in purported violation of an 1866 treaty.[3] At a time of "tribes disenrolling people" and adhering to U.S. blood-quantum standards as the primary criteria for citizenship, Harris said she "felt sorry for [Depp] because he got rejected."⁴ As someone, she says, whose own "relatives are captives"—her great-grandfather emigrated from Spain to Mexico, where he was captured by her tribal sister Iola Hayden's Comanche great-grandfather—Harris empathized with Depp's search for an Indigenous identity off-screen and appreciated his determination to showcase a Comanche character on-screen. So, she decided, as she audibly grinned a gesture of maruawe into the phone that day, to be like "real Comanche women: we're gonna capture Johnny Depp!"⁵

Harris's phrasing seriocomically recognizes the strength and determination of traditional Comanche women. With her use of "real," she positions herself in a cultural genealogy of recognized Comanches, or those whom Comanche Nation citizens and descendants already acknowledge as fellow Comanches, as compared to fictive Comanches like Depp's imagined character of Tonto. At the same time she playfully undermines authenticity debates on what constitutes "real Comanches" in a popular discourse that often confines the "real" Indigenous to the distant past. Moreover, mainstream media largely negates representational space for Indigenous women and, when it does show Comanches, privileges hypermasculine warriors of the nineteenth century.

On May 16, 2012, Harris adopted Depp, thus inverting the formulaic on-screen capture of white women by Indian men in Hollywood westerns like the fictive Comanches in John Ford's *The Searchers* (1956). Harris and her "captive" also became co-stars of a modern-day Indian captivity narrative.⁶ Published Indian captivity narratives are accounts of, and often written by, non-Natives captured by Natives dating back to the 1600s. In general, the "captivity narrative," Kathryn Zabelle Derounian-Stodola explains, "encompasses any story with a captor (usually from a minority group) and a captive (usually from a majority group)." Derounian-Stodola observes that "the Indian captivity narrative is arguably the first American literary form dominated by women's experiences as captives, storytellers, writers, and readers." There is, for example, Mary Rowlandson's best-selling 1682 book *A True*

10. LaDonna Harris in traditional Comanche clothing. Photo by Wakeah Vigil (Comanche). Courtesy of Americans for Indian Opportunity.

History of the Captivity and Restoration of Mrs. Mary Rowlandson.[7] Or, for the first publication in Texas by a former captive of Texas-based Natives, there is former Comanche captive Rachel Parker Plummer's 1838 account, *Rachael Plummer's Narrative of Twenty One Months Servitude as a Prisoner among the Commanchee Indians.*

In contrast to the narratives written or inspired by white female captives of Native men, the Harris-Depp story comes with an authorial twist: Harris co-writes her captivity account of Depp. Nineteenth-century Anglo-Comanche captives Rachel Plummer, Nelson Lee, Sarah Horn, Herman Lehman, and siblings Theodore "Dot" Babb and Bianca Babb Bell authored or co-authored published captivity narratives, and Tejano Comanche captive Macario Leal gave his recorded account in 1854.[8] Their Comanche captors did not. Harris's take on the adoption represents the Indigenous captor's perspective. She redirects the conversation and opens space not just for recognizing Comanche representation in a movie but also for centering Comanche perspectives in the discourse about Depp's controversial role as Tonto. Ultimately, as Harris intercedes and complicates the conversations between competing camps either supporting or protesting production of *The Lone Ranger* and Depp's Tonto, she constructs an irremovable Comanche imprint on both the Comanchería and Hollywood that effectually declares, "Comanches were here. Comanches are still here."

Lone Ranger producers had decided early on to make Tonto a Comanche, thus eliminating "mystery regarding which Native American nation Tonto belongs to."[9] Executive producer Jerry Bruckheimer explained, "It made complete sense to us geographically, historically and culturally that since the Lone Ranger is from Texas, Tonto should have been born into the great nation that had lived on those lands for generations: the Comanche."[10] Asked if it was important to incorporate Indigenous culture into the film, executive producer Chad Oman similarly replied, "Absolutely. I'm from Wichita Falls, Texas, which is the heart of Comanche territory and around where the movie is set."[11] Although Bruckheimer's rationale for Tonto's nation depends on the Lone Ranger's home, he and

Oman recognize the historical borderlands power of Comanches over other tribal possibilities. However, once Harris captured Depp off-screen—and as the film's Comanche consultants recognized and embraced Depp's Comanche-specific role and Comanches engaged the fictional Tonto's Comanche affiliation—tribal specificity became more significant in Indian Country discourse, and Tonto's Comancheness increasingly transcended its representation in the film's fictional 1870s account. "Comanches," including Comanches and others' imagined ideas of who Comanches were and are, became a much bigger part of the conversation about Depp and Tonto.

This chapter analyzes contemporary Comanches' contributions to the Indigenous identity controversy resulting from Disney's "decision to assign the role of the Indian character Tonto not to an actor unquestionably Native but to Johnny Depp."[12] Adopting a storytelling approach grounded in tribal traditions and values, I recognize "cinematic Comanches" like Depp's Tonto not only as on-screen performers and characters but also as off-screen cultural critics and social actors who, like Harris, maneuver through thorny layers of representing the Indigenous. *The Lone Ranger* built on to the representational resurgence of screening and writing "Comanches" into the U.S. imaginary discussed in chapter 1, but the film's production also prompted possibilities for Indigenous intervention into representational reclamation both on-screen and off. Specifically, I ask how Harris and other cinematic Comanches created opportunities to assert self-determination and make kin with Depp, build relations with Disney, and expand the convoluted discourse on producing Comanche representation and cultural knowledge.

Continuing Comanche efforts to claim shares of representational jurisdiction, both Harris's decision to adopt and the adoption itself represent the Comanche tradition of performing a legacy of agency. As she later reported, she told Depp, "Since no one claimed you, and since you are playing a Comanche, I want to claim you [to] be our Comanche."[13] From generation to generation this legacy has been embodied and enacted by Comanches who construct and narrate their own histories and intervene in others' narratives about Comanches, be they already federally recognized or celluloid or otherwise. As an elder who adopted Depp, Harris established a cross-cultural relationship representative of what anthropologist Mary Weismantel calls "making kin," a process informed by Indigenous cultural and familial protocol on constructing relationships not wholly dependent on biological definitions of kinship.[14] In *LaDonna Harris: Indian 101*, Harris explains, "relationship is the kinship obligation" in which "everyone/everything is related to us *as if* they were our blood relatives." "Reciprocity is the cyclical obligation" that "is based on very long relational dynamics in which we are seen as 'kin' to each other."[15]

By rhetorically recasting the adoption as captivity, Harris invoked Comanche history and asked the public to reorient their attention toward the Comanche kin-making tradition of taking captives. Comanches' borderlands economy of taking captives, as historians James Brooks, Brian Delay, Joaquín Rivaya-Martínez, and others illustrate, was integral to repopulating and strengthening the tribe.[16] In the 1830s and 1840s alone, Comanches captured hundreds of Mexicans. Some were sold, but the majority reportedly stayed. "Most captives," Delay argues, "eventually became family," which "strengthened not only the Comanche economy, but also the community itself." Continuing a history of the "captive-turned-Comanche phenomenon," Harris brought Depp into her family.[17] In effect, she expanded what anthropologist Christina Gish Hill calls the "kinship web," in which relationships are built on "reciprocity, and the respect inherent in it."[18] "Harris views relationships," Chickasaw scholar Amanda Cobb once wrote, "as an ever-widening spiral" with "all things as being part of a web of relationships."[19]

Harris's traditional Comanche worldview of relationships and reciprocity form a foundation from which to conceptualize and actualize the capture of a Hollywood celebrity. Rather than suggest that Harris and certain other Comanches had simply "gone

Hollywood" with Depp and Disney, I contend that Comanches made moves toward bringing Depp into Comanche ways of cultural kinship relations. Rather than work from biological relations or the U.S. government–imposed blood-quantum system, Harris recreated a traditional mode of kinship in the twenty-first century. She took Depp in as a son to honor his on-screen efforts, to build and develop relationships, to express Comanche self-determination in kinship, and to increase the cultural capital of the Comanche Nation. Harris also built on to the traditional Comanche view of familial capital. "Comanches always felt," she says in *LaDonna Harris: Indian 101*, "a form of wealth is to have relatives, relatives who looked after you and cared for you."

Before returning at length to a Comanche way of making kin, I provide some of the backstory leading up to the adoption. First, I present an Indigenous critique of Disney's pre- and early-production hype of Depp's Tonto in news and social media. Then I focus on the cultural politics and reception of the adoption and conclude with thoughts on postadoption collaborative events between Comanches, Depp, and Disney. In all I work with what media scholar Jonathan Gray calls "entryway paratexts," the prefilm release texts that "hold considerable power to direct our initial interpretations" and that "draw many of the battle lines that surround media consumption"—in this case of *The Lone Ranger* and its Comanche representations. As textual entities that address or relate to the main "text" (usually the actual film) under consideration, entryway paratexts (e.g., Harris's adoption of Depp, Disney's promotional materials, and social media posts) become significant sites of making meaning and assumptions about a movie and its characters long before its official release in theaters.[20]

Resurrecting Tonto

To account for what trained the media spotlight on Depp's characterization of Tonto, I turn to the moment when Disney and Depp officially announced their new role. On September 24, 2008, nearly two thousand movie industry insiders and reporters crowded into the Kodak Theatre in Hollywood for the Walt Disney Studios Showcase to catch the latest news and sneak previews of forthcoming movies. Amid pomp and circumstance for their audience, Disney unveiled production plans for such films as *Princess and the Frog, Cars 2*, and *Toy Story 3* and screened footage of forthcoming films *Up, Bolt*, and *Race to Witch Mountain*. The most prominent spotlight, staged during the event's finale, belonged to Johnny Depp. Disney chair Dick Cook announced the "Depp trifecta" of roles, including reprising Capt. Jack Sparrow in a fourth installment of *Pirates of the Caribbean* and the Mad Hatter in *Alice in Wonderland*.[21] The other role for "the main man at the Mouse House" seemed to confound everyone.[22] As the University of Southern California marching band played the classic *Lone Ranger* theme music, Gioachino Rossini's *William Tell Overture*, Depp appeared onstage dressed as Jack Sparrow with the iconic Lone Ranger mask.

Afterward Disney confirmed that Depp would play not the title character in the new reboot of *The Lone Ranger* but Tonto, arguably the most celebrated and condemned Indigenous American character of all time. The Tonto of the mid-twentieth century is celebrated for his righteous principles, Hollywood stardom, and TV portrayal by the Mohawk actor Jay Silverheels in the 1950s but is condemned for his sidekick subordination, pidgin English, and ideological submission to the white Lone Ranger and, by extension, white America. Tonto was an empowering and rebellious "Uncle Tomahawk" all rolled into one character, as embodied and projected by Silverheels, a highly respected Native actor in Indian Country. "Although I've never met an Indian who admired Tonto," Comanche critic Paul Chaat Smith reflects, "I've also never met anyone who had an unkind word for the actor who played him on television."[23] The conundrum shows Native reception both associating and distinguishing between a fellow Native and his on-screen role. For his decades of work and dedication to improving Indigenous roles, Silverheels became the first Native actor to receive a star on the Hollywood Walk of Fame in 1979.

For Depp Tonto represented a significant chapter of his child-hood, during which he saw "the great Jay Silverheels" play a character "getting the unpleasant end of the stick" in the Lone Ranger–Tonto relationship.[24] "Why," Depp recalls asking himself, "is the f—ing Lone Ranger telling Tonto what to do?"[25] Depp therefore set out to change the power dynamic by giving Tonto far more agency and wit than previously allotted in Hollywood. He even used the character's name in his musical moniker Tonto's Giant Nuts on the soundtracks for Robert Rodriguez's *Once upon a Time in Mexico* (2003) and Depp's executive-produced documentary *West of Memphis* (2012).

The Hollywood press's initial reactions to Depp's decision to rep-resent Tonto carried relatively little fanfare when first announced in 2008. Some reporters briefly expressed shock ("I never saw this coming," wrote one reporter); misunderstanding ("Johnny Depp is playing The Lone Ranger," said the same writer); and borderline indifference (buried late into an article titled "Johnny Depp Is Back as Captain Jack" is the afterthought, "He'll also be Tonto in a *Lone Ranger* movie").[26] Other news sources tidily skirted over the contentious politics of race and blood quantum in Indian Country and justified the casting decision by meshing Depp's off-screen and on-screen identities. Upon learning Depp is "going to play Tonto," one site's contributor exhaled, "I'm glad he's part Cherokee so there's more basis to this pick."[27] MTV UK similarly reasoned, "Alas, Johnny won't be rocking a white cowboy hat, he's set for the role of trusty sidekick Tonto. Depp's grandmother was a full blooded Cherokee and Johnnys [*sic*] embraced his native American roots before in his self-directed movie *The Brave*," in which he stars as an Indigenous character.[28] For a while Depp's IMDB bio curiously included "some Navajo as well."[29] Although many consider Depp predominantly white despite the actor's self-identification as Indigenous, such fleeting nods to Depp's purported Native ancestry affirm casting him in the role of the unequivocally Indigenous Tonto.[30]

Native media critics tended to show more insight into the

politics of on- and off-screen indigeneity. Writing for the former site NativeVue, Carol Levine questioned, as many Natives did, why someone "from the flourishing crop of talented Native actors" was not cast. She responded to her casting question by collapsing multicultural talent and blood: "Yet, let's be honest, there isn't an actor of any ethnic background who could add the savoir faire to the patently uncool Tonto that Depp can. And lest we forget, he is of Native blood and has always proudly acknowledged this."[31] For the Caddo critic Michael Sheyahshe, casting Tonto requires more than "Native blood." Citing the IMDB biographical references to Cherokees and Navajos, Sheyahshe respectfully complicates the conversation with a pointed but rarely asked series of inquiries to actors claiming indigeneity: "While [I] do not dispute his ethnicity [including Indigenous ancestry] in any way, I must question whether [Depp] is actually a part of these Native communities. Was he raised near one of the tribal communities . . . ? Did he have relatives that demonstrated specific Indigenous culture to him? Has he taken part in . . . tribal communities, either socially, culturally, or ceremonially?"[32] Rather than shut down the debate about Depp's claims to Native ancestry, Sheyahshe expands it into a tribal-specific and, generously, a pan-Native realm.

Critic Ungelbah Daniel-Davila (Navajo) argues that the "crux of the issue is not that a non-Native is playing Tonto, but that Tonto continues to exist." Personally, when I first heard the news in 2008 that Depp would play Tonto, I blogged about Native actor Gary Farmer and his co-starring role with Depp in Jim Jarmusch's post-western *Dead Man* (1995). "Perhaps," I speculated wildly, "Farmer will re-appear as a pseudo-Lone Ranger in whitefaced disguise and take out the subservient Tonto once and for all?"[33] Daniel-Davila writes, "I'm glad Depp was cast as Tonto and I can't think of anyone better to portray him. Tonto is a character that is and always has been a simulation of indigenous-ness." "For a 'real Indian' to play Tonto," she adds, "would be a disgrace, and I'd like to believe that no self-respecting Native actor would have chosen that role."[34]

Cree actor Adam Beach, though, did express strong interest in the role. As a First Nations co-star of *Smoke Signals* (1998), *Flags of Our Fathers* (2006), *Law and Order: Special Victims Unit* (2007–8), and other film and TV productions, Beach told Canadian talk show host George Stroumboulopoulos, six months before *The Lone Ranger* was released, that he "wanted to [portray Tonto] really bad" and had auditioned for the role about a year earlier. After saying Depp's early performance in *21 Jump Street* inspired his acting, Beach expressed support and jovial resistance for Depp's casting as Tonto. Depp is "well respected by everybody, so everybody says, 'yay!' [flashes thumbs up], but for me," he grins, "I'm like, 'Man, stay away from my territory.'" Respectfully calling out the *Twilight* series and the casting of its main Native character, Beach says, "The lead guy [Taylor Lautner] is supposed to be a Native American, but he's not. And it's nothing against his performance. But . . . you can't give that message to Native people to say, 'You are not good enough to be a lead-role status in our trilogy.'"[35]

In all the early reports from news outlets in the media borderlands offer a sneak preview into the emergent voluminous discourse surrounding the film, including the subsequent unsettling and simplistic approval of the casting for some (generically framed as "Johnny Depp says he has Indian blood, end of story") and disapproval for others ("Johnny Depp is not of Indian people, end of story").

#TheLoneTonto

During Disney's paratextual hype of *The Lone Ranger*—beginning with announcing the film in 2008 to the film's trailers in 2012 and 2013 to its premiere in summer 2013—a new precedent may have been set in terms of the volume of Indigenous critique concerning a film. Before the days of Twitter and Facebook, Kevin Costner's Lakotas in 1990 and Michael Mann's vanishing Mohicans in 1992 garnered considerable Indigenous praise and ire. Now, along with Stephanie Meyers's topless *Twilight* wolf pack in 2008 and James Cameron's ten-foot-tall blue Na'vis in the 2009 *Avatar*, Verbinski's and Depp's representation of Tonto would soon captivate and repulse Native peoples on social media.

After the initial surprise at Depp's casting as Tonto faded, social media chatter concerning the character's representational indigeneity was relatively quiet until four years later, when a lone production photo began to circulate. On March 8, 2012, executive producer Jerry Bruckheimer tweeted the first publicity pic of Depp as Tonto on location in Albuquerque—where he would become a Comanche captive just two months later. The photo ignited a major firestorm of critiques and confusion in Indian Country. In contrast to previous thinly headbanded, heavily buckskinned Tontos, Depp sported a crow headdress atop a broad Southwest-style headband and white face paint with black horizontal stripes. "This isn't going to be your grandfather's Lone Ranger and Tonto," Bruckheimer tweeted the day before.[36] A month later Depp publicly confirmed in an *Entertainment Weekly* exclusive what some critics had already suspected about his character's visual inspiration: "I'd actually seen a painting by an artist named Kirby Sattler, and looked at the face of this warrior and thought: 'That's it.'"[37] Depp and his makeup artist Joel Harlow were searching one day for "images on the Internet of warriors" when they were "struck" by Sattler's painting, called *I Am Crow*.[38] Depp knew the bird flew behind the Native figure's head in the painting, but the actor decided, "Tonto's got a bird on his head. It's his spirit guide in a way."[39] To quote the TV series *Portlandia* and its catchphrase of two fictional interior decorators, Depp "put a bird on it."[40]

Right after Bruckheimer's tweet came news headlines such as "Johnny Depp as Tonto: How Racist Is That?" and "Stunned by Tonto: A New and Improved Version?"[41] Twitter raged with the spreadable power of hashtags.[42] Facebook feeds overflowed. "Android phones lit up across Turtle Island," wrote Paul Chaat Smith, "as we stared at the glowing screens and prepared to render judgment."[43] Across the Comanchería and social media, my tribe, my relatives, and my friends agreed, disagreed, agreed to disagree, and all the standpoints in between about the new Tonto.

In sum the discourse swirled into an ambivalent ebb and flow of expressed excitement and outrage, delight and disgust, and curiosity and disinterest.

Retweeted more than seven hundred times, "filtered to over 1.6 million web pages," and reprinted in countless publications and social media posts, Bruckheimer's pic drew swift reactions.[44] Upon seeing the photo, Lakota journalist Dana Lone Hill claimed, "There was going to be a stir—an uprising, perhaps—among the American Indian community's social networks."[45] Cherokee critic Adrienne Keene called it a "horrific image" in her blog post "Johnny Depp as Cultural Appropriation Jack Sparrow . . . I mean Tonto."[46] "That bird," Navajo writer Natanya Ann Pulley wrote in her "An Open Letter to Johnny Depp's Tonto," "might pluck your eyes out, man. The moment it hit my Facebook newsfeed the updates from my friends went nutso."[47] "In rapid succession," Paul Chaat Smith recalled thinking it was "outrageous, shocking, wait, is that a bird?, and okay, pretty fabulous."[48] *Indian Country Today* writer Ray Cook (Mohawk) countered by calling the "Tontomania" clamor a waste of time, in his divisive and dismissive argument that media representations do not matter in comparison to more pressing issues like health care and poverty.[49] A year later filmmaker Chris Eyre (Cheyenne-Arapaho) similarly reflected on the Tonto "debate" in Indian Country as a "ridiculous use of our time" since, he contended, *The Lone Ranger* is "just entertainment."[50] Eyre's observation suggests frustration with the polarizing discourse after, in 2012, he had recognized it and called for a deeper dialogue. "It's too easy to bash this," the filmmaker said of Depp's Tonto. "There's too many shades of grey. And it's unintelligent to not look at Depp's relationships with Native actors and his contributions to Indian country."[51]

Discourse about Depp's Tonto on Twitter and other sites and Comanche-centered events with Depp challenged Cook's dismissal and Eyre's frustration with cinematic conversations in Indian Country. *Lone Ranger* discussions had the potential "to advance the conversation" on the current state of Indigenous portrayals.[52]

Recognizing the remake of a Hollywood film and TV franchise known for historically marginalizing Natives, numerous critics perceived a continuation of Disney's problematic history with Indian representations, such as in *Peter Pan* (1953) and *Pocahontas* (1995).[53] Critics also called attention to Disney's casting yet another actor not readily recognized by most as undeniably Native to play an undeniably Native co-starring role. Critics cognizant of the history of performing indigeneity in the United States accused the production of appropriation and redface in casting Depp—despite reports he may be, however remotely, Native.[54] The bird headpiece was not helping matters.

In accordance with Hollywood's historically loose, racialized standards for passing as Indian, Disney had green-lighted Depp's decision to play Tonto after learning he would not play the white title character. The corporate approval joined a representational economy of examples, such as Chuck Connors's title character in Arnold Laven's *Geronimo* (1962), Taylor Lautner's Jacob Black in Catherine Hardwicke's *The Twilight Saga* (2008–12), Charles Bronson's Harry Starr, a Comanche, in the *Bonanza* episode "Underdog" (December 13, 1964), and, for double the fun, William Shatner as twin Comanche-Anglo brothers in Razzie recipient José Briz Méndez and Gilbert Kay's *White Comanche* (1968). Other examples include white characters "gone Native" like star and director Kevin Costner's Lakota character in *Dances with Wolves* (1990), Daniel Day-Lewis's Hawkeye in Michael Mann's *The Last of the Mohicans* (1992), and Sam Worthington's Jake Sully in James Cameron's *Avatar* (2009).

The conversation about Depp's Tonto also turned to his relations with the Navajo Nation, where *The Lone Ranger* began filming scenes as Bruckheimer tweeted the photo. On April 12, just ten days before public confirmation of Tonto's visual inspiration and tribal affiliation, Navajo Nation president Ben Shelly and vice president Rex Lee Jim went on set in Monument Valley and gifted Pendleton blankets to Depp, Armie Hammer, Bruckheimer, and Verbinski. Navajo Nation surgeon general Dr. Gayle Diné Chacon appeared too, to give Depp a leather pouch adorned with a symbolically protective arrow. As Indigenous hosts, the Navajo Nation took and released photos of Depp shaking hands with Shelly and standing with Chacon. The story was picked up by news sources like *Indian Country Today* and *People*, and the press circulated the photos, which were met with reactions ranging from enthusiasm for coming together to accusations of Disney using the Navajos for self-gain.

The tribe's Broadcast Services and its director Kee Long had generously granted the filming privilege to Bruckheimer and Disney, an important reminder of Indigenous territorial jurisdiction. As Bruckheimer told *Navajo Times* reporter Cindy Yurth, many Navajos worked on the film or behind the scenes as "extras, production assistants, drivers and security guards." He referred to Navajos as very "gracious, friendly and wonderful" and acknowledged "what a privilege it has been" to film in Diné Bikéyah/Navajoland.[55] In appreciation to Navajo leadership, Depp later quietly donated $25,000 to the Office of Navajo Nation Scholarship and Financial Assistance. In their letter of response to Depp, Shelly and Jim "appreciated the time you took to listen. We appreciate that one issue you took to heart was our Nation's youth and ensuring they would see a prosperous future unfolding for them."[56] Depp's new relations with the Navajo Nation inspired the "Johnny Depp Zone" fan club to reach out. Each year on Depp's birthday, the club donates funds to a charity that they believe Depp would support. In 2012 they gave $7,750 to the volunteer organization Project Pueblo, which teams with the nonprofit Forgotten People to bring running water and solar lights to the Bennett Freeze area of the Navajo Nation. Depp replied in kind, "Having spent some time with the beautiful people of the Navajo Nation, I am sure that your efforts here will prove to be hugely influential and in admiration of your continued benevolence, I will be making a donation for the very same purposes in your name."[57] Forgotten People president Raymond Don Yellowman (Navajo) said his organization was "pleased to see the generous donation," which he called a "great gift to the future generations of our Navajo people."[58]

Amid the gift giving, handshakes, and photos between Navajos, Depp, and Disney and the subsequent critiques, something else quietly unfolded on set in Navajoland. Two months after Bruckheimer's lone Tonto tweet traveled the world's electronic networks came news about a lone Comanche, who once was likened to the masked Lone Ranger for bringing social and political justice to Indian Country and prompting U.S. politicians to ask, "Who was that woman?"[59] Set to "capture" Johnny Depp in spring 2012, LaDonna Harris arrived from Albuquerque to the nearby *Lone Ranger* set in Puerco Valley. Through William Voelker and Troy, the on-set Comanche consultants for *The Lone Ranger*, she had reached out to Depp, who in turn invited her to visit the set. After conversing with the actor, Harris reciprocated by inviting him to her home, where she captured and adopted Depp into her maternal Comanche family at a private traditional ceremony. "I reached out," Harris recalls, "and Johnny was very receptive to the idea."[60]

Around thirty-five people attended, including her daughter Laura Harris, staff from their nonprofit organization Americans for Indian Opportunity (AIO), and Verbinski, Bruckheimer, and Disney publicist Michael Singer. As Laura Harris explains of the adoption ceremony, "We didn't send out a press release." She adds that the adoption "wasn't Disney's idea. This was solely my mother's idea." She also cites the late Winnebago tribal leader Reuben Snake as saying, "Every Indian ought to adopt one white person just to teach them and help them to learn about our experience in the United States."[61] The sentiment reflects the lifelong intercultural bridge-building work of the elder Harris, who previously adopted former president Richard Nixon adviser Bobbie Kilberg and also worked with TV producer Norman Lear and actors Max Gail, Candice Bergen, Alan Alda, Mike Farrell, and others.[62]

Voelker and Troy led the adoption ceremony and gave Depp the name Mah-woo-meh, a fitting name from the Numu tekwapu, or Comanche language, for the actor to embody and represent the rest of his days, both on-screen and off. One English translation of Depp's name is "He can change."[63] As Depp's new Comanche *pia*, or "mother," Harris also explained, Mah-woo-meh can mean "shape-shifter." The name evokes the actor's ability to "change into all of these entities," including his shift to a Comanche character in *The Lone Ranger*, which at the time of the adoption was still in production.[64] To determine Depp's real-life Comanche name, Voelker and Troy worked at the cultural confluences of on-screen and off-screen realities as Comanches, by performing a traditional naming ceremony, and as film consultants, by carrying forth a tradition of producing cinematic Comanches for the camera.

Just two days after the adoption ceremony, guitar legend Carlos Santana released his album *Shape Shifter* "to honor the First People of the land."[65] *Shape Shifter* is all the more relevant here because its cover art depicts Comanche artist Rance Hood's painting *Coup Stick Song* (1980). Raised by "his maternal grandparents, who taught him Comanche ways and values," Hood has been an accomplished artist since the early 1960s.[66] The art on Santana's album features a warrior on horseback singing of "how many coups he will touch in battle, with his coup stick."[67] In 2008 Comanche artist Apryl Allen released her album *Na Unu Nahai (Shape Shifter)*, which features songs in both Comanche and English. Some tracks include spoken word by Comanche elder Videll Yackeschi, whose brother Bud taught my first Comanche-language class years ago in Walters, Oklahoma. As another name for shape-shifter in the Comanche language, *Na Unu Nahai* represents Allen's efforts to honor her Comanche legacy, as she notes, "in the best way she can, through her music."[68] When translated as shape-shifter, Mah-woo-meh suggests a further reconfiguration and reclamation by Comanches of a name often popularly relegated to fictive stories in Hollywood, like writer Tony Hillerman and director Chris Eyre's shape-shifting Navajo witches in *Skinwalkers* (1986, 2002) and writer Stephanie Meyers and director Catherine Hardwicke's shape-shifting Quileute wolf pack in *Twilight* (2008).

Mah-woo-meh is a creatively apt moniker for an actor known to perform variable looks, sounds, and movements through his decades of cinematic characters. The roles of the "Hollywood shape-shifter," as CNN once dubbed Depp, range from the animated Edward Scissorhands (1990), demon barber Sweeney Todd (2007), and eccentric chocolatier Willie Wonka (2005) to *Alice in Wonderland's* Mad Hatter (2010); *Pirates of the Caribbean's* Jack Sparrow (2003); *Dark Shadows's* vampire Barnaby Collins (2012), which premiered just six days before Depp's adoption; and the color-changing chameleon *Rango* (2011), for which the film's director Gore Verbinski called his star "the real-world chameleon, Mr. Johnny Depp."[69] As Mah-woo-meh started filming the reenvisioned cinematic Comanche named Tonto in 2012, the actor admitted, "I have . . . many voices in my head. There are a lot of characters in there."[70]

Contrary to critics who presumed Depp entered uncharted territory as Tonto, the actor's filmography represents long-standing relations with cinematic indigeneity. In his self-directed film adaption, *The Brave* (1997), Depp shape-shifts into Native character Raphael in an impoverished Indian community. Long before reshaping Tonto, Depp, with his brother Dan, worked on *The Brave* script and refashioned Raphael from the novel's "stupid drunk Indian" into an intelligent and sober Indigenous character. The film co-stars Marlon Brando, who Depp calls a "great mentor, father and friend."[71] Depp attributes his learned understanding of cinematic Indigenous injustice from Brando. "I learned more about this through . . . Brando," Depp says, that "in the history of cinema, the Native American has been portrayed as a savage."[72] In *The Brave* Depp also worked closely with Cody Lightning (Cree), who plays Raphael's son. Cayuga actor Gary Farmer says that Depp and Lightning "formed a real bond" on set. "My time on that set was so special," Farmer remembers, as he saw "Johnny be a dad to Cody" a year before Farmer played Lightning's father in the Native film *Smoke Signals* (1998).[73]

In Jim Jarmusch's postwestern *Dead Man* (1995), Depp and Farmer join together as a somewhat inverted Lone Ranger–Tonto duo in a nineteenth-century anti-Indigenous American West, or "hell," as one character bluntly puts it. Farmer's tribal outcast, Nobody, finds Depp's character, William Blake, a meek accountant, wounded from a gunshot and wanted for killing the gunman. Mistaking Blake for the famous British poet reincarnated and whose poetry he studied as a child in a colonizing boarding school, Nobody leads the accountant on the rest of his dying journey away from bounty hunters and into becoming, he tells Blake, "a killer of white men." He tells Blake that a gun, not a pen, will be his new weapon, as "your poetry will now be written with blood." Throughout *Dead Man* attempts to challenge the ideas of historically unjust Native representation, which Mah-woo-meh too was "trying to reshape . . . and retell," Farmer once said, "with a new vision" for Tonto and other old stories.[74]

Depp's ties to other on-screen Indigenous relations date back to the actor's screen debut in *Nightmare on Elm Street* (1984). Depp plays white teenager Glen Lantz, who eventually succumbs to the bladed hand of Freddie Kruger. Depp's character subtly positions himself with ideas of Nativeness through non-Natives' visual and musical texts of Indigenous subjects. Lantz's bedroom wall art includes Edward S. Curtis's famous 1903 photograph of Chief Joseph, the Nez Perce leader popularized for his "I will fight no more" speech. Nearby is a poster for the white Australian band Midnight Oil, long known for singing songs concerning Indigenous injustice, such as their Top 40 hit "Beds Are Burning," about returning land to the Pintupi people in Australia.[75] Since early in his career, Depp himself posed for publicity shots in an "American Indian Movement: Still Strong" T-shirt. Depp's alignment with indigeneity also recurs through his tattoos, from his first one in 1980 of a Native male "chief" in a headdress to honor Depp's ancestry to the three tattoos he added soon after his adoption into Harris's family in 2012 of a zigzag, a snake symbol (Comanches are known by some as the snake people), and the Comanche seal to recognize his honorary Comanche status.[76]

Additional Indigenous relations continue to play out on-screen. In Michael Mann's *Public Enemies* (2009), Depp's gangster character, John Dillinger, dates Marion Cotillard's Menominee French character, Billie Frechette. Inspired by the real-life relations between Dillinger and Frechette, Cotillard, a French actor, prepared for the role by visiting the Menominee reservation.[77] At one point in the film, Cotillard's character tells Depp's Dillinger she's Menominee. "Most men don't like that," she reflects, to which he suavely replies, "I'm not most men." In Emir Kusturica's surrealist French American film *Arizona Dream* (1993), co-starring Depp, Jerry Lewis, and Faye Dunaway, an opening dream sequence shows a loving Inuit family in their Alaskan igloo. The camera cuts to New York, where Depp's lead character, Axel, awakes from the dream. In a voice-over Axel speaks the film's first words of English: "'Good morning, Columbus.' These were my mother's eternal words reminding me that America was already discovered and that day-dreaming was a long way from life's truths." In *Arizona Dream*, filmed during the quincentenary of the Italian explorer's first (in)famous voyage, her words could imply she greets her son as a settler continuance of the colonizer Columbus, yet the line richly reroutes popular "day-dreaming" perceptions of Columbus as discoverer.[78] Like Depp told reporters twenty years later at *The Lone Ranger* premiere in Russia, Natives were "originally called the human beings before Columbus f—ed up and called them Indians."[79]

Depp also played characters prone to Columbus-inspired "Indian" talk. In *Finding Neverland* (2004) Depp portrays real-life British playwright J. M. Barrie and his relationship with a family that inspired his creation *Peter Pan*, including who Barrie called "savages," and Disney's 1953 film version, which produced the stereotypical song "What Made the Red Man Red?"[80] Depp's Barrie dons a stereotypical Indian headdress at a dinner party and later wears a feather and headband and speaks broken English in a game of cowboys and Indians.[81] In Verbinski's animated animal western feature, *Rango* (2011), Depp's title character, a bumbling and eventually heroic chameleon, becomes sheriff of an old western town. At one point he compliments his deputy Wounded Bird's "Injunuity . . . no pun intended." Gil Birmingham (Comanche descendant) plays the deputy who comes from the "Crow Nation," a precursor to Tonto's headpiece and a problematic name, given the sovereign Crow Nation in Montana.

At Mah-woo-meh's adoption ceremony, Harris and many other Comanches (though certainly not all) embraced the actor as a new relative and respected his new name as recognition of the actor's *puha*—a Comanche term for "medicine," "personal strength," or "talent"—in entertaining the masses through a host of characters. Continuing the Comanche tradition of expressing gratitude, Harris provided gifts to her new son, who in turn gave them to attendees at the ceremony, including AIO employees and Comanche artist Nocona Burgess, whom Depp once called "a wizard with a paintbrush."[82] Depp deemed his own new name "quite apt" and felt "great pride in that choice." "[The adoption] was an honor beyond all honors," Depp said afterward.[83] The actor and father of two compared the "ceremony itself" to "something [almost] as intense as the birth of my kids."[84]

Among those attending was the late Johnny Wauqua, chair of the Comanche Nation at the time, who read the following proclamation:

Whereas the tradition of sovereignty of the Nʉmʉnʉ [Comanche people] since time immemorial long predates the existence of the United States; and whereas the historic Nʉmʉnʉ practice of taking captives is a long standing and vital tradition of the Nʉmʉnʉ; and whereas Numu Wiape [Comanche woman] LaDonna Harris on behalf of her Tabbytite family has called forward a man of extraordinary talent and Tubitsi Puha [True Medicine] of unique entertainment spirit who has enriched millions of people through the world, I, Johnny Wauqua, Chairman of the Comanche Nation do hereby call forward Mr. Johnny Depp, here and after known by the Nʉmʉnʉ as "Mah woo meh" taken this day as a ceremonial member of the Tabbytite/Harris family and do further call upon Mah woo meh, also known as Johnny Depp, to serve as the Goodwill Ambassador of the Comanche Nation (Schonchin).[85]

Harris and Depp sincerely appreciated Wauqua's unexpected proclamation and recognition. The tribal chair's wording is embedded
within Comanche nationalist and familial discourses of sovereignty,
captivity, medicine, and kinship responsibilities. His rhetoric illustrates the propensity for Comanches' critical-creative meshing
of the on-screen and off-screen realms, as well as Comanches'
"flexibility of membership," to borrow from borderlands historian
James Brooks, in historical and modern contexts.[86]

As critics and proponents in Indian Country and the United
States added to the hype surrounding Depp-as-Tonto, Harris calmly
entered the fray and through, as Wauqua says, "the historic Numunu
practice of taking captives," complicated matters by adopting Depp
as her son and thereby blurring the identity politics of indigeneity and the tribal-specific politics of performance. An astute
off-screen actor, Harris acted neither to legitimate the actor's
ancestral claims as "Cherokee or maybe Creek" nor to appease
or anger critics whose arguments and counterarguments regarding
Depp's Tonto portrayal hinge on his ancestry and appearance.[87]
Instead, she captured him in expressive agreement with a tribal
legacy of agency, which contrasts to misleading media reports
that either omitted the names of those who decided or stated that
Disney planned the adoption.

The adoption also entailed acts of teasing and humor that are
not meant to detract from the seriousness of ceremony. When asked
to account for why she adopted Depp, Harris responded with a
line that humorously resonates with the importance of Indigenous
representation. Harris said with a grin, "We made him a Comanche
so he'd act like one."[88] A classic line from a classy Comanche,
it represents how acting is not confined just to cinema and the
arts. In everyday vernacular people say things like "Act right,"
"Act your age," "Don't act up," and "Get your act together"—all
said with jurisdictional convictions of what constitutes (in)correct
behavior. But Harris's line, including the analogous word "like,"
bridges the off-screen and on-screen in a way that destabilizes
static definitions of acting in a role as only on-screen, and acting

Comanche as only having one off-screen way of being. In the documentary *LaDonna Harris: Indian 101*, she says absolute truth is nonexistent "in the Comanche philosophy because everybody was an individual. But people can't understand how you can be an individual and be collective at the same time."[89]

In *LaDonna Harris*, directed by Comanche filmmaker Julianna Brannum and produced by Comanche captive Depp, Harris shows her own political "acting" skills. A biopic about Harris's Comanche upbringing, marriage to former U.S. senator Fred Harris, political activism across the United States, and global Indigenous networking, Brannum's film showcases Harris's implementation of "Indian 101" to educate U.S. politicians on federal Indian policy. Harris recalls, for example, asking a prominent U.S. politician to support an Indigenous forum she was planning. "I don't think we can do that," he replies, "but tell me, can you people vote?" When she and two friends in the room "burst into laughter" to call isa kwitapʉ (Comanche for "bullshit") on his ignorance, Harris explains, "It embarrassed him so that he did fund us."

As acts of building relations and kinship, Harris repeatedly taught Indian 101 lessons at her dinner parties, where she assembled senators, tribal officials, grassroots leaders, and movie stars—in short, "anyone that might have an impact on Indian policy." "You always had a great time and socialized and laughed," Michael Mahsetky (Comanche) says in Brannum's film, but "bottom line: LaDonna wants to make sure that these people leave her house knowing about the current Indian issues" and "how they could have a role" in effecting change. Harris also called out mining companies' exploitation of impoverished tribal communities. When tribes and the federal government did not know the percentage of Indigenous-owned energy resources, she made up statistics: "35 percent of all the coal west of the Mississippi and 75 percent of all uranium in the country was on Indian land." "Everybody believed her," her daughter Laura Harris remembers, "because there was nobody to dispute her." "It turns out," she adds, "she was actually right." For Native nations to gain control over their lands' resources, Harris formed the Council of Energy Resource Tribes, a multi–Indigenous-nation consortium on tribal interests.

Even after decades of activism and building relationships, some still couldn't understand why she adopted Depp. Harris counters, "Why not adopt him?"[90] That concise comeback represents a form of resistance from Natives who are repeatedly asked to explain actions deemed outside of popular expectations of performing Indianness. She confounds those trying to reconcile romanticized Comanches of the past with modern-day Comanches and their eclectic communicative and performative sovereignties. Replacing the "why" with "why not," Harris performs agency by asking listeners to understand the adoption as a continuance of Comanche tradition, foreclosing their desire to unfairly question the sovereign right of Comanche self-determination over who can be accepted into one's family.

Harris's decision to capture a global celebrity like Depp in the twenty-first century harkens back to the sociopolitical savvy, agency, and creativity that sustained Comanches as a borderlands superpower, built on a multitude of practices including taking captives, Harris's ancestors among them. For Harris, "Welcoming Johnny into the family in the traditional way was so fitting. He's a very thoughtful human being and throughout his life and career, he has exhibited traits that are aligned with the values and worldview that Indigenous Peoples share."[91] In these days of always-connected, always-on digital media, when sounds and images and ideas are incessantly produced and disseminated, Harris both stays current in the media climate and recognizes what it means to be culturally and politically astute by continuing the old Comanche tradition of capturing and adopting non-Comanches. At a time when some tribes disenroll their citizens and cling to scientific fictions of blood quantum as the sole citizenship criteria for Comanches and other nations, she calls for circling back to older ways of understanding Comanche kinship responsibilities while creating new opportunities for a future of respectful interdependence.

News media hyped the private ceremony and communicated

surprise, if not shock waves, across Indian Country, the United States, and the world. To cinematic Comanches, however, Comanche relationships with Hollywood celebrities were nothing new. As discussed in chapter 1, generations of Comanches have worked in film, in front of and behind the camera, from Quanah Parker and his children in early silent films to Comanche filmmakers and consultants today. Comanche Nation officials also have hosted invited Native actors, such as Adam Beach, Gary Farmer, Irene Bedard (*Pocahontas, Smoke Signals*), Chaske Spencer (*Twilight, Winter in the Blood*), and Rudy Youngblood (Comanche star of *Apocalypto*) and non-Natives Mel Gibson (director of *Apocalypto*), Chuck Norris (*Walker, Texas Ranger*), and Peter Weller (*Robocop*). Comanche relations extend elsewhere too, such as when LaNora Parker, Quanah's great-granddaughter and Nocona Burgess's mother, adopted Native musician Micki Free. In politics Vermont senator Bernie Sanders visited Comanches at the Comanche Nation Fair in 2019. Sanders called it a very moving experience.

Comanches also come up in celebrity discourse of potential relations that might have been. Following Harris's well-known adoption of Depp, actor Leonardo DiCaprio entered the captivity conversation. After he recognized Indigenous peoples and Indigenous land rights in his 2016 acceptance speech at the Golden Globes awards show for his performance in *The Revenant* (2015), Nocona Burgess posted in social media, "Comanches call dibs on DiCaprio!" A Comanche would have surely called dibs on Kevin Costner if he had not moved film production of *Dances with Wolves* from Oklahoma, where the original novel was set, to South Dakota, because of its higher buffalo population. Sicangu Lakotas adopted Costner instead at the 1990 Washington DC premiere of the film. After Larry David, the creator of *Seinfeld* and *Curb Your Enthusiasm*, took a DNA test on *The George Lopez Show* in 2009 and was bizarrely told he is "37 percent Native American," he was stunned. He asked Lopez, "What do you mean? I'm a Comanche?"[92] Of all the Native nations, the native New Yorker first picked Comanche. If the consumption of media—from Hollywood films and television series to award-winning popular history books and novels—is any indication, then Comanches have become serious contenders for the honor of being the most famous, or infamous, Natives in the U.S. imaginary. In his 2013 novel *The Son*, adapted into a popular TV series on AMC with Comanche adviser Juanita Pahdopony, Philipp Meyer summed up the captivation when one of his nineteenth-century Comanche characters declared to a new white captive in his camp, "Everyone in the world wants to be Nʉmʉnʉ."[93] Sure, it's literary hyperbole, but such sentiment illustrates the centrality of Comanches in the U.S. imaginary, not to mention in the Comanche imaginary, marked by a profound insider pride and strength in being Comanche.

Comanche adoptions of actors do have a longer history. Closely corresponding to Harris's adoption of Depp, for example, the late Baldwin Parker, grandson of famous Comanche leader Quanah Parker, adopted soap opera star Maree Cheatham (*Days of Our Lives* and *General Hospital*) in the early 1980s. The daughter of a Muscogee Creek mother and Choctaw/Scots-Irish father, Cheatham had "dreamed as a child of being carried away by an Indian."[94] After growing up hearing stories of Quanah Parker, she was honored to be brought into the Parker family for her portrayal of Baldwin's great-grandmother Cynthia Ann Parker, Quanah's white captive mother, in a Parker family pageant written by the late Vincent Parker—who, incidentally, also went to Hollywood to make a feature film about his great-grandfather Quanah. In pageant performances in the 1980s, including the first in a rodeo arena in Cache, Oklahoma, Cheatham wore a dress sewn by Comanche elder Anna Tahmahkera, who also gave Cheatham a Comanche name.[95]

Despite Comanches' cinematic and televisual history of relations, Harris's decision to privately adopt Depp in her home became another source of public controversy, conflict, and confusion over how family, tribe, and Hollywood claim to represent themselves and indigeneity. Reactions varied, to say the least. Many recognized Harris as an undisputed elder and longtime champion for Indigenous rights who enacted her sovereign right to capture.

Choctaw author and filmmaker LeAnne Howe aptly deems it "a case where art becomes life. Depp plays Comanche and is then adopted by respected Comanche elder LaDonna Harris."[96] Brannum calls Harris's adoption of Depp "strategic and brilliant" for bringing increased recognition to Comanches and Indigenous initiatives.[97]

For some there was no gripe with Harris, but rather a concern that her actions excused Depp from critique and legitimated his controversial casting as Tonto. As Adrienne Keene says of the adoption, "It's really complicated for me" because Harris is "very well respected in Indian country. But my reaction is mixed, because I feel like others will say the adoption excuses Johnny from any sort of criticism for his portrayal of Tonto."[98] For example, if Comanches like Harris and Wauqua embrace Depp in his Comanche role, the logic goes, then who are non-Comanches to say otherwise? Yet for some Comanches, the Harris-Depp relationship was not enough to fully excuse Depp. In his op-ed for the *Wichita Eagle* newspaper in Kansas, Comanche filmmaker Rod Pocowatchit thinks it is "cool to say that Depp is now one of my tribal brothers" but adds that Comanches and others should protest Depp being cast as Tonto and that "an unknown native [should] have the part."[99] Disney, however, would likely have never green-lighted *The Lone Ranger* blockbuster without Depp as a principal actor and executive producer and without his proven box office draw.

Other Indigenous critics lambasted Harris and chalked up the adoption to a publicity stunt. Right after the adoption in May 2012, the Blackfeet author and musician Gyasi Ross wrote, "Johnny Depp has never done anything for Native people and was adopted 100% on the basis of his celebrity status." "We need to stop being groupies and," he advises in a rhetorical encroachment on individual tribal sovereignty, "start having some standards about our Nations."[100] Over a year later, perhaps wanting to finally shut down the conversation, the Rosebud Sioux citizen Sonny Skyhawk wrote an article for *Indian Country Today*. Founder of the advocacy organization American Indians in Film and Television, Skyhawk calls the adoption "a farce and a photo opportunity for LaDonna Harris and nothing more." He also groups together the Indigenous casting of Depp's Tonto, Filipino American actor Lou Diamond Phillips's Cheyenne character on the Netflix series *Longmire* (2012–17), and Puerto Rican actor Benicio del Toro's Blackfoot title character in Arnaud Desplechin's feature film *Jimmy P: Psychotherapy of a Plains Indian* (2013). He then turns to the problematic colonized criteria of Indian blood quantum for authenticating indigeneity and Native cinematic roles. Both Depp and Phillips claim Cherokee ancestry. Both also were adopted, partly in response to their on-screen Indigenous roles—Depp by Comanches with *The Lone Ranger*, Phillips by Lakotas in 1991 with *Young Guns I* (1988) and *Young Guns II* (1990) and by Northern Cheyennes in 2014 with *Longmire*.[101] Skyhawk, though, cites Del Toro as perhaps "the only one of the three that has indigenous blood. Just sayin'."[102] Not said by Skyhawk is the significance of the adoption to Depp and many Comanches. Nor does he, like Ross and Cook, see larger, long-term possibilities for Comanches and other Native peoples inspired by Harris's actions.

Observing the battle lines of praise and protest over the captivity, Comanche filmmaker and writer Jason Asenap calls for a moment of culturally reflective pause in his op-ed "In Defense of Comanches": "Let's all of us, in Indian Country, take one big collective deep breath now." More pointedly, he calls for non-Comanche "naysayers" unfamiliar with Comanche history to recognize the tribe's "long history of taking captives and making them Comanche." Citing the whiteness and Indianness of Comanche celebrity Quanah Parker, Asenap adds, with tongue in cheek, "when cavalry soldiers were being chased by Quanah they didn't stop and ask for his Certificate degree of Indian Blood" to prove he is Comanche.[103]

For Asenap the captivity of Depp "is a grand opportunity for Indian Country to build bridges of communication." Depp "gets an opportunity to learn about a tribe who accepts him and his goodwill and heart," and the Comanche Nation "gets to have a say, albeit a small one, in how they can be portrayed in the future by having opened this line of communication." Following Harris's commitment to making kin, Asenap says, "I welcome the notion that Depp will now keep in mind his new Comanche family." In his call for respecting Comanches' communicative sovereignty in relation to the representational politics of Comanche and Indigenous portrayals in film, Asenap suggests that Harris's act of adoption may mark not simply a case of Comanches gone Hollywood but rather the "beginning of a beautiful friendship and dialogue" in Indian Country.[104]

Postcaptivity

Both relationships and communications continued to develop in a subsequent series of prefilm release interactions between Comanches and Depp, all of which were set into motion by the actor's commitment to his Comanche-specific character, Voelker and Troy's consulting work on *The Lone Ranger*, and Harris's captivity of Depp. The first major event occurred four months after the adoption and nearly four years to the day after Disney announced Depp would play Tonto. On September 29, 2012, the tribe hosted Depp at the twenty-first annual Comanche Nation Fair at the tribal complex just outside of Lawton, Oklahoma. Comanche Nation chair Wallace Coffey, who calls Harris his sister, recalls Depp asking him, "'Ah-tah [Comanche for "uncle"], will you not advertise it?' I said, 'Word of mouth?' He said, 'Word of mouth.'"[105] Most non-Comanches did not know, but news traveled quickly among Comanches, who showed up in droves to the parade, though such attendance is common each year. The actor served as grand marshal at the fair's annual morning parade. Seated next to Harris in a new convertible Chevy Camaro on a very rainy day, Depp waved to hundreds of onlookers with one hand and held an umbrella over his adoptive mother with the other. Then, upon Depp's request, he visited with Comanche youth and their parents for a two-hour question-and-answer and autograph session. Young Comanches asked questions like "Why are you so sexy?" and "Will you come back to visit?" To the latter he replied, "Of course." Depp also encouraged the youth to work hard and embrace their ancestral "warrior spirit" to achieve their dreams. As Dana Attocknie (Comanche) reports in closing, "Depp made time to shake hands, take pictures and lift up little kids to take pictures after he spoke."[106]

Led by Harris throughout the day, Depp had lunch at Sia (Comanche for "feather"), an eagle aviary and feather repository operated by *Lone Ranger* consultants Voelker and Troy; visited historical Comanche leaders Quanah Parker's and Ten Bears's grave sites; met Fort Sill's commanding general; and exchanged gifts with Coffey and Harris. "He didn't go anywhere without LaDonna. He loves LaDonna," observed Asa Attocknie (Comanche).[107] As part of the adoption/captivity and his acceptance into Harris's family, Depp received traditional Comanche clothes from Coffey. As Depp's *ara* (uncle) in a Comanche web of kinship, Coffey explains, "I completed that cycle of adoption by putting [Comanche] clothes on him." He says the clothes "identify him as being part of a Comanche family."[108] Following maruawe-like protocol of one reporting for another, Coffey also asked Comanche actor and Comanche Nation Fair guest Gil Birmingham to be a "witness" to the dressing. In return Depp gifted his own painting of Quanah Parker, which now hangs in the Comanche National Museum and Cultural Center. In all the actor stayed "focused on Comanches" the entire time, Brannum attests. He "never once took out his phone" as she, Harris, and others hosted their new relative.[109]

Over the next several months, more hype and protest of *The Lone Ranger* unfolded. The first trailer debuted on October 3 during the week after Depp's Comanche Nation Fair visit. Subsequent trailers premiered in December 2012 and April and May 2013. In April 2013 Depp delivered "greetings and salutations" in a prerecorded message to attendees at the thirtieth annual Gathering of Nations powwow in Albuquerque. Seated in a room adorned with lit candles, guitars, and Alice Cooper memorabilia and wearing a jacket embroidered with the name "Mah-Woo-Meh," he spoke of his new relatives: "I received so much in being adopted by the Comanche Nation under the guidance of my amazing Comanche *pia*, the beautiful LaDonna Vita Tabbytite Harris, and, of course, the late chairman Johnny Wauqua. It is also an honor unlike any I've ever known to spend time with the new chairman Wallace Coffey, the brilliant William Voelker and, of course, Troy from Sia."[110]

In May Disney collaborated with the American Indian College Fund (AICF) to sell tickets at $1,000 each to an advance screening of *The Lone Ranger* in Anaheim, California, with all of the revenues going to support Indigenous students. AICF president Cheryl Crazy Bull said her organization was "pleased to be the beneficiary of this event because our scholarships are an investment in a healthier, more prosperous future for tribal students and their families."[111] Reactions to Disney's community-outreach efforts ranged from viewing it as genuine goodwill to deeming it shameless self-promotion for trying to boost box office numbers. What went relatively unknown was Harris's push for the AICF collaboration. As Laura Harris recalls, Depp "asked us advice about things," including ways to give back to Indian Country. She cites Disney's initial intent to donate the Anaheim ticket sales to the Make-a-Wish Foundation, but LaDonna and Laura Harris spoke with Depp and "were able to change that to the American Indian College Fund."[112]

On the day before the Anaheim showing, Depp returned to Lawton on the summer solstice of June 21, 2013, for an advance screening of *The Lone Ranger*. After months of planning the Comanche Nation—mainly its elected officials of the Comanche Business Council and the director of Special Projects, Donna Wahnee—attracted Hollywood celebrities, Indigenous dignitaries, and a global media spotlight on the longest day of the year. My cousin Julianna Brannum and I drove in that morning from the part of the Comanchería known as Austin, Texas. Following Interstate 35 to Highway 287 in Fort Worth to Interstate 44 in Wichita Falls and Lawton, we went straight to the Comanche Nation–hosted luncheon at the Best Western Hotel, located next to the Comanche Nation Casino and, at the time, the Comanche Nation Tourism Center in Lawton. Coffey emceed the occasion, with speeches by professional boxer George "Comanche Boy" Tahdooahnippah, lieutenant governor of the Chickasaw Nation and then president of the National Council of American Indians Jefferson Keel, Navajo Nation president Ben Shelly, Disney executives, and others.

Later limousines arrived to the hotel en route to Carmike Cinemas, carrying Coffey, Harris, Depp, Bruckheimer, Verbinski, and *The Lone Ranger* Indigenous actors Birmingham and Saginaw Grant (Sac and Fox). In nearly triple-digit temperatures, they walked the red carpet to the theater's front doors, as Wild Band of Comanches, one of the most recognized drum groups in North America, sang songs for the large crowd and to honor Depp, whom they called their Nʉmʉ pavii, or Comanche brother. Harris and Depp walked arm in arm a few steps behind Coffey and his wife, Debra, and ahead of *The Lone Ranger* entourage. Then Depp stayed outside for nearly two hours, visiting with fans and fielding questions from reporters. "It really does feel like home after being here last year," he reflected at the premiere. "It's good to be back. The Comanche people really welcomed me into their nation."[113] Finally, Depp joined Coffey and his *Lone Ranger* colleagues inside the theater, where he reciprocated by welcoming hundreds of Comanche attendees to the premiere in each of the screening rooms. On behalf of the tribe, the Coffeys and Wahnee presented signature Comanche Nation blankets to Depp, Birmingham, Grant, Verbinski, and Bruckheimer.

By the next day photos of Depp on the red carpet traveled the Associated Press wire around the world. Numerous photographers had attended, but one stood out in staking a Comanche claim to representational jurisdiction. Credit for a photograph of LaDonna Harris and Johnny Depp walking arm in arm went to "HAUS/AKM-GSI." The latter is short for AKM Images and GSI Media. HAUS is short for professional Comanche photographer and my cousin Marc Hausman. A son of *The Son* consultant Juanita Pahdopony, Hausman captured Depp's image on film and further added to cinematic Comanches' contributions amid *The Lone Ranger* hype. Comanches were framing the publicity from the inside out.

From the luncheon to the premiere and its photographed

11. LaDonna Harris and Johnny Depp, at *The Lone Ranger* premiere,
Comanche Nation. Courtesy of Marc Hausman and BackGrid photo agency.

aftermath, Comanches ran the show that day. Through a Comanche-hosted advance screening of a movie starring a Comanche character portrayed by a Comanche captive, Comanches curated the day's festivities. When I asked Coffey how the Disney premiere in Lawton came to be, he replied, "I asked." It was part of the then tribal chair's efforts to "develop a relationship" with Disney.[114] "It took a lot of work for us," Coffey said of the tribe's off-screen efforts to showcase the on-screen, "just to convince Disney that this needs to be done." "Indian Country," he continues, "needs to be given consideration to a special screening, not just the fact that it's a Lone Ranger movie but that it has a Comanche presence."[115] As one reporter in attendance concluded, the premiere capped "off a significant chapter for the Comanche Nation, which lent a lot of information and technical support for the making of *The Lone Ranger*."[116]

Conclusion

Depp's visits to Oklahoma would likely not have happened without LaDonna Harris's captivity of the actor—without her making kin with a cinematic Comanche. Like the legacy of agency performed by Quanah Parker and other Comanche leaders before her, Harris carries on the long-standing tradition of engaging pop culture and Hollywood celebrity. With every captivity by Harris and other twenty-first-century Comanches' contributions to cinematic discourse and performance, the descendants of the eighteenth- and nineteenth-centuries' Comanche empire strike back against colonial forces that wished the Indigenous to be vanished and destroyed. Today's Comanches, descended from a borderlands superpower, move from cultural survival and preservation to creatively and fluidly continuing the art of making kin. Recognizing the ancestral agency of her people as a borderlands superpower, Harris sends forth a critical and creative message to all: if one uses the Comanche name, then expect Comanches to confront, critique, celebrate, or otherwise engage them. In short, expect Comanches to take notice and, sometimes, even captives.

Expect Comanches, too, as evident from the volume of involvement in and around *The Lone Ranger*, to take notice when movie producers attempt to represent Comanches and bring representational visions of justice to the big screen. At the premiere in Lawton, Comanches practically filled the five screening rooms that simultaneously showed, after years of hype and protest, *The Lone Ranger*. We turn next to that night. From that solstice night in Comanche country, I recount how Comanches saw Comanches on-screen pursuing representational justice as Mah-woo-meh, Tonto, and *The Lone Ranger* rode across the media borderlands in the newest chapter in Comanchería cinema.

CHAPTER 3

Performance

Seeking Representational Justice

> The Lone Ranger: If we ride, we ride for justice.
>
> Tonto: Justice is what I seek, Kemosabe.
>
> —*The Lone Ranger* (2013), directed by Gore Verbinski

On June 21, 2013, just before the lights went out at the Comanche Nation film premiere of Disney's *The Lone Ranger* in Lawton, Oklahoma, in walked numerous cinematic Comanches to each of the five screening rooms already filled with Comanche viewers. Comanche Nation chair Wallace Coffey and *Lone Ranger* executive producer Jerry Bruckheimer, director Gore Verbinski, and actors Johnny Depp, Saginaw Grant (Otoe-Missouria), and Gil Birmingham (Comanche descent) filed in to thank everyone for attending. Coffey also discussed Depp's adoption into LaDonna Harris's Comanche family and how, as Depp's new uncle in the Comanche kinship web, he dressed the actor in traditional Comanche clothing to complete the adoption. Coffey then asked "brother Gil," as he called Birmingham, to say a few words to their people. The Comanche descendant, who assisted in dressing Depp and played Comanche warrior Red Knee in *The Lone Ranger* after collaborating with Verbinski and Depp in the 2011 animated feature *Rango*, stood alongside his cinematic relations and looked out at the all-Comanche audience. After cracking a joke that "it was a true honor to see Depp in his skivvies," Birmingham got serious for a moment. "I hope," he says of *The Lone Ranger*, "we've done justice for our people."[1]

Birmingham articulates an enactment of maruawe. In a communicative exchange between cinematic Comanches of actors and audience, Birmingham greets and reports back to Comanche people, who applaud in response to his desire for on-screen justice

12. *Left to right:* Jerry Bruckheimer, Gore Verbinski, Saginaw Grant, Debra Jo Childs Coffey, Wallace Coffey, Johnny Depp, and Gil Birmingham at *The Lone Ranger* premiere, Comanche Nation. Courtesy of Marc Hausman and BackGrid photo agency.

for off-screen people. The Comanche-to-Comanche moment is intimately set in belonging and community, where Birmingham represents a Comanche actor with both tribal ties and Hollywood experience. In 2014 the Comanche Little Ponies Society, including my relatives Benny Cable and Benny Tahmahkera, honored Birmingham by welcoming him into the warrior society, which opens powwows with Comanche gourd dancing to honor veterans.[2] Like Depp's expressed deep appreciation for being adopted into a Comanche family, Birmingham says he feels "tremendous gratitude and a distinct privilege to be honored by the Comanche Little Ponies Society." Cable, among the Comanches who dressed Birmingham in gourd-dancing regalia, recalls that the actor was "humbled and proud to be accepted."[3] As a Comanche actor with dozens of TV and film credits—from his debut as a bodybuilder in a Diana Ross music video (1982) to his Native characters in *The Lone Ranger* TV movie (2003) and *The Twilight Saga* (2008–12)—Birmingham is well aware of the politics of casting and performing Native characters, including the advance mixed and contentious reactions to Disney's

The Lone Ranger and Depp's Tonto. In response he told Comanches at the premiere, "I know Johnny's full intent was thoughtful and respectful all the way along . . . with this portrayal for an iconic character."[4] Notably, Birmingham's hoped-for justice is paired with a subsequent recognition of Depp's intent, not necessarily a defense of Depp's performance.

Birmingham's expressed hope for justice through *The Lone Ranger* starts to uncover a lens into the dichotomous tension between intent and performance, which is at the core of this chapter's cinematic inquiry about *representational justice* in the film's production of portraying indigeneity, namely Comanches. I imagined Depp's intent, too, as heartfelt and had hoped to see justice delivered on-screen since the news broke in 2008 that Depp would play Tonto. At the same time, given the problematic history of Indigenous characters in feature films, I also did not expect too much from a Hollywood system that skewed indigeneity and wanted to reboot an eighty-year-old *Lone Ranger* franchise notorious for Indigenous injustice with its marginal, monosyllabic sidekick Tonto.[5] I went in to the Comanche Nation premiere with ambivalence and, perhaps predictably, emerged from the screening with ambivalence. Following the late cultural theorist Stuart Hall's encoding/decoding model of reading representations, the result, for me, became a *negotiated* stance, which tries to recognize where producers and principal actors are ideologically and performatively coming from (encodings) and how the performative implications of their ideas and intentions play out on-screen (decodings).[6]

In this chapter a Comanche-centered critique of the film and its on-screen performativity of "Comanches" take center stage. With negotiated ambivalence in tow, I travel through the media borderlands to consider where the film works and where it comes up short in representing justice. Personally, I like Comanche critic Marti Chaat Smith's concise characterization: *The Lone Ranger* has its "moments."[7] In efforts toward representing Comanches justly in the film (and in these pages), I translate the moments as on-screen Comanche agency, complexity, and nuanced cultural citations and details, all of which are significant but unable to overthrow the film's larger preoccupation with upholding systemic ideas of Indigenous erasure and settler-colonial superiority.

Disney's 2013 version follows similar story lines from *The Lone Ranger* intertextual history and its essential elements (e.g., the Ranger's silver bullet) along with updated citations from previous westerns and added Comanche-specific moments.[8] With a rather conventional plot and unconventional Comanche lead, the first film opened in 1933 in San Francisco, the same year *The Lone Ranger* debuted on radio. From inside a Wild West show's diorama, a very elderly Tonto comes to life and narrates, in flashback, his late 1860s adventures in Comanche territory/Texas with young lawyer John Reid, portrayed by Armie Hammer, whom Tonto transforms into the masked Lone Ranger. The two fight, as director Verbinski puts it, "for justice in a very unjust world." The unjust include the villainous partners Latham Cole, a railroad magnate, with whom he calls the "notorious outlaw and Indian killer" Butch Cavendish. In the pursuit of colonizing power and capital, the pair seeks to control the Transcontinental Railroad and extract silver by train from Comanche country. To protect their unlawful assets, they massacred Comanches years earlier after befriending Tonto as a boy who naively showed them the silver in exchange for a pocket watch. Years later Cavendish and his gang ambush and kill Texas Rangers, including John's brother, Dan Reid. They leave John Reid for dead. Tonto, now a traumatized outcast seeking revenge for his people, heals Reid, as he did in the original TV series in 1949. Cole later recruits the U.S. Cavalry, led by Capt. Jay Fuller, a vain General Custer–like character, to join him in illicitly securing the silver and killing the rest of the Comanches standing in the way. To usurp Comanche lands Cavendish's gang also raids white settlements, including Rebecca Reid's (Dan's widow), disguised as Comanches, to build anti-Indigenous sentiment and break a peace treaty between the tribe and the United States.

Bound by their shared contempt for the men responsible for killing their relatives, the title character and Tonto, in classic *Lone*

Ranger fashion, eventually defeat the villains. They "ride for justice," as Reid says, and save the day, but for whom and whose interests? The film critiques ruthless U.S. capitalism and military force again the Indigenous, but the depicted Comanches are gone, save for the Comanche outcast Tonto, and the white settlers continue building and populating their towns on expropriated Comanche homelands. As the late Patrick Wolfe once wrote on the "logic of elimination" of Native peoples, "settler colonizers come to stay: invasion is a structure not an event."[9] In *The Lone Ranger*, with the elimination of Comanches, the settlers expand their reach (with the help of Tonto and the Ranger) toward further transforming Comanche territory into a majority-white Texas. In line with my ambivalent reading of the film's performativity of Comanches, how does *The Lone Ranger* support and disrupt the "structure" in representing the Indigenous and settler in the Comanchería media borderlands?

In response I address representational justice and injustice in the film's interpellated scenes of Comanche history through the lens of intertextual Comanche citations. By Comanche citations I mean a genealogy of what informs the discursive and visual representations of the film's Comanches set against Comanche cultural history and a Hollywood territorial backdrop long fraught with white producers' claims to jurisdiction over marginalized Indigenous representation.[10] I filter the coding of Comanche citations through the film's representations of Comanche rhetoric (in English and, thanks to the Comanche consultants William Voelker and Troy, the Nʉmʉ tekwapʉ [Comanche language]), raids (by non-Comanches playing Comanche and playing off of Comanche raiding history), and massacres (of on-screen Comanches, twice), all centered around whom I identify as the film's four Comanche bands: (1) the outcast Tonto rejected by his Comanche people as a "band apart," or outcast; (2) the outlaws Cavendish and his gang playing Comanche raiders in disguise; (3) Tonto's silenced and massacred childhood female band; and (4) Chief Big Bear's ousted male band who also performs a rapid vanishing act on-screen.

I conjoin these four bands into a conversation on justice and injustice of who and what signifies late nineteenth-century Comanches in the narrative of the twenty-first-century *Lone Ranger*. Rather than group all Comanches into one tribal monolith, I opt for a "band" analysis modeled on our tribe's internal band structure, to illustrate a more nuanced reading of Indigenous representations and their heterogeneous relationships with one another. In comparison to a nation or tribe as a sovereign collective entity, bands are smaller sovereign units generally demarcated by groups of families, within the nation, inhabiting particular areas together. Here the bands are remixed into on-screen representational groups of "Comanches."

To account for producers' intent and implications in performing portrayals of "Comanche" bands, I read the representations intertextually by migrating through the media borderlands of textual influences on *The Lone Ranger* to expand analytic possibilities in what Thais Morgan dubs an "apparently infinite play of relationships with other texts" and Richard Bauman describes as the "relational orientation of a text to other texts."[11] Instead of solely confining analysis to the 149 minutes of footage in *The Lone Ranger*, this multitextual method considers the production of Comanches through what John Michael Corrigan calls Verbinski's "intertextual collage of metacinematic tropes that informs and structures the film's narrative frame."[12] Like interculturality in first contact histories between cultures in the borderlands, intertextuality is, following Mikhail Bakhtin, "a dialogic contact between texts" in which, Julia Kristeva adds, "any text is constructed as a mosaic of quotations" and the "absorption and transformation of another" text.[13]

In the dialogic back-and-forth, I continue to practice maruawe by reporting on representational jurisdiction through both a tribal-specific lens and the "inescapable interdependence" of intertextuality.[14] Although narrowing in on the tribal specificity of Comanche representation may sound restrictive and bordered, the approach opens up hermeneutic space and possibilities in the media borderlands to reshape and undermine the symbolic borders of critical interpretation of a tribe and film. In this case *The Lone Ranger* is read through an intertextually eccentric series of moments in search of justice in the Comanchería borderlands.

Representational Justice

Although no book or film can fully recreate history, writers and filmmakers go forth to tell their takes on the past. "Everyone from historians to novelists to Hollywood directors," Juanita Pahdopony and Brian Daffron once observed, "try to depict or re-enact the Comanche in battle. Yet, can any of them truly do the Comanche justice?"[15] This chapter is no exception. The on-screen cinematic Comanche battles in warfare, words, and other enacted signifiers in *The Lone Ranger* prompt the question of what constitutes the performance of "Comanche" in the name of representational justice and injustice.

Justice, however, is a highly subjective and slippery term for what counts, by and for whom, as just and fair. One need only look at a history of Native America and the complex entanglements between federal, state, and tribal sovereignties to know that administered justice to one may be grossly unjust to another. Where, for an obvious example, is justice for Native peoples in the U.S. history of forced displacement and land theft? In *Lone Wolf v. Hitchcock* (1903), the U.S. Supreme Court ruled in favor of Congress and its bid to exercise plenary power in going against the 1867 Treaty of Medicine Lodge. The court ruled that the United States has jurisdiction over Indian lands and supported Congress' decision to open up two million acres of land to settlers, all of which, according to the 1867 treaty, belonged to the Kiowas, Comanches, and Apaches.[16] Examples such as this one abound and beg the question, to quote the late John Trudell (Santee Sioux) in a CNN interview, "How did my land become somebody else's country?"[17]

Recognizing a "radical heterogeneity of justice discourse" in contestations involving nation, sovereignty, race, gender, and class, Nancy Fraser asks, "How do we know which scale of justice is truly just?"[18] Or as historian Waziyatawin asks, in the context of tribal-state-federal relations, "What does justice look like?" For her Dakota people and Dakota homelands, it means "reparative justice" through truth telling of genocidal history, confronting contemporary sites and systems of celebratory colonization, returning the land to Native peoples, relocating the people back to the land, and "creating an oppression-free society" of "sustainable, healthy, and peaceful co-existence" for all.[19]

African American art historian Sarah Lewis asks of photography and mediated optics, "What does it take to work toward representational justice?" Situated at the "nexus of vision and justice" through African American visualities, representational justice for Lewis implies practicing critical "visual literacy." It involves the "effort to craft an image to pay honor to the full humanity of black life" and "to affirm the dignity of human life."[20] "Honor" and "dignity" are also two recurring terms in Depp's expressed sense of justice. Yet their performativity can play out in very different ways, not surprising, given diverse experiences, sensibilities, and idiosyncrasies of artists and other human beings. One's intent to honor by representation does not always align with its reception. Otherwise, "Indian" mascots and racist monikers like "R—sk—" would still be all the rage across the United States.

In conversation with Lewis, Palestinian filmmaker Kamal Aljafari similarly talks of "cinematic justice" as a process of representational reclamation. Such justice, for Aljafari, means "reclaiming cinematic territory that was taken away from us [Palestinians]" by Israel. In his 2015 film *Recollection*, for example, Aljafari works with previous Israeli film footage of Jaffa in Tel Aviv. Gil Hochberg calls it a "citational engagement with these Israeli cinematic fantasies" to express a "subversive imitation" of colonial imagery. In *Recollection* Aljafari keeps the land on-screen but visually erases the Israeli actors and centers, in close-ups, the marginalized Palestinians who had occasionally showed up in the background of Israeli film frames. In her analysis of Aljafari's films, Hochberg talks of the filmmaker's "cinematic justice" as a "model of repair that involves exposing the failure of the colonial fantasy to do away with the colonized, who not only continue to invade the cinematic frame, but who move further from its margins to its centre."[21]

The models of justice by Waziyatawin, Lewis, and Aljafari call for centering, humanizing, and healing their respective peoples through deep cultural recognition, principles, and creativity. Representational justice for cinematic Comanches is similarly ambitious in scope. It involves centering Comanches in production, performance, and perception against a cultural history of unjust, colonizing portrayals, but through whose epistemological "scale of justice" are Comanches represented? In *The Lone Ranger* producers encode liberal intentions of justice in representing Comanches through their expressed off-screen objectives to honor Native peoples on-screen, to reconfigure Hollywood Indigenous portrayals, and, in effect, to reshape public perceptions of Comanches and other Natives. Yet how the justice-oriented objectives play out on-screen produce an ebb and flow with and without Comanches in the film's representational development and underdevelopment of Comanches, for whom justice is both reached for and elusive.

Justifying Intent

"From the first time," says Depp, that he and Verbinski "had script meetings with [screenwriter Justin] Haythe, the main thing was 'Are we doing right by the Indian? Are we doing this right? Let's not make any mistakes here.'"[22] As guiding questions in a shared vision of constructing cinematic Comanches, Depp contrasts the "right" of representational justice with the "mistakes" of injustice. Two days before the Comanche Nation premiere of *The Lone Ranger*, Depp justified his Tonto role and acknowledged naysayers and critics of his work. When asked if his Tonto appropriated Indianness, the Comanche captive asserted he had "done no harm [read: injustice] and represented—at the very least the Comanche Nation—in a proper light [read: justice]."[23] Depp and the rest of his *Lone Ranger* "think tank" knew "we had to make a film that's going to entertain," yet they recognized the "agenda" to "bring back in Hollywood cinema the respect and the dignity that the Native Americans deserve, as they've been mistreated forever and ever in television and cinema." "Hollywood," Verbinski adds, "has a long legacy of sort of getting it wrong in terms of representing Native Americans."[24] Depp acknowledged he could not "eliminate" the mistreatment and wrongs but at least could "reinvent the relationship" between his Tonto and Hammer's Lone Ranger and make a "dent" in the representational injustice of Natives in media borderlands.[25] "Johnny is creating a Tonto, unlike any we've seen before," said Bruckheimer during production, "a character with multiple levels, with great humor but a really moving core of pathos and emotion."[26] In sum producers expressed intent to respect, humanize, and empower the Indigenous on-screen.

In the intertextual development of his character's search for justice, Depp drew inspiration from both non-Native actors like Buster Keaton (*The General*, 1926) and Dustin Hoffman (*Little Big Man*, 1970) and Native actors like Jay Silverheels (Tonto in 1950s television) and Gary Farmer (Depp's co-star in *Dead Man*, 1995). When asked of Farmer's influence on the development of Tonto, Depp replied, "I suppose probably somewhere in the back of my mind, because I had fallen so deeply in love with Gary Farmer and his performance, I'm sure that that seeped in somewhere along the lines." Depp calls their *Dead Man* collaboration an "amazing learning experience, watching Gary work and his passion for the reality and to keep all of the ceremonial things accurate. He represented a large group of people."[27] Depp's Tonto even lifts a line that Farmer's Native character, Nobody, says to Depp's white character, William Blake, in *Dead Man*. When Nobody tries to remove "white man's metal" (i.e., a bullet) from Blake's heart, the Native seriocomically scolds him twice as "stupid f—ing white man." Later Nobody asks him, "What name were you given at birth, stupid white man?" Minus the f-bomb, the line aligns with the Disneyfied version echoed verbatim two decades later in *The Lone Ranger* when Tonto calls the title character "stupid white man" for thwarting his efforts to kill the villain Cavendish. In both films the one-liner speaks back not only at naive white characters but also at systemic representational injustice long leveled in Hollywood at Comanches and other Natives. In support Tonto repeatedly one-ups his "less-skilled, less-bright, less-brave, less-everything sidekick," such as when he drags the Lone Ranger on a cart through horse manure.[28] Incidentally, the droppings were real.[29]

For the Lone Ranger character, Haythe calls John Ford's *The Man Who Shot Liberty Valance* (1962) "one of my favorite movies" and "my direct cross-connection to the Lone Ranger character—a purely good man who wanders into a more complicated world, a world of shades, of grays and corruption," as illustrated in violent revisionist western films like Sam Peckinpah's *The Wild Bunch* (1969).[30] As in *The Lone Ranger, The Wild Bunch* is set in Texas and the outlaws want silver. Verbinski was similarly "interested in taking Jimmy Stewart from *The Man Who Shot Liberty Valance* and throwing him into this Peckinpah movie. Colliding those worlds."[31] The collision of traditional and revisionist westerns suggests wanting a complicated white hero, but one inspired by films that happen to marginalize the Indigenous.

For example, *Liberty Valance* stars Jimmy Stewart as Ransom Stoddard, who, like John Reid, is a lawyer trained in the eastern United States and highly resistant to wielding a gun. Ford's film reduces Native representation to two references. In a lengthy political speech to nominate Stoddard for Congress and to advocate for statehood, a settler character cites the inferior past of the former "savage redskin roaming our beautiful territory with no law to trammel them except the law of survival, the law of the tomahawk and the bow and arrow." Later someone says Peabody can "talk the ears off a wooden Indian," reducing the Indigenous to an "inanimate piece of *kitsch*" in a moment of "racism by erasure."[32] Sergio Leone and Sam Peckinpah rarely show Native characters. The absence is all the more curious to serve as cinematic influences for a *Lone Ranger* production team vocally determined to reshape representational presence and reception of Native peoples in Hollywood.

In preparing his vision of representational justice for *The Lone*

Ranger, Depp welcomed "the opportunity to play the classic character of Tonto," but not as the traditional marginalized sidekick. Enacting his Comanche name Mah-woo-meh (Shape-shifter), Depp wanted "to take that shape" of Tonto, he explains, "and mess around with it a little bit."[33] He desired "to try to, almost in a weird way, embrace the cliché [of savagery] so it's recognized by people who have been conditioned to [viewing] how the Native American has been represented in film." His performance became "kind of a trick, in a weird way, to suck them [viewers] in and then switch them around and take them on a different path."[34] Depp's Tonto "employs the trickster," one critic argues, "as a form of playful indeterminacy."[35] Within Depp's dually designated "weird way," the actor suggests he temporarily embraced injustice to bring justice by rerouting Tonto into a multidimensional representation that debunks savagery and humanizes a Comanche character.

Depp explicitly expressed his circuitous commitment to justice for Comanches and other Natives in both film performance and narrative. Off-screen, the actor said playing Tonto "was a role that I wanted to bring justice to."[36] On-screen, his character said, "Justice is what I seek" in his cryptic eye-for-an-eye message on avenging the killers of his Comanche relatives in *The Lone Ranger*. As seekers of Indigenous representational justice, both Depp and his Tonto perform utterances to reframe and speak back at a documented unjust cinematic history of producing, portraying, and perceiving marginalized monosyllabic, one-dimensional Hollywood Indians.[37] Depp and Tonto also speak toward a cinematic present and futurity of seeking justice, a corrective via cinematic Comanches. On-screen and off, Depp doubly demarcates a desire to perform representational justice, the former by an adopted Comanche actor on his fictional Comanche role ("I wanted to bring justice to" representing Tonto), the latter by his fictional Comanche character in a cinematic narrative ("Justice is what I seek" for massacred relatives). Depp's soundbites suggest responses to what constitutes representational justice for him in and through film.

Depp said repeatedly in interviews that he wanted to not only entertain audiences but also enlighten them about Native human beings and history in a respectful way. Depp suggests his vision of doing *justice*—a term, not coincidentally, uttered eight times in *The Lone Ranger*—means "to give as much back to the human beings, the Native Americans as possible; to show they have a fantastic sense of humor" and, he continues, "to try to, in my own small way, right the many wrongs that have been done to those people."[38] Depp similarly says elsewhere that "the idea was to give something back to the human beings." The something suggests an intent toward representational justice both for fictional Native characterization in film and for real-life Natives caricatured and dehumanized by the skewed history of Hollywood portrayals of Indianness. Depp recognizes dated representations of Natives as dehumanizing "sidekicks or savages" and says he wants "to flip it completely on its head" by representing the Indigenous humanely with "integrity and dignity."[39] "It was my way of trying to give back and," to borrow again from legal discourse, "redress" cinematic mistreatment.[40]

Speaking Comanche

The Lone Ranger producers' expressed encoded intent translates into key decoded areas of on-screen performance. For one the film attempts to articulate representational justice through speech acts of injustice as well as in speaking the Nʉmʉ tekwapʉ, or Comanche language. The result represents a spoken semblance of justice when set against a cinematic history of racist monikers and misnomers, such as "savage" and "Indian."

The film's Comanche rhetoric, including discursive and audible references to Comanches, tells a story of jurisdictional clashes between who narratively has the power to name and represent indigeneity. The first clash unfolds just after the film opens, in 1933 at an amusement park in San Francisco, just past the Golden Gate Bridge, which began construction the same year. An Anglo boy named Will, wearing a Lone Ranger mask, hears a carny's loud invitation to "witness the Wild West as it really was." Encapsulating *The*

Lone Ranger producers' intent to entertain and enlighten audiences, the carny then directs his attention to Will: "Fun and educational for you, young sir." Upon entering the tent, Will spots a diorama of a stuffed bison. The camera cuts to a close-up of the plaque: "The Mighty Buffalo: Lord of the Plains." The brief visual interpellates the popular phrasing of Comanches as "Lords of the Plains," after white historians Ernest Wallace and Adamson Hoebel's book *The Comanches: Lords of the South Plains* (1952).[41] Predating the recent academic historical turn to "Comanche empire," the moniker "Lords of the Plains" is attributed to Comanches' acquisition of and rise to dominance on the horse, not necessarily to our sustenance from the "mighty buffalo." "Lords of the Plains" can be found stamped on the official seal of the Comanche Nation flag and tribal license plates, T-shirts, and travel mugs at the Comanche Nation gift shop and on hoodies and skateboards at the Comanche-owned business Intertribal Visions Unlimited, to name a few.[42] For a moniker coined by non-Natives, it sure gets around among Comanches claiming shares of the signifier. Its curious placement in *The Lone Ranger*, with the singular "Lord" affixed near a single stuffed buffalo in the exhibit, may be a cinematic first. Although the moment is easy to overlook, as Will seems to do, it is culturally packed as an insider "joke" if one goes by the light chuckles I heard among Comanche viewers at the tribe's premiere.

From there Will moves on to glance at an exhibit of a stuffed grizzly bear before stopping at the next exhibit, where the Comanche named Tonto, a frozen old man with a crow headdress, stands with raised tomahawk in hand by a tipi in front of a painted mountainous backdrop. Dually pointing toward Comanche and pan-Indian subjectivities, Depp's Tonto debuts in a conflation of identity markers to represent the Indian's past and passing, as once was and now no more than a frozen curiosity. When he hears young Will crunch on a peanut and sees his mask, Depp's very elderly and stuffed Tonto comes to life and mistakes Will for "Kemosabe," Tonto's nickname for the Lone Ranger.[43] The resurrection follows similar acts of previous cinematic Native characters, such as a plastic Indian toy-turned-human in *Indian in the Cupboard* (1995) and Sacajawea in a museum diorama in the *Night at the Museum* series (2006, 2009, and 2014). The awakenings trade a frozen pastness of indigeneity for present-day fantasy.

Tonto's placard reads, in parallel structure to the first exhibit, "Noble Savage: In His Natural Habitat." European Renaissance writers in the sixteenth and seventeenth centuries conceptualized the "noble savage" to locate the Indigenous outside of Western "civilization."[44] The exhibit's subtitle, "In His Natural Habitat," is typically an animalistic association and could pair just as well with "The Mighty Buffalo" diorama. Tonto, film critic Eileen Jones says, is here "represented as one with the animals slaughtered in order to make the West safe and comfortable for white settlers, immobilized and 'ennobled' in a museum-like setting arranged to convey history as a romantic adventure narrative."[45]

Whereas some critics panned the "Noble Savage" diorama as dated and literally reiterated racism, another interpretive possibility emerges.[46] What if *The Lone Ranger* engaged the racist logic of noble savagery to upend it? For producers to position Tonto, physically and rhetorically, among wild animals suggests an awareness of how such exhibits in the United States further dehumanized and committed symbolic injustice against the Indigenous. For example, the 1915 Panama-Pacific International Exposition also took place in San Francisco, where the public saw James Earle Fraser's statue *The End of the Trail*. It shows a male Indian on horseback, head lowered as if mourning the loss of his people, land, and way of life, frozen "at the edge of the Pacific."[47] San Francisco also is where Ishi, known as the "last wild Indian," spent his last years on display at the Museum of Anthropology. In an interview Depp said the film's diorama was inspired by the history of Native performers as spectacles in traveling road shows. "Ooh, look at the wild Indian," he imagined non-Native customers saying.[48] Paired with Depp's aforementioned intent to "embrace the cliché [of savagery]" before rerouting viewers' popular expectations of Indianness, the seemingly stuffed and static "Noble Savage" may have served as a premeditated "trick," to recite Depp, for thawing his Comanche character into multidimensional motion.

The opening engraved nods to "Lord of the Plains" and "Noble Savage" set the stage for juxtaposing terms, in just and unjust contexts, directed at Comanches throughout the film. *The Lone Ranger* includes seventeen uses of the term "Comanche," twelve of which are uttered by non-Natives and five spoken by Tonto, the Comanche outcast. That "Comanche" is repeatedly spoken, mostly by non-Native characters, locates the film's tribal specificity, but the disproportionate use of who speaks "Comanche" furthers the jurisdictional clash and split in rhetorical representation and agency over who speaks the signifier. For example, the first utterance of Comanche is by the white railroad magnate Latham Cole. It occurs approximately seven minutes into the film, in Tonto's narrated flashback to the new settlement Colby, Texas, in 1868. The year marks the near cusp from a vast Comanche empire to an encroaching reservation era ratified in the 1867 Medicine Lodge Treaty, followed by the first Comanches' arrival to the reservation in 1869. As Irish and Chinese workers lay track for the Transcontinental Railroad, Cole tells Colby's citizens of his mission to unify "this great country of ours by iron rail." He next addresses in the crowd two attentive Comanches, Red Knee and a character listed in the credits as "Red Knee's Young Warrior," portrayed, respectively, by Comanche descendant Gil Birmingham and Navajo citizen and Kiowa actor Malachi Tsoodle-Nelson. Evoking the first appearance of two Comanche men on horseback in Clint Eastwood's *The Outlaw Josey Wales* (1976), Red Knee and his apprentice also represent a traditional pair of anticipated "warriors coming back from somewhere," as Juanita Pahdopony explains of enacting maruawe, "and reporting what they observed" to Comanches.[49] "To the Comanche," Cole explains, "I say you have nothing to fear. Long as there is peace between us, all land treaties shall be honored." Whereas Comanches do not appear in *Josey Wales* until nearly ninety minutes in, their early appearance in *The Lone Ranger* suggests promise for rich character development. But hoped-for

13. Gil Birmingham as Red Knee and Malachi Tsoodle-Nelson as Red Knee's Young Warrior, in *The Lone Ranger*.

justice at the film premiere fell far short, as Red Knee and Young Warrior promptly and quietly exit the frame fifteen seconds in. They return to their Comanche people, but over an hour passes in the film before they reappear.

Other references to "Comanche" include Tonto's, all spoken to the Lone Ranger. First, after healing the Ranger, the Comanche outcast introduces himself: "I am Tonto of the Comanche." Second, at a saloon in pursuit of the villains, Tonto plays on the Ranger's ignorance of Comanche customs when he takes Reid's drink and gulps it. "Comanche gesture of respect," Tonto lies. Next, after the raid at Rebecca's settlement, Tonto is solemn when he sees one of Cavendish's men wearing a familiar necklace. He tells Reid it is "Comanche. Very sacred." When Reid questions why Cavendish made "it look like the Comanche violated the treaty," Tonto humorously speculates that Cavendish "want[s] to make it look like Comanche violate treaty." Finally, when Reid thinks he and Tonto have been captured by Apaches, Tonto recognizes their captors and corrects him: "Comanche." In all five scripted references, "Comanche" circulates for Tonto as political stances of tribal-specific personhood, trickery, sacredness, matter-of-fact insight, and tense tribal recognition.

In the original 1930s *Lone Ranger* radio program, writer Fran Striker created Tonto early on "solely for the purpose of giving the Lone Ranger someone to talk to."[50] In the 2013 film the lone Tonto won't stop talking to him. That Tonto's Comanche references reactively depend on a white character's attention highlights a curious absence: Tonto never really starts talking "Comanche" with other Comanches. The closest acknowledged interaction occurs when Comanches capture the Lone Ranger and Tonto trespassing in Comanche territory, and Chief Big Bear (Saginaw Grant) later tosses Tonto's pocket watch toward Tonto after the chief repaired it. Tonto's closest discursive recognition of a Comanche relative comes after the Lone Ranger hears him talking to the horse Silver in the Nʉmʉ tekwapʉ, or Comanche language. "My [Comanche] grandfather," Tonto explains to the Ranger, "spoke of a time when animals could speak when you get them alone. Some still do." As Chadwick Allen pointedly observes, "Tonto lacks an Indigenous interlocutor. He ritually feeds the stuffed crow mounted on his head, he exchanges witty banter with the horse Silver, he chides the hapless white man into becoming a hero, but he never once speaks to another Native person."[51] Even in the flashback scenes to his boyhood, Tonto communicates not with other Comanches on-screen but with Cole and Cavendish. Despite being an outcast from the tribe, couldn't Tonto at least say "marʉawe" to a brother? Or perhaps the incommunicado goes with the territory of being a Comanche outcast.

On a representationally just note, *The Lone Ranger* includes several moments of speaking the Nʉmʉ tekwapʉ by different Comanche characters. Big Bear exclaims "*kima*" (or "come") to rally his warriors. Red Knee's Young Warrior colloquially shouts "*weechaw*" to rally them again. Red Knee, played by Comanche actor Birmingham, bellows "*ekạsaapana*" (or "soldier") to signal a charge into battle against the Custer-inspired Captain Fuller. Birmingham's pronunciation was also heard by elder Auntie Juanita Pahdopony as "*Itsa muura*," which she translated as "It's a mule or It's an ass!"[52] I like the layers of that aurality: a Comanche elder hearing a Comanche actor and character calling the Custer-like captain an "ass"! Other Comanche sounds from Big Bear's band of "full Comanche war whoops and traditional songs" came from, says dialogue supervisor Douglas Murray, "a loop group recording session near Lawton, Oklahoma, in the home of the Comanche Nation." "Voelker," Murray explains, "was instrumental in getting us access to fluent Comanche speakers, and some of the best singers and drummers."[53]

A longer example of the Nʉmʉ tekwapʉ occurs when Comanches capture the Lone Ranger, and Red Knee shoves him into Chief Big Bear's tipi, where the chief and five other Comanche men are seated. When the Lone Ranger explains who he is, they say nothing. Assuming they do not know English, he gestures confusing sign language and slows his speech to follow a history of what Comanche linguistic anthropologist Barbra Meek calls "Hollywood Injun English": "Me, Spirit Walker, from great beyond."[54] Comanches intervene. "*Tapay. Kweenuhma*? [Sunstroke?]" Big Bear asks Red Knee. His reply in Comanche is captioned on-screen in English: "Or his mind is poisoned with whiskey." Big Bear's and Red Knee's Comanche lines are likely translated on-screen to allow a non-Comanche-speaking audience to be in on the Comanche humor at the clueless title character's expense. The humorous exchange also echoes insider mediated communications between Comanche code talkers in World War II when they called Adolf Hitler *posah thaivo*, or "crazy white man!"

Interestingly, Grant's Big Bear is not the first cinematic Comanche chief in *Lone Ranger* history to speak the Nʉmʉ tekwapʉ on-screen. In 1938, just two years after Grant was born, the Comanche language was spoken in *The Lone Ranger* film series episode "Wheels of Disaster." The Lone Ranger (Lee Powell) rescues a non-Comanche Tonto (Victor "Chief Thundercloud" Daniels) from none other than a band of enemy Comanches. In one scene the Comanche character Chief Dark Cloud (Philip Armenta) says "*wahatu*" to another Comanche character who holds up two fingers in response.[55] The pronunciation closely resembles a word for "two" in the Nʉmʉ tekwapʉ: *wahaitʉ*. In the earlier series episode "Red Man's Courage," Comanches say *haa* for "yes" and *thaivo* for "white man" in reference to the Lone Ranger. The series was co-directed by Jack English and William Witney, the latter of whom was born in the Comanche capital of Lawton, Oklahoma. When I asked Witney's son Jay Dee Witney if his father had decided to include the Comanche language in the film, he replied, "My guess would be yes." Although the elder Witney moved away from Lawton at a young age, his son attributes the linguistic agency to his father's interests: "He loved and studied American and Native American history; he also knew some phrases and words of the languages."[56]

In contrast to most Comanche lines spoken by Big Bear's band, Tonto's use of the Nʉmʉ tekwapʉ represents speech acts of the unscripted. "As a result of Johnny's great interest in who we are culturally," Comanche consultant William Voelker explains, "he has added words in Nʉmʉnʉ that were not part of the original script where it seemed appropriate to call on our language." For example, he sings quietly in Comanche in one scene. Right before Tonto cites his Comanche grandfather, Tonto also talks playfully in the Comanche language to the white horse Silver to figure out if the "horse is stupid, or pretending to be stupid." Later, upon seeing one of Cavendish's men wearing a "very sacred" Comanche symbol as a necklace, Tonto offers up a prayer to *taa Ahpʉ*, or "our Father," in the Comanche language in a solemn moment. Depp's unscripted Comanche lines are captioned only in pan-Native terms as "Native language," but certain viewers picked up on the specificity. Former Comanche Nation College language instructor Todd McDaniels, for one, told the *Boston Globe*, "The words were there. The pronunciation was shaky but adequate."[57] Still, the unscripted moments reveal a creative collaboration and shared agency between Depp and Voelker, the work of whom makes it on-screen in the final product.

The inclusion of the Comanche language also signifies a sonic semblance of justice. "Johnny quickly revealed what a sensitive person he is," Voelker says, "and a quick bond developed between us." The unscripted and uncaptioned "Comanche" talk represents a cinematic and cultural commitment from Depp to Nʉmʉnʉ, or the Comanche people.[58] At the film's Los Angeles premiere, Voelker called Depp "a man of great integrity" who has "embraced our culture . . . with mind, heart, and spirit."[59] Twenty years earlier Depp expressed commitment to another Indigenous language in Emir Kusturica's film *Arizona Dream* (1993). Co-starring Depp, Jerry Lewis, and Faye Dunaway, *Arizona Dream* includes scenes with Inuits. "I was learning," Depp recalls, "to speak all these words in Yupik, in Eskimo" in preparation for his role, "and Jerry said, 'Oh no, we don't need to do that, we don't need to learn the Eskimo language. We just make it up. We just invent it as we go along.'" Depp remembers watching "this legend" on set speaking his version of a "made-up language."[60] Dubbed "The King of Comedy," Lewis represents an older Hollywood generation with earlier twentieth-century Tontos and comedy acts like the Three Stooges speaking "Indian" gibberish and broken English.[61] Depp's intent to learn a few Yupik lines carries forth in his commitment to speak the Nʉmʉ tekwapʉ in *The Lone Ranger* and with accountability to his new Comanche relatives. Other recent productions in which the Comanche language is spoken with Comanche consultants on set, such as *Magnificent Seven* (2016) and *The Son* (2017–19), reveal a growing interest in cultural accuracy.

Raiding Comanches

Like the audible rhetoric, Verbinski's visual language in *The Lone Ranger* illustrates intertextual efforts to reshape representational justice toward Comanches. The film's raid scenes, in particular, cite previous western films' invocations of nineteenth-century Comanche history but liberally rewrite the history to represent Comanches as excessively innocent. Following a cultural history of real and reel Comanche raids off-screen and on, the scenes initially take viewers into familiar imagined territory in the media border-lands, suggesting the Comanches are raiding again, before rerouting who is raiding whom. The decoded raids eventually challenge popular perceptions but, in the process, disavow Comanche history and an integral dimension of the Comanche empire.

When bar and brothel owner Red (Helena Bonham-Carter) informs Tonto and Reid that "the Comanche violated the treaty" by "raiding settlements up and down the river," the pair rush to Rebecca's home and find it in flames from presumably Comanche raiders. Viewers soon learn, however, that the raiders are Cavendish and his gang dressed up as Comanches, reminiscent of whites in redface as Paiutes (linguistic relatives of Comanches) in *The Lone Ranger* TV episode "Backtrail" (1951).[62] Cavendish's "Comanche" band raids not only white settlements but also ideas of Comanche identity. The appropriated raiding plays off of Comanche history by violently playing Comanche, a tribal-specific trope of what Philip Deloria and Rayna Green call "playing Indian."[63] In effect, Cavendish's band breaks a peace treaty presumably between the settler colonial U.S. government and the Comanche Nation. The treaty had demarcated nonviolent relations ("As long as there is peace between us," Cole sneers to Comanches, "all land treaties shall be honored") and territorial jurisdictions ("[Comanches] keep to their side of the river," Rebecca says before the raid, "and I keep to mine"). Now Cole, somehow vested with the political authority to legislate, extols to the U.S. press, "From here on, all treaties with the [Comanche] Indian Nation are null and void." The declaration frees him to push his construction through what the film designates, in an on-screen caption, as "Comanche Territory," where he uses the extended tracks to secure and transport the silver from Comanche land.

The raiding scene begins as Rebecca and hired African American worker Joe wrap up a day's work on the Reid farm. Her son, Danny, and their small dog play in the river. Rebecca then spots a Comanche, Red Knee, in the far distance. He looks toward her from atop his horse on the other side of the river. Like he did near the film's start, Red Knee soon rides off without a word and out of view. After Rebecca and the others ride a wagon back to the main house, she stands at the well for a drink of water. The camera slowly pans to the left across the field from Rebecca's point of view. The mood turns ominous. The cicadas go quiet, and the scene nears silence before birds suddenly scatter and fly from a bush in the distance. "Get yourselves inside!" shouts Joe as he grabs a gun and stands guard outside. Rebecca rushes inside with Danny and tells her Mexican American housekeeper, Pilar, to close the windows. Rebecca aims a rifle through a front peephole and begins firing at Cavendish's "Comanches" fast approaching on horseback. Joe shoots at the incoming raiders before one of them kills and prepares to scalp him. Another pseudo-Comanche soon shoots and kills Pilar. Rebecca and Danny are taken captive.

From the scene's start Verbinski cites the Comanche raiders from *The Searchers* and their reconfigured invocation in *Once upon a Time in the West*. In both *The Searchers* and *The Lone Ranger*, white settlers see doves scatter, step inside to close the shutters, and grab rifles; even the same looking dog barks. In *The Searchers* the Comanches (or "Comanch'" as John Wayne snarls) are undoubtedly encoded *and* decoded as the raiders of the Edwards family settlement. Comanches loom large as imagined menacing figures in line with settler-dominant understandings of nineteenth-century Texas borderlands history. Ford's Comanches become legible in an imagined presence through the film's tonal shift to chilling stillness, the birds' jarring movements, and female settlers' stern and worried faces. Ford especially focuses on the settlers' emotional fear of anticipated doom before the scene closes with the appearance of the Comanche leader Scar and his signal to attack. The film later cuts to the aftermath of the house in ruins amid deceased settlers.

In contrast to Ford's tensely slow and quiet pace of representing the Comanche raiders, Verbinski rapidly cuts to the "Comanches" approaching furiously on horseback. The split-second shots reveal another layer of playing Comanche. Registering another Indigenous presence, the riders are momentarily played by Blackfeet stuntmen. Whereas the rapid cuts of Comanche raiders work to build dramatic tension, the pace also blurs and masks, nearly, the identity of the riders to produce triangular raiding relations between Comanches,

Cavendish's gang, and Blackfeet stuntmen. That the professional hired riders are also Native represents a subtle performative and historical moment of relations in the Greater Comanchería media borderlands and in the Comanche-constructed Greater Comanchería map (see introduction), which includes Blackfeet homelands in Montana.

Twelve years later, in *Once upon a Time in the West*, Comanches are visually absent, but Leone invokes their preceding presence in *The Searchers*. Leone reconfigures Ford's "savage" Comanches into another group of societal others: white bounty hunters. He heavily cites Ford's raid scene but amplifies the visual violence against the settlers—an Irish family named McBain—by showing their deaths at the hands of actor Henry Fonda's character, a sadistic killer named Frank. The McBains prepare for a festive occasion outdoors. The patriarch goes to the well for water and his daughter sings "O Danny Boy" as she sets the table.[64] Then comes, as Leone biographer Christopher Frayling observes, "a series of sinister portents—cicadas suddenly going silent, partridges flying away from the sage brush, sage hens squawking excitedly." The sonic citations from *The Searchers* "herald not the arrival," as Frayling says, "of Comanche warriors at the Edwards ranch (as in *The Searchers*) but the appearance of a gang of hired killers."[65]

Leone's filmmaking was clearly influenced by Hollywood westerns like Ford's *The Searchers*. For *Once upon a Time in the West*, Leone says, "The basic idea was to use some of the conventions, devices and settings of the American Western film, and a series of references to individual Westerns—to use these things to tell *my* version of the story of the birth of a nation." In addition to *The Searchers*, the cinephilia of references, Frayling notes, includes *Johnny Guitar* (1954), *The Iron Horse* (1924), *Shane* (1952), and other westerns. Leone, though, rejected any critique of using filmic "citations for citations' sake." Rather, he wanted a "kaleidoscopic view of all American Westerns put together," an ambitious objective applicable to Verbinski and his cinematic western mosaic depicting the formations of U.S. nationhood in *The Lone Ranger*.[66]

Through referents to classic Hollywood westerns, such as the bandit and gunfighter, Leone "wanted to present a homage to the Western at the same time as showing the mutations which American society was undergoing at the time."[67] According to Frayling, "Westerns had become too formulaic and talky" in Leone's adulthood.[68] Leone tried to "play with the conventions of the American Western," Edward Buscombe argues, "rather than slavishly imitate them." Like Verbinski recognizing the popular *Lone Ranger* TV series as "squaresville" in a black-and-white world, Leone pushed for constructing a more complex cinematic world with shades of grey.[69] He cast, for example, Henry Fonda in a heinous family-killer role after the actor had "symbolized justice and goodness" in *The Grapes of Wrath* (1940) and other films.[70]

In *The Lone Ranger* Verbinski pays homage to Ford and Leone, recognized exemplars of U.S. and Italian westerns, but some reviewers did accuse the director of using citations for citations' sake. "Where," one critic asked, "is *your* movie, Mr. Verbinski?" "*The Lone Ranger*," the same critic adds, "takes artistic theft to a whole new level."[71] "Theft" is harsh, as if the answer to who is raiding whom is Verbinski as thief of previous films' signifiers. Although the borrowing is blatant, Verbinski, in an effort to revive the western genre, offers both an ode to his white directorial inspirations and a challenge to the reception of relations between manifest destiny and genocide for a twenty-first-century audience.

Verbinski's intertextual play suggests unoriginality to some, but his citational work with previous westerns opens up routes for how the signifier "Comanche" functions in the richly intertextual *Lone Ranger* storyworld. By situating Comanches into the representational realm of savage raiders and initially appearing to replicate *The Searchers'* Comanches as raiders, Verbinski makes it look like Comanches are the perpetrators. Then he shifts the cinematic western pendulum from reconfiguring Comanches as Ford's guilty raiders in the 1950s and the inspiration for Leone's ruthless violence in the late 1960s to become subjects of noble innocence and not the raiders in 2013. Verbinski symbolically invokes cinematic Comanche ancestors of earlier generations, but this time Comanches are not the bad guys.

The liberal decision, however, to situate Cavendish's band as the Comanche raiders comes at a price. It unjustly represents Comanche visual absence. By rewriting Comanches into innocence, *The Lone Ranger* disavows a documented history of the Lords of the Plains as raiders and an opportunity for Red Knee and other Comanches to garner more screen time. The film's creative rewriting of who is raiding whom disavows in the process a real part (and a possibility for an on-screen reel part) of Comanche history. Even in the film's encoded attempt for shades of gray, Comanches in *The Lone Ranger* suggest a conundrum in what to make of history and cinema's revisionist interpretation. To some critics, when it comes to cinematic Comanches in the *longue durée* of history, it's like a catch-22: damned if you do represent us as the villains, damned if you don't.

Encoded efforts to represent the Indigenous justly, by highlighting unjust non-Native deception, continues after the initial raid scene. Tonto and the Lone Ranger ride up to see the Reid homestead in ruins.[72] They soon hear a scream coming from the barn and rush inside to see a terrified Pilar held captive by the white character Frank, one of Cavendish's men, in Comanche-inspired face paint and clothing.[73] Frank also tries on settler women's clothing and holds a pink parasol. "Not an Indian," Tonto reports to the Ranger, who thought Comanches must be the raiders of "settlements up and down the river" in a narrative "trick" to the audience of who raids whom.

"This ain't what it looks like, mister," Frank tells them in reference to his concern with what he's wearing, and not that he's holding a Mexican American woman captive. As Pilar escapes through a side exit, the Ranger demands Frank reveal where Rebecca and Danny are or else he will "let the Indian do what he wants to you." Frightened and curious, Frank stutters, "Wh-what does he want to do?" Tonto holds up a duck foot but says nothing. A gunshot is then heard from outside the barn, which momentarily distracts Tonto and the Ranger. Frank jumps through a glass window to escape and tells his two fellow outlaws outside of a "lunatic Indian" who "was gonna violate me with a duck foot."

The scene's emphasis on Frank's suggestive homoeroticism downplays the violent and sudden death of Pilar from the heard, not seen, gunshot. The killing of Pilar is doubly unjust on-screen. Not only is she murdered but also unjust is how she is shown, and not shown, on camera in death. She was killed off-screen one moment; then the camera keeps its distance as she lay motionless on the ground. Verbinski foregrounds instead her killers, Cavendish's men Barrett and Jesús ("the Spaniard," Tonto says) still dressed as "Comanche" in horned buffalo hat, breastplate, and other signifiers. In the film's book adaptation by Elizabeth Rudnick of Disney Press, Pilar's death goes unnoted. The closest mention is a vague "BANG! BANG!" and reference to the "sound of the gunshots."[74] Pilar exits and seemingly vanishes. The scene in the film also portrays disturbing tonal shifts as Pilar's murder and lifeless body are positioned between crude homophobic "jokes" about a duck foot. Chronologically, Pilar shakes with fear; the Ranger, Tonto, and Frank exchange suggestively sexualized remarks; Pilar is killed off-screen; and Frank notes the threat of violation by Tonto's duck foot. The Mexican maid becomes another cinematic example of an expendable Brown female. Like the African American character Joe earlier, Pilar is identified by name but has very little screen time and dies abruptly, rendering her practically unknowable and ungrievable in the Comanchería media borderlands.[75]

The scene also registers another momentary Comanche signifier: the aforementioned pink parasol. It appears twice, first with Frank when he finds it at the Reid settlement, then with Tonto and the Lone Ranger, who take it from Frank. The object and its changing ownership suggests a playful Comanche specificity (to recall chapter 1's question of hakaru maruumatu kwitaka, or who is shitting whom), but the parasol's appearance also is grounded in Comanchería borderlands history and subsequent art in the media borderlands.[76] In retaliation for Republic of Texas officials killing thirty-five Comanches who gathered for peace talks in March 1840 in San Antonio, the Comanche Buffalo Hump led raids in southeast Texas. On August 6 Comanches ransacked John Linn's general store in the Linnville Raid near present-day Lavaca, Texas. As Linn describes the scene and stolen goods, "These [hats and umbrellas] the Indians made free with, and went dashing about the blazing village, amid their screeching squaws and 'little Injuns.'" Linn likens Comanches to dehumanized "demons in a drunken saturnalia, with Robinson's hats on their heads and Robinson's umbrellas bobbing about on every side like tipsy young balloons."[77] Another observer said Comanches "were singing and gyrating in divers [sic] grotesque ways."[78] T. J. Owen's 1889 engraving depicts Comanches with their stolen loot arriving to Plum Creek, where armed white Texans awaited them.[79] Howard Terpning's painting *Comanche Spoilers* (1986) depicts Comanche men riding away from Linnville on horseback with their loot. As Terpning says, "The men rode with women's parasols, stovepipe hats, ribbons and all kinds of goods stolen from the warehouse." Like in Owen's work, the parasols stand out. They also represent the making of a practical tradition of shading oneself from the hot sun, as subsequent scenes reveal. For example, in the painting *Horseman, Anadarco [sic], I.T.* (1890), Julian Scott represents the likeness of possibly a Comanche or a Native man from a neighboring tribe on horseback holding a red umbrella near the Anadarko Agency in Oklahoma.[80]

After the raid in *The Lone Ranger*, the Lone Ranger and Tonto ride together on a horse through the desert, with the recaptured pink parasol in the Ranger's hand. As archaeologist and Comanche collaborator Severin Fowles observes, Verbinski "quietly retranslated" the scene from Comanche history and Terpning's painting.[81] Like the stolen parasols in 1840 in the Comanchería, the parasol in *The Lone Ranger* helps to signal the heroes' territorial transition into what the film captions as "Comanche Territory."[82] Armie Hammer recalls the scene: "So I am sitting on a horse behind Johnny Depp, holding this pink umbrella, and I'm thinking that this is the craziest thing ever. And what does this have to do with

14. Johnny Depp as Tonto and Armie Hammer as the Lone Ranger, with pink parasol, in *The Lone Ranger*.

The Lone Ranger?"[83] It doesn't. In a clever visual gesture to tribal history, it's about Comanches.

Massacring Comanches

After the raid and deaths at the hands of Cavendish's faux-Comanche band, more killings are soon revealed in scenes encoded to show white injustice against Comanches but that problematically and unjustly silence those killed: Comanche women. As Tonto and the Lone Ranger continue their search for Rebecca and Danny, pink parasol in tow, an arrow soon whizzes in with the classic "pfft!" cinematic westerns sound, which was once humorously mimicked by the late Oneida comic and actor Charlie Hill.[84] It pierces the Lone Ranger in his shoulder, prompting a madcap shriek. The shooter, like the Comanche-identified arrow in the western *Red River* (1948), is unseen but still registers a Comanche presence.[85] The duo is taken captive off-screen by Chief Big Bear's Comanche band.

Nearly ninety minutes into the film, viewers finally see a Comanche village. Held in a cell-like enclosure, Tonto and the Lone Ranger see Comanche men dancing around a fire to the drumbeat of a song, recorded in the aforementioned session with

15. Joseph Foy as Young Tonto, in *The Lone Ranger*.

Comanches in Oklahoma. Tonto calls it a "death dance. They are preparing for war with the white man," as if readying themselves for—spoiler alert—representational death. Reflective of the Greater Comanchería borderlands, the on-screen Comanche extras are portrayed by Eastern Shoshones, Navajos, Taos Pueblos, Jemez Pueblos, Chiricahua Apaches, and other Natives.[86]

The Lone Ranger is removed from the cage and shoved into Big Bear's tipi. In a scenic detour from Tonto as the film's narrator, Chief Big Bear explains to Reid, surrounded by Comanche men, the origins of Tonto's transformation into, as the chief calls him, a "band apart."[87] Tonto is a Comanche "no more," Big Bear declares on behalf of his people and their sovereign right to recognize who is in and who is out of the tribe. Representing an act of cinematic Comanche agency, Big Bear tells the story of Tonto's trauma as a boy.

In the ensuing flashback Joseph Foy makes his big-screen debut as the boy Tonto and enters an engaging intertextual history. Foy is Mescalero Apache and a Comanche descendant with the Klinekole family. Despite all the critiques of "injustice" in casting the ambiguous Depp, and not a Comanche or Native actor, as Tonto, critics seemed unaware that an actor with Comanche relations portrayed the young version.[88] Foy had previously auditioned for Jon Favreau's feature film *Cowboys and Aliens* (2011), in which white settlers and Natives partner up Lone Ranger–Tonto style to fight the aliens. Foy did not secure a role, but his audition was kept on file. "They called us for this movie [*The Lone Ranger*]," Foy's father, Jimmy Foy, explains, "and asked to see Joseph." He recalls it was a "10-minute audition" before casting director Elizabeth Gabel said, "We want him." Over 275 others reportedly auditioned for the young Tonto role, in Los Angeles and New Mexico.[89]

"Many moons ago," Big Bear tritely begins his voice-over flash-back, a young Tonto "found two white men" (Cole and Cavendish) hurt from an unknown cause and "brought them to his village to be healed." With a pet crow perched on his forearm and leading the men laying over his horse, Tonto arrives to be greeted by six Comanche women and two Comanche girls. Verbinski shows one close shot, for less than two seconds, of the Comanches. The camera cuts to a wide shot of the village to reveal over two dozen Comanches—all appear to be women except three boys—and numerous tipis. The next shot shows several women going about daily caretaking tasks and one Comanche serving food to the two men. (Their final appearance is later after they have been killed.) In all the Comanche women garner approximately seventy-three seconds of screen time, with all but five seconds kept at distant long shots. No explanation is given for the absence of Comanche men, possibly from Big Bear's band. Big Bear knows young Tonto's story well but does not say, for example, if men were away hunting, as Peta Nocona and other Comanches were during the real-life Pease River massacre in 1860, when Texas Rangers massacred mostly Comanche women and children and "rescued" Cynthia Ann Parker.[90]

While eating food prepared by the Comanche women, Cole and Cavendish see silver in the river, presumably the same body of water Rebecca references as a jurisdictional boundary in Comanche territory. They then privately trade a "cheap pocket watch from Sears Roebuck," Big Bear recalls, with Tonto in exchange for the whereabouts of "more silver than any white man had ever seen."

16. Comanche women, in *The Lone Ranger*.

Wanting all the silver and "to keep the place a secret," Cole and Cavendish proceed to cold-bloodedly kill everyone back at the camp—the women, children, and even the crow. Tonto returns to the camp to see his relatives motionless on the ground.[91]

Following Pilar's cold-blooded murder, the massacre of expendable Brown bodies continues with Comanches. Producers screen blatant injustice to build sympathy and support for Comanches, yet the performance on-screen unjustly silences and erases Comanche women. *Lone Ranger* co-stars Ruth Wilson's and Helena Bonham Carter's white female characters receive considerable screen time and story lines, albeit highly marginalized in comparison to the numerous starring male characters. In contrast, the Comanche women are unnamed and move just a few steps, share a somber but curious look, and say nothing. Verbinski tries to show injustice in the narrative toward Comanche women and that Native "people were here before us," as he says in a settler-to-settler ("us") interview, but the director also leaves the women silenced and slaughtered on-screen. Earlier in the film, when Tonto prepares to kill Cavendish, Tonto references the "screams of my ancestors in the desert wind" at the hands of Cavendish and Cole, yet not even screams were uttered on camera against the loud gunshots. When the women do appear on-screen, they are muted and motionless targets before they quickly vanish from the film.

Absent is any indication of Comanche women's prowess in tribal history. Chiricahua Apache educator and curator Nancy Marie Mithlo recognizes the predominance of male representation and the erasure of women on-screen and off. "Johnny Depp's Tonto portrayal is the *least* offensive matter to consider," she contends. "The greater issue is, where are the voices of our Native women?" Mithlo, whose relatives also include Comanches, observes a major critical absence in *The Lone Ranger*. When her daughter asked what she thought of the film, Mithlo replied, "All the Native women were dead hon, there's something wrong with that."[92] There is no suggestion in *The Lone Ranger* that the twenty or so Comanche women fought back against Cole and Cavendish. Gunshots are heard, but the camera stays on young Tonto with his new watch outside of the camp. As Comanche elders like my auntie Juanita Pahdopony says, "We had women that were very powerful who were warriors."[93] Eric Tippeconnic's painting *Comanche Woman* shows a woman warrior aiming a rifle on horseback. "Comanche girls were introduced to horses at an extremely young age," Tippeconnic explains, "and while their roles were different than men, they were also skilled riders." "Comanche women," he adds, "fought with the same ferocity displayed by their male counterparts in the martial defense of their homes and Comanchería"—not that viewers would ever know that from *The Lone Ranger*.[94] Nor would they know that, historically, Comanche women also served as "political mediators" who signified "native codes of peace and war."[95] Like Michael Burgess says in the episode "Lords of the Plains" of reality TV series *Texas Ranch House*, "In our old way, when we traveled with a woman, it meant we weren't looking for war." He pauses and grins, "Generally."[96]

In *The Lone Ranger* the dominant sight of silenced and massacred Comanche women strewn across the land is a vast underperforming contrast to the multidimensional, humanizing content of Indigenous women by Native filmmakers like Julianna Brannum (Comanche),

Ramona Emerson (Navajo), Sydney Freeland (Navajo), and Elle Maija-Tailfeathers (Blackfeet/Sami). *The Lone Ranger* shows scant attention to Native women and intertextual awareness of films featuring strong Native women, like the late Misty Upham's character, Lila, in *Frozen River* and the work of Indigenous female filmmakers. *The Lone Ranger* reinforces a representational jurisdiction over selectively privileging a few Indigenous men and silencing Indigenous women in its historical story line at a time today when tribes continue to strive for territorial, legal, and familial jurisdictions and for justice for missing and murdered Indigenous women (MMIW).

During the film's production, real-life Native women and allies continued to lead movements toward social justice. In December 2012, for example, First Nations women and a non-Native ally from Saskatchewan launched the Idle No More movement, which has since sparked millions of Natives and non-Natives "to join," as the movement's vision articulates, "in a peaceful revolution, to honour Indigenous sovereignty, and to protect the land and water." In March 2013 then president Barack Obama signed into law the Violence against Women Reauthorization Act, including a provision in which Native nations' law enforcement can prosecute non-Natives for certain acts of abuse and domestic violence. In June 2013 Mi'kmaq women began antifracking protests against a Texas-owned company in New Brunswick and held their ground as they were pepper sprayed and hit with rubber bullets by the Royal Canadian Mounted Police. In May 2014 Diane Humetewa (Hopi) became the first Native woman to serve as a U.S. federal judge.[97] Yet *The Lone Ranger* shows no recognition of such leadership, courage, and determination and instead privileges and reinforces the male-dominated western genre of the twentieth century. In response to her critique of Native women representation in the film, Mithlo offers this directive: "If you want to move the dialogue on race forward, even and especially in the entertainment industry, you've got to include women—behind the scenes and on camera." Mithlo continues, "For all of his apparent good will to erase stereotypes, Mr. Depp is not the individual who can change centuries of bias, hate and discrimination. In fact, no one man can accomplish this, but I'm pretty confident a Native woman could."[98]

Rather than turn to such perspectives by Indigenous women, *The Lone Ranger* draws narrative inspiration for Tonto's backstory in intertextual hypermasculine violence. In Leone's spaghetti western *Once upon a Time in the West*, a genre and film not known for empowering female leads, Harmonica, the character of Lithuanian American actor Charles Bronson's, is one of Tonto's closest cinematic relations. Like Tonto as the last Comanche by the end of *The Lone Ranger*, Harmonica is the "last descendant" of his unnamed tribe. After playing several cinematic Indian characters, Bronson plays Harmonica, who Leone calls a "half-breed." "Since he [Harmonica] is an Indian" from an "ancient race," Leone rigidly reasons, "he already hates the white man," especially Fonda's character, Frank.[99] Leone's and Verbinski's films represent what film scholar Janet Walker calls "traumatic westerns."[100] Like Tonto's search for vengeance against murderous outlaws and capitalistic settlers, Harmonica suffers from childhood trauma and seeks retribution against the perpetrators. Just moments before the film's end in a flashback, Leone shows a young Harmonica (Dino Mele) holding and balancing his older brother (Claudio Mancini) on his shoulders until, finally, collapsing in exhaustion. The camera slowly pans out to reveal Harmonica's brother had a noose around his neck and now dangles lifeless from a post. Like Tonto, Harmonica may feel tremendous guilt for the death of family as he "implacably pursues his revenge" and eventually executes eye-for-an-eye vengeance against the killer Frank.[101] In the flashback Frank sadistically stuffs a harmonica in Mele's mouth as he balances his brother. Now, as Frank lay dying, Harmonica returns the instrument to Frank's mouth, which brings a chilling last-breath realization to Frank of the identity of his killer. Similarly, near the end of *The Lone Ranger*, Cole asks Tonto, "Who *are* you?" Tonto answers by tossing to Cole the pocket watch he received from him as a boy. "Bad trade," Tonto tells him, as Cole dramatically falls to his death into a river with his trainload of silver, like Frank dropped to his death with his harmonica. In a nod to Leone's "Indian," the 2009 *Lone Ranger* script had Tonto play a harmonica.[102]

Massacre Redux

As the flashback narration concludes, Big Bear says that Tonto "was left to wander the Earth alone," as Nobody says verbatim of himself after his tribal banishment in *Dead Man*. Tonto's "mind is broken," Big Bear adds, evident by how Tonto bears his shame and wears it with the proverbial monkey on his back, transmuted into a crow on his head. The Lone Ranger tells Big Bear, "I know you didn't raid those settlements. If you let me go, I can prove it. There doesn't have to be a war." Big Bear disagrees. Captain Fuller suggests he had already murdered other Comanches off-screen. Cole's and Cavendish's orchestrated masquerade as pseudo-Comanches fooled Fuller into thinking Comanches were the raiders. As the captain smugly told Cole, "What they [Comanches] have done to the settlements, we have given back tenfold." "Now the Cavalry," Chief Big Bear laments to the Lone Ranger, "cut down our children."

Just before the Comanches exit their camp, the Lone Ranger pleads again for them not to fight. "It makes no difference," Big Bear says. "We are already ghosts." Big Bear's foreshadowing his people's doom follows his telling the Ranger, "There is no more tribe to return to. Our time has passed."[103] Despite his repeated efforts to dissuade violence, the Lone Ranger, along with Tonto, is buried up to his neck in sand by Big Bear's Comanche band. In Clint Eastwood's *The Outlaw Josey Wales* (1976), cinematic Comanches led by Ten Bears (Will Sampson, Muscogee Creek), named after the real-life historical Comanche leader Ten Bears, similarly bury two captives. But the citation of the cinematic Ten Bears band's survival does not extend to Big Bear's perishing band.

Big Bear's defeatist and doomed rhetoric trails the Comanches into battle against the U.S. Cavalry at the silver mine, presumably near where the Comanche women were slaughtered years earlier. On horseback Comanches strike first with a barrage of arrows that hit a number of soldiers. The act momentarily suggests the Comanches may "win" for once. As Comanches descend the mountain and charge, the Custer-like Captain Fuller commands his men to hold their ground. Finally, they unveil rapid-fire Gatling guns and fire indiscriminately. Comanches are quickly "mowed down," as the hired visual-effects company MPC puts it, through ragdoll physics animation in Disney's efforts at simulated realism. Red Knee and Red Knee's Young Warrior, the first two Comanches shown near the film's outset, are visually lost in the dehumanizing fray of ragdoll special effects of fallen Comanches. The warriors rapidly "flop into death," MPC impersonally says of the impersonal "Comanche massacre."[104] With Red Knee and Young Warrior presumably gone, Big Bear's close-up death is the lone exception. He runs at Fuller, who pierces the chief with his saber. In a matter of moments, all the Comanche men—save for outcast Tonto—are gone. Vanquished and vanished, Comanches fulfill Big Bear's fatalistic prediction as a tribe "no more" whose "time has passed." To return to Pahdopony's and Daffron's questioning if any filmmakers "can . . . truly do the Comanche justice" in representing "the Comanche in battle," such justice eludes in *The Lone Ranger*. The Comanches predict ("we are already ghosts") and enact (they ride downhill into rapid gunfire) their roles in a violent elimination.

Meanwhile, as the violent scene unfolds, John stands blindfolded on a platform on railroad tracks before a cavalry firing squad. He was captured and sentenced to death by Cole and Fuller after bringing in Cavendish. Tonto, disguised as a Chinese railroad worker, emerges from the silver mine and sets off an explosive device. Tonto liminally, and comically intended, reappears as he cuts through in-between bullets and arrows on a handcar to rescue the Lone Ranger. To his right are the cavalry, Cavendish, and Cole; to his left, the Comanches, a fitting scene for the liminal Comanche outcast who is neither fully in nor fully divorced from his Comanche tribe.[105] Tonto and the Ranger soon jump from the handcar in a mine shaft and roll downward to the river. Realizing the fate of Big Bear's band, Tonto mourns his people for a moment as he picks up his bird from the water like he did years earlier after the first massacre. Then he spots Silver standing in a tree and plays it for laughs: "Something very wrong with that horse."

Verbinski juxtaposes a mass killing with Tonto's slapstick hand-car rescue of, and loyalty to, the Lone Ranger and not with Tonto assisting Comanches. Critics were appalled at the film's tonal shifts between the gravely serious and slapstick comedy. One critic says, "It's like having Johnny Depp do a jig at Little Bighorn National Monument and calling it entertainment."[106] Citing the scene's shifts, another critic claims the film "plays like [Dee Brown's] *Bury My Heart at Wounded Knee* reconceived as a Disney theme-park ride."[107] Elsewhere Depp too cites Brown's sympathetic 1970 book on Native history and John Ehle's sympathetic and tragic 1988 book *Trail of Tears: The Rise and Fall of the Cherokee Nation* as "the classics" he studied for *The Lone Ranger*. Both non-Native authored books tell an outsider history of Indigenous victimhood and pastness, which may help to explain why the film's falling Comanches vanish in defeat and are excluded from the film's present-day 1933 with the elderly Tonto.[108]

In her review "The Fantastic Failure of *The Lone Ranger*," Eileen Jones observes the shifts, or "the 'unevenness,' the collision of genre elements," as a recurring critique by reviewers. "But there's no indication," she counters, "that he [Verbinski] ever meant to create a tightly controlled genre narrative. He almost never does." The tonal shifts align with citational derivations from previous westerns. For example, Depp's comedic tone, new transportation, and subsequent train theft hark back to Buster Keaton's humorous handcar and stolen train performance in the silent film *The General* (1926). Tonto's rescue of the Ranger by handcar, as Gatling guns obliterate Comanches, also draws specifically from another cinematic duo and sequence. In Leone's film *Duck, You Sucker* (1971), an Irish explosives expert named John uses dynamite to create a chaotic and violent diversion, then rides up on a motorcycle to save Mexican revolutionary Juan just in time from a firing squad. The camera soon cuts to Gatling guns gruesomely massacring Mexican peasants trapped below ground in deep pits. Like the cold-blooded slayings earlier of Pilar and the unnamed Comanche women in *The Lone Ranger*, Big Bear's band quickly vanishes as well.[109] With them goes additional possibilities for representational justice.

Conclusion

After all is screened and done, what are we to make of the fate (read: the fall) of Comanches in *The Lone Ranger*, save for one tribally excommunicated Tonto as the last of the Comanches on-screen? When the lights came up at the Comanche Nation film premiere, I remember thinking that there's more depth to Depp and his Tonto than critics had recognized. I also thought of how depth alone does not make a movie great. Personally, I liked Depp's culturally idiosyncratic and, at times, culturally grounded take on a Comanche outcast and trickster. Given the individualism of Comanches, it was plausible—the trauma, drama, comedy, determination, loss, heroism, and all else that may come with being human. Yet given the collectivity of Comanches, Tonto's loner status left him a band apart without the relations and interlocutors that are foundational to Comanche sovereignty, kinship, and nationhood. Even when they shared space in the village and war scenes, Tonto and the Comanches never really restored their broken relations. It left something of a gaping wound in a tragicomic film where justice was sought, and wanted, but remained elusive for Comanche nationhood. My negotiated ambivalence remains too, years after first seeing *The Lone Ranger* with Comanches in Lawton.

I know producers promised to "do right" by the Indian. They labored hard to make a new Tonto the star and to represent Comanches as excessively innocent and inoffensive recipients of injustice in the late nineteenth century. They fought for a film to be made that could humanize and respect the Indigenous. Thanks in large part to historical research, the film's Comanche consultants, Native actors, and Depp's dedication to crafting his Comanche character, Tonto and the other cinematic Comanches in *The Lone Ranger* perform "moments" of justice in Comanche speech, visuality, and motion. In the end Bruckheimer, Verbinski, Haythe, and Depp appeared to achieve their version of justice for Comanches through the uncanny Tonto and his performance of Indigenous stardom over secondary sidekick status, victory over victimhood, agency over apathy, and humor and wit over mere stoicism and static.

Despite good intentions for justice, the end product still honors a shared Hollywood and U.S. pop cultural legacy of Indians under erasure. All the Comanches but Tonto are scripted to cultural doom as expendable and ready to vanish abruptly. Redeeming acts of a collective sense of Indigenous-led justice fall short. Absent is a history of how a people of pride and power became an empire as once again the Comanches on-screen exited into the representational downfall of previous films. The on-screen Comanche performances are narratively marginalized and marred by an unsettling sympathy, victimhood, and Edenic innocence, all of which leaves viewers with fleeting salutes, disavowed empire, and reified logics of barely grievable, if not ungrievable, Indianness. How many times must a people fall in feature films and other mainstream media before more expanded, developed, and alternative stories of cultural resurgence and rising are produced and represented?

The film's moments of justice circulate in a much longer 149-minute movie. From their first appearance at Cole's first speech to the village captivity scene and Tonto childhood flashback to their demise in war, the Comanche characters, excluding Tonto, receive less than ten minutes of screen time. In comparison the settler majority, be they children, Texas Rangers, harlots, homesteaders, outlaws, railroad executives, soldiers, or otherwise, are represented throughout. The film's closing credits reveal the stark contrast in who predominantly performs a story populated with far more white characters on-screen for far longer periods than nearly all Native peoples and other peoples of color. The end credits start with Depp, followed by ten consecutive white actors, eight of whom are male.[110] Those credited as Comanche characters, all male, are listed twelfth (Grant's "Big Bear"), twentieth (Birmingham's "Red

Knee"), twenty-sixth (Foy's "Young Tonto"), and seventy-second (Tsoodle-Nelson's "Red Knee's Young Warrior").[111]

As the credits rolled at the film's Comanche Nation premiere, we watched Depp's elderly Tonto shuffle out of the "Noble Savage" exhibit and into the proverbial sunset, slowly heading to somewhere in a suit and bowler hat with suitcase in hand. I'd like to think the fictional character was heading home to Comanche relatives, but who would they be? After the massacres he presumably, and tritely, became the last of the on-screen Comanches, representing in the media borderlands before an all-Comanche crowd in attendance. Birmingham's expressed hope, at the outset, for justice for Comanche people, which includes more than sixteen thousand Comanche Nation citizens plus countless descendants, is a hope that I think many of us, as Comanche viewers, shared and, given the history of Indigenous representation, remained cautious about as we began to watch *The Lone Ranger*. The film finally ended, but the conversations it sparked for Comanches had just begun. The next chapter continues seeking justice by centering the voices of real Comanches viewing and discussing reel Comanches on-screen. I turn to how Comanche viewers responded afterward to *The Lone Ranger* in the production of a larger conversation and body of criticism in the Comanchería media borderlands.

CHAPTER 4

Audience

Comanches Viewing Comanches

That movie was crazy!
—LaDonna Harris on *The Lone Ranger*,
Comanche Nation premiere

Opening scene: Theatre #4, Carmike Cinemas, Lawton, Oklahoma,
June 21, 2013.

During our first viewing of *The Lone Ranger* with hundreds of
other Comanches at our tribe's premiere on the summer solstice
in 2013, Comanche relative and filmmaker Julianna Brannum and
I witnessed something on-screen near the film's end that the press
never recognized. After over two hours of watching Johnny Depp's
Tonto wear a dead crow on his head, the likes of which I've never
seen in any historical photographs of Comanches, Tonto morphed
into a new look, long seen in old photos of Comanches. As the
elderly Tonto concluded his narration from within "The Noble
Savage" diorama at a 1933 carnival in San Francisco, Depp's self-
identifying Comanche character exchanged the crow, breastplate,
buckskin, and moccasins for a dark bowler hat, suit, and dress shoes.
The transformation by Mah-woo-meh's Tonto elicited a curious
moment of shared recognition and reception in Comanche kinship
through his likeness to a historic leader of Comanches. The relatively
few critics who acknowledged the costume change suggested the
mainstream suit represented another example of Indigenous assimilation into white society, an ironic critique still leveled at the same
Comanche leader during the so-called fall of Comanches. For some
of us, including from the Quahada band of Comanches in attendance
that evening at the premiere, we saw Hollywood once again take
representational inspiration from one of our relatives.[1]

Recognizing the sudden change in costume by Depp's Tonto,

17. Quanah Parker, circa 1890.

Brannum leaned toward me and whispered, "That's Quanah Parker!" Cousin to cousin, critic to critic, I nodded in agreement at the semblance of maɾʉawe and the resemblance between Depp's Tonto, last of the film's on-screen reel Comanches, and Quanah Parker, last chief of the off-screen real Comanches.

This quiet reactive moment of maɾʉawe, or reporting, between two Comanches reroutes the discourse on the visuality of Depp's

18. Johnny Depp as the elderly Tonto, in *The Lone Ranger.*

Tonto. One could call the comparison "crazy," to redirect Comanche elder LaDonna Harris's response to the film, but the expressed visual recognition has support. It comes from one of my all-time favorite photos: an 1889 or 1890 sepia-toned photograph of Quanah. The coloring and Parker's posture and signature stern stare toward the camera add to the visual variety in snapshots and filmic scenes of Quanah's looks, and looking, over the years. It marks a momentary shift in dress from breechcloth and leggings to suit and hat, like Tonto's visual change, but no matter the visuality or reception of it, Quanah is still being Comanche.

Taking a cue from Parker's recursive looks back at the camera, Brannum continues a tradition of looking, and speaking, back in her response at another camera's close-up on cinematic Comanches. She also once saw close-up, during her film shoot at Quanah's famous residence the Star House in Oklahoma, the suit he likely wore in the photo. "I came across an old armoire in Quanah's main bedroom," she recalls, and "there was his old suit" inside, "tattered and dusty" on a hanger.[2] The scene she describes brings to mind when Depp's Tonto first emerges from his dioramic tipi with the suit on a hanger and uses an old tennis racket to dust it off.

A year before "That's Quanah Parker" was uttered, additional connections between Parker, Depp, and Tonto unfolded. At Depp's heartfelt, traditional adoption ceremony in May 2012 into Harris's family, the Quahada Comanche artist and my cousin Nocona Burgess gifted a cigar box to Depp. The top of the box is adorned with an original painting by Burgess of his great-great-grandfather Quanah Parker in, what else, a derby hat, akin to the historical one in the sepia photograph. This came from Burgess, a highly respected artist whom Depp personally once called a "wizard with a paintbrush."[3]

Then, within days of wrapping production of *The Lone Ranger* in September 2012, Depp—accompanied by several Comanches, including his new *pia* (mom), LaDonna Harris—visited Quanah Parker's grave at Fort Sill in Comanche country. It was reportedly an emotional experience for the adopted Comanche. During his visit in Comanche country, Depp also gifted his original art, a large mixed-media triad of what he boldly says depicts Quanah, Jesus, and himself, to the Comanche Nation, where it now is on display in the Comanche tribal museum. Parker's own mixed heritage as Comanche and Anglo likely resonates with Depp, a longtime self-identifier as white and "Cherokee or possibly Creek." Although no Cherokee or other Indigenous genealogists have confirmed Native ancestry for Depp, the actor does live up to his newfound Comanche name Mah-woo-meh, or "Shape-shifter," especially at the end of *The Lone Ranger*, when Depp shifts in his Comanche look from the controversial crow headpiece to the Quanah Parker–like suit and bowler hat. The moment represents a modern Comanche visuality that reflects an overarching intent by Depp to perform a Comanche characterization, as I argue in chapter 3, into a symbolic and political space of representational justice.

This intertextual recognition, whether strategically intended by the film's producers or tactically inferred by Brannum, illustrates who certain Comanches saw as visual inspiration in that moment, which others perhaps never did. Tonto in the suit and hat signifies, as open and polysemous (and potentially "crazy") signifiers are wont to do, endless potential meanings as determined by each viewer. "All images," Roland Barthes once wrote, "are polysemous," with "the reader able to choose some [signifiers] and ignore others."[4] Whereas Tonto's suit-and-hat look reminded some of us of Quanah Parker, other Comanches in the same viewing room may have sensed other visual comparisons or none at all. Regardless, seeing "Quanah" reveals one way of how Comanches can view a 2013 film through an interpretive lens informed by late nineteenth-century Comanche visuality and history in the Comanchería media borderlands. In this chapter I look at off-screen Comanche critics' additional ways of looking at on-screen Comanche characterizations and enacting maruawe by reporting their thoughts in the media borderlands.

Comanches as Cultural Readers

Brannum's spontaneous and affirmed articulation "That's Quanah Parker!" in conjunction with other reviewers' lack of that recognition illustrates what is at the crux of this chapter: the receptive conjunctures and disjunctures in interpretation and ongoing expressions of jurisdiction in the receptive territories of the media borderlands. Comanches, like other peoples, represent who Black feminist media scholar Jacqueline Bobo calls "cultural readers." Following Bobo's analysis of African American women's critical and complex discursive engagement with Alice Walker's 1982 novel and Steven Spielberg's 1985 film adaptation of *The Color Purple*, I recognize cinematic Comanches as culturally specific and competent readers engaging with *The Lone Ranger*. Cinematic Comanche critics also engage with far more. "Reading," as Robert Warrior (Osage) argues, "highlights the production of meaning through the critical interaction that occurs between a text as a writer has written it and a text as readers read it."[5] Often for the Comanche readers cited in this chapter, *The Lone Ranger* was a brief catalyst, a momentary sidekick, for opening up a larger discourse of Comanche history and practices. Comanches' ways of reading a film are informed by individual and shared epistemologies, experiences, and other contexts impacting and shaping views and understandings. These "ways of seeing" compose "cultural competency," which Bobo describes as "the repertoire of discursive strategies, the range of knowledge, that a viewer brings to the act of watching a film and creating meaning from a work."[6] Armed with this repertoire, cinematic Comanche critics counter the relative erasure of Comanches in mainstream receptive discourse through a tribal-specific mode of representational "reclamation of social, political, and cultural texts" in the media borderlands.[7] This is "looking at Us looking," as Rosa Linda Fregoso says of Chicana/os with film, including "Us as spectators, as viewers between 'the look of the camera' and 'the images on the screen.'"[8]

Contemporary Comanche readers also follow a tribal history of producing Comanche criticism in the media borderlands. In 1867, for example, Yamparika Comanche leader Ten Bears critiqued U.S. officials and their policy of territorial containment: "You said that you wanted to put us upon a reservation, to build our houses and make us medicine lodges. I do not want them. I was born on the prairie where the wind blew free and there was nothing to break the light of the sun. I was born where there were no enclosures and where everything drew a free breath." In 1910, standing before a large crowd at the State Fair of Texas, Quanah Parker responded to incorrect media accounts of the death of his father, Peta Nocona. His father, he explained, was not killed in an 1860 battle with Texas Rangers but died two or three years later. "I want to get that," he says repeatedly, "in Texas history straight up."[9] His daughter Laura Parker Birdsong, in 1912, said she had written an unpublished manuscript "in a true light" about her father's life at his request because newspapers in the media borderlands got "so many things out [of] shape."[10] Turning to film, Comanche educator Augustine McCaffery responded to the 1956 western *The Searchers* and its problematic Comanche representations: "Why can't those Indians shoot better? Why are those whites so accurate? It confused me, because my uncles and my dad were all good shots."[11] Comanche viewers of the 2006 reality series *Texas Ranch House* told guest star and former Comanche tribal administrator Michael Burgess they "liked" his realistic inclusion of the Comanche language, hand-rolling a Bull Durham smoke, and sharp rhetorical comebacks.[12]

Continuing to chart the contours of representational jurisdiction through open-ended questions, as I have done in this book through on-screen and off-screen happenings in Comanchería cinema, I now ask, *Who is reading whom?* Or, *Who is viewing whom?* If this chapter's subtitle is any indication, the simple answer would be "Comanches viewing Comanches," but there are more multidirectional routes between reception and representation than just an off-screen Comanche audience watching on-screen Comanche characters. As critics of all persuasions vie for receptive territory—that is, for space to be heard in the media borderlands—the paths of who says what and when, where, how, and why they say it are constantly in motion. "Everybody's got an opinion," as Depp somewhat dismissively told reporters in response to his controversial portrayal of Tonto.[13] However, not everybody got equally heard, Comanches among them. In response this chapter highlights and synthesizes a number of Comanche and non-Comanche voices from independent and mainstream media sites to fill in some of the gap of who gets heard.

Following cultural theorist Stuart Hall, I recognize audiences, including Comanches, as actively making meaning from texts, not passively absorbing and agreeing with a potentially ascribed meaning.[14] Comanches engage in what media scholar John Fiske calls "audiencing," a process of how viewers make meaning in specific contexts and settings.[15] Visual theorist Gillian Rose recognizes the specificity of audiencing through which an "image has its meanings renegotiated, or even rejected, by particular audiences."[16] Through a multivalent Comanche lens of critique, the particularity in this chapter acknowledges the criticism by predominantly white film reviewers and *Lone Ranger* producers' reactionary defense to critique before concentrating at length on cinematic Comanches' shared and divergent responses to *The Lone Ranger*. To center Comanche responses to and around the film and the film's generative mainstream discourse is to move toward considering the film as a Comanche-centric "cultural forum" for discussion of representation and for considering the forum's members as an "interpretive community" of Comanches in the media borderlands.[17]

Previous Indigenous audience–reception studies have assembled forums and communities for conversation on media representations of Native peoples. As Joanna Hearne observes, such studies "have generally involved focus groups."[18] JoEllen Shively asked a group of Anglos and Natives their opinions of *The Searchers* and its Comanche characters. S. Elizabeth Bird recorded Native and non-Native responses to the television drama *Dr. Quinn, Medicine Woman*. Sierra Adare assembled a group of Native participants to discuss Indians in *Star Trek, Quantum Leap*, and other sci-fi TV series. Sam Pack observed a Navajo family's engagement with film and television in his article "Watching Navajos Watch Themselves."[19] In this chapter I add to scholarship on texts (audience perspectives) about texts (film), but I have not conducted a focus group study or questionnaire. Nor am I interested in making generalizations about Native peoples or any single tribe based on responses in small groups. Instead, I turn to where Comanche critics appear in news media recordings and narratives to glean receptive insights into the politics of Comanche representation.

By critics I mean Comanches who shared thoughts in recorded media on cinematic Comanches in *The Lone Ranger*. Among them is Paul Chaat Smith in an article he wrote amid the hype and well before the release of *The Lone Ranger*. As discussed in the previous chapter, Depp repeatedly told the press he wanted to bring justice to Native representation in cinema by engaging and reinventing its past and present through Tonto. He also repeatedly told reporters that he wanted his Tonto performance to inspire Indigenous youth, Comanches and others, to be proud of their heritage and to embrace their "warrior" identities. What was sorely lacking in the one-sided soundbites in the press was picked up on by Smith. Unlike most U.S. reporters, Smith—a Comanche curator and writer at the National Museum of the American Indian (NMAI) in Washington DC—spoke to and of Native readers. Noting Depp's intent "to right what he [Depp] considered a pop culture wrong" in Native representation in the media borderlands, Smith turns to ask Native readers, "What do we want from Johnny Depp? And why do we care so much?" Smith quickly answered with more queries: "Because it leads to questions like this: Is Johnny Depp Native American? How much, and what kind? Hey, and what tribe was Tonto anyway? Nobody knows. Not really."[20] Smith underscores the politics of Indigenous identity and uncertainty, off-screen (Depp) and on-screen (Tonto), in Indian Country as commonly expressed—however justly or unjustly—through tribal specificity, blood quantum, and kinship for the nonfictional (Depp) and fictional (Tonto).

I extend Smith's line of inquiry to ask what Comanches saw and wanted from *The Lone Ranger*'s characterizations of those inspired by ideas of our ancestors and, in recognizing the integral work of the film's Comanche consultants William Voelker and Troy, inspired by ideas articulated by those today in our Comanche Nation. Like former Comanche Nation chair Wallace Coffey told an interviewer before the advance screening, "I am curious to see how the citizens of the Comanche Nation respond."[21] To illustrate part of what was said among Comanches about *The Lone Ranger*, my case study turns toward listening to recorded responses in several media borderlands sites, including news reports, television, radio, and social media. Namely, I enter the receptive territorial sites of published film reviews, *Lone Ranger* producers' responses to criticism, and film premieres before engaging at length two web and radio series' inclusion of Comanche guests, featuring *Lone Ranger* consultant William Voelker and filmmaker Jason Asenap finding common ground and educator and playwright Terry Gomez and film producer and artist Jhane Myers, two strong Comanche women strongly disagreeing about *The Lone Ranger*.

All these media sites, occurring in the summer of 2013 near the film's nationwide U.S. release on July 3, make inroads into what was said by Comanches about Comanches in the reception of *The Lone Ranger*. The interrelated media texts represent the aforementioned conjunctures and disjunctures between cinematic responses, among Comanches viewing Comanches, in a media borderlands terrain of intratribal and intercultural coexistence and clashes in film criticism. Despite the agreement and disagreement—and arguments and counterarguments—in cinematic critique, the Comanche perspectives herein command to be heard. They comprise a collective refusal to be erased from the media landscape, a stark contrast to the glaring Comanche absence in most mainstream criticism of *The Lone Ranger*.

"Comanche" under Erasure

Media scholar Jonathan Gray contends that film "reviews hold the power to set the parameters for viewing, suggesting how we might view the show (if at all), what to watch for, and how to make sense of it" in the politicized scope of receptive jurisdiction.[22] Reviews constitute media paratexts, or "textual entities," that can persuade others how to approach (and not approach) the film. In the case of *The Lone Ranger*, the published mainstream film criticism spoke loudly and represented multiple camps of thought in what was said and, more often, not said about the on-screen cinematic Comanches. In response to a film in which non-Tonto Comanches briefly appear on-screen before twice vanishing, most reviews also continued a written erasure of Comanches.

First, one camp of critics largely lambasted the film and pulled no punches in plot-inspired puns. Reviewers reveled in calling the film a "train wreck," "a scrap heap of train wreckage," "a train wreck of tonal clashes," and "a cinematic train wreck" that should "ride off into the sunset and be forgotten forever."[23] Discursively derailed locomotives aside, *Rolling Stone* called the film an "obstacle course of cinematic horse turds," a degrading reference to co-starring horse Silver's dropped feces that Tonto drags an unconscious John Reid through at one point, which Comanches in our screening room found amusing. Tonto's crow also got conflated with Edgar Allen Poe's poetic raven. "In a just world," one review concluded, "*The*

Lone Ranger would end with the bird on Depp's head croaking, 'Nevermore.'"[24]

Calling for cinematic mercy, one recurring response in reviews questioned why Disney ever agreed to remake an old western and excessively fund it in the first place, especially after Disney's big-budgeted and box office underperformers *John Carter* (2012) and *Cowboys and Aliens* (2011).[25] "*The Lone Ranger* is a work of tremendous hypocrisy," one reviewer surmises, "as it villainizes industry, big business, and the pursuit of wealth, when the evidence, from casting on down, shows that all three things seem to comprise the film's reason for being."[26] Even Mark Wahlberg (former rapper Marky Mark of my teen years) weighed in on Disney and *The Lone Ranger*: "They're spending $250 million for two dudes on a horse? Where's the money going?"[27] Two days before the film's U.S. release, one site ran this damaging headline in response to initial reviews by a select few advance viewers: "'The Lone Ranger' Reviews: It's as Awful as Everyone Thought It Would Be."[28] "Everyone" is a hyperbolic dissuader for potential viewers to stay away. Celeste Headlee's review politely advised readers, "Please Don't See 'The Lone Ranger.'" Or, as the Cherokee critic Adrienne Keene titled her review of the film, "I Saw *The Lone Ranger* So You Don't Have To."[29]

Such critiques drew the defensive ire of the movie's producers and principal actors. In interviews with Yahoo UK, Depp and Armie Hammer both suspected U.S. critics of penning reviews in advance. "I think," Depp said, "the reviews were written seven to eight months before we released the film." He also conjectured, "The reviews were written when they heard Gore and Jerry and me were going to do 'The Lone Ranger.'" Hammer's response was more graphic and laden with violent metaphors: "This is the deal with American critics: they've been gunning for our movie since it was shut down the first time [in 2011], that's when most of the critics wrote their initial reviews. If you go back and read the negative reviews, most of them aren't about the content of the movie, but more what's behind it." U.S. critics, Hammer surmised, "decided to slit the jugular of our movie." Jerry Bruckheimer claims that critics "were reviewing the budget, not reviewing the movie" and expects critics to rereview "it in a few years and see that they made a mistake."[30]

In the swirling layers of receptive back-and-forth, critics responded to producers' responses to other critics' responses to *The Lone Ranger*. One wrote, "Johnny Depp blames the media for ruining *The Lone Ranger*. Not the controversy surrounding Tonto. Not the massive budget. And definitely not the fact that it wasn't very good."[31] Another critic challenged producers' perception of his newfound jurisdictional power: "It's admittedly very flattering, gentlemen, that you think the critical establishment is responsible for the catastrophic domestic box-office performance of 'The Lone Ranger,' but it's also hilarious." He then adds, "If film critics could destroy a movie, Michael Bay and Adam Sandler would be working at Starbucks."[32]

In further defense of *The Lone Ranger*, producers also spoke of Native reception to the film's Native representation. "Tonto is a heroic figure," Bruckheimer explained, "but Natives are going to have to decide that for themselves. I can't see the story through somebody else's eyes."[33] Bruckheimer appeared to have no problem expressing not only "somebody else's" thoughts but also framing Native responses into a singular, and hence misleading, verdict. "We have the Native American community," he proclaimed to Fox News two days before the film's U.S. release, "which is so behind this movie, it's fantastic." The assertion went unchallenged.[34] Hammer spoke similarly over two months earlier: "The Indians—the Native Americans—are like, 'This is great. We love it.'"[35] Considering that *The Lone Ranger* was not yet in theaters when Bruckheimer and Hammer spoke their verdict on Indigenous viewership, both appear to express their perceived support from those Natives who were on set during production and problematically suggest the praise extends to other Natives, as if the opinion of a few represents the other 99.9 percent of Indian Country. Bruckheimer's and Hammer's "Native American" samples sound as highly questionable and skewed as recent media outlets' polls that express vast Native support of stereotypical Indian mascots.[36] Hammer even dares to paraphrase what he thinks "the Indians" are saying and reinforces a homogeneity of indigeneity, the antithesis of my thesis.

The rhetorical moves do not surprise in a popular U.S. discourse that favors the monolithic nomenclature "Native American" over tribal specificity and intratribal heterogeneity. Some critics, for example, experienced tribal confusion over who is depicted in *The Lone Ranger*. A reviewer for the *Austin Chronicle* thought the film's Natives were "Cherokees." Another site called Depp's Tonto a "Cherokee role." Both possibly confuse Depp's off-screen identification with Cherokees with his on-screen rogue Comanche character.[37] Or possibly, as I can attest to in personal experiences over the years, they jumble the Oklahoma C tribes—Comanche, Cherokee, Choctaw, Chickasaw, Caddo, and Cheyenne and Arapaho. Numerous critics also spelled Comanche with two *m*'s, despite the official and widely accessible name of the Comanche Nation.

Occasionally, reviewers note Tonto's Comancheness, suggesting tribal affiliation actually matters to some (i.e., more than just me and the Comanches I quote). Opting for the collective singular, *Rolling Stone* called "the Comanche" the film's plural "doomed heroes" (read: the valiant-but-vanishing Indian trope).[38] Kevin Gover, the Pawnee director of the NMAI, talked of Tonto as "Mr. Depp's wacky Comanche" and "another memorable, offbeat character" in Depp's filmography.[39] *National Post* reviewer Chris Knight similarly observed Tonto as "so deeply, weirdly Deppian that his Comanche warrior is more enigma than insult."[40] For Depp's performance to be recognized as "wacky" and "weird" is nothing new in his oeuvre of films, but both Gover and Knight, ambivalent as they are in their reviews (and as I am with the descriptor "doomed heroes"), afford receptive space for ambiguity, at least for those who embrace the enigmatic and do not feel compelled to solve Depp's Comanche Tonto.

One critic was far less open to representational ambiguity. British critic Jonathan Foreman engaged at length with the film's

Comanche specificity to reinscribe an unapologetic anti-Comanche perspective. Rewinding the rhetoric on Comanches to sensationalized terrorist talk from dated and clichéd scholarship and popular accounts, Foreman scolded Depp and *The Lone Ranger* for not depicting Comanches as bloodthirsty savages hellbent on destruction. The British conservative tabloid *Daily Mail* ran Foreman's verbosely titled article "The Truth Johnny Depp Wants to Hide about the Real-Life Tontos: How Comanche Indians Butchered Babies, Roasted Enemies Alive and Would Ride 1,000 Miles to Wipe Out One Family."[41] Using twenty-nine words to paint an extremist picture, the lengthy title resembles the sensational, twenty-eight-word title of the 1839 publication *A Narrative of the Captivity of Mrs. Horn, and Her Two Children, with Mrs. Harris, by the Camanche Indians, after They Had Murdered Their Husbands and Travelling Companions.*[42] Despite being published almost two centuries apart, both texts sensationalize what constitutes "Comanche."

Foreman's egregious and misguided published response also follows the recent hyperbolic fare of S. C. Gwynne's 2010 Pulitzer Prize finalist, *Empire of the Summer Moon: Quanah Parker and the Rise and Fall of the Comanches, the Most Powerful Indian Tribe in American History.* That's twenty-three words, for those keeping score on verbose accounts of Comanche violence. Foreman extends his reading of Gwynne's work into the cinematic to support a few meager references to the film. Masking as film review, the article reads more as a litany of what the Crow Creek Sioux writer Elizabeth Cook-Lynn calls "anti-Indianisms." For example, Foreman contends that Comanches "are presented in the film as saintly victims of a[n] Old West where it is the white settler—the men who built America—who represent nothing but exploitation, brutality, environmental destruction and genocide. Depp has said he wanted to play Tonto in order to portray Native Americans in a more sympathetic light. But the Comanche never showed sympathy themselves."[43] The wording conflates off-screen and on-screen Comanches, but the unsympathetic descriptor appears to refer to real-life historical Comanches.

Foreman also tries to right the wrongs he perceives of Comanche representation: "By casting the cruelest, most aggressive tribe of Indians as mere saps and victims of oppression, Johnny Depp's Lone Ranger perpetuates the patronizing and ignorant cartoon of the 'noble savage.'" That quote, paired with the earlier "saintly victims," recognizes part of the film's problematic, if not patronizing, portrayal of Comanches, but the majority of the article rehashes the limited and fetishized understanding by Gwynne (and Foreman) of Comanche torture methods and killings informed by settler-colonial sources. Whereas Foreman props up *The Lone Ranger* to construct an ultraconservative anti-Comanche stance, he also takes the time to note how "brilliantly" the Anglo writer Larry McMurtry portrays heroic white Texas Rangers in *Lonesome Dove*, curious praise for a writer known, along with Gwynne, for penning "ultraviolent Comanche" representation.[44]

Comanches Viewing Comanches in the Media Borderlands

Comanche responses to *The Lone Ranger* and its portrayals of Comanches paint a far more progressive portrait of reception. Running the receptive gamut from praise to scorn to mixed shades of gray in a three-dimensional network of reception, Comanches talk of Comanches as a people always-already worthy of discussion and reflective of agreement and disagreement. To present a comparative and intertextual look into Comanche reception, I turn to interviews with Comanches who viewed advance screenings of the film and hence "hold" jurisdictional shares of "the power to set the parameters for viewing" Comanches.[45] I concentrate on four sites featuring Comanche opinions near the film's release in summer 2013: the film's red-carpet premieres in Lawton and Los Angeles on June 21 and 22, the Al Jazeera web TV series *The Stream* in Washington DC on July 16, and a *Native America Calling* call-in episode in Albuquerque on July 3. Spanning nearly four weeks across sites in the media borderlands in Indian Country and the United States, these outlets represent a growing interest among media producers, at least some, who want to know what a tribal-specific people think of tribal-specific representations of themselves.

By tuning in Comanches' ways of looking at Comanches in the film, I repeatedly hear tribal-specific replies situated in relation to our people's history and futurity of how on-screen and off-screen Comanches are perceived. Following this temporal thread in representation and reception through expressed Comanche culturality, I gather responses into coexisting and, at times, clashing glimpses into a significant historical moment for cinematic Comanches. In all, Comanches show agency in speaking for themselves about our tribal representation in the media borderlands. From invoking ideas on Comanche filmmakers and our history with Texas Rangers to tipi poles as representational texts and the well-being of future generations of Comanche viewers, the interviewees and invited guests momentarily intervene in, and repeatedly reroute, *The Lone Ranger* discourse into a Comanche-centric conversation.

RED-CARPET PREMIERES

Depp's attendance at the Comanche Nation premier increased media presence in Lawton, but it also increased opportunities for reporters to speak with the adopted Comanche's new relatives. Among those traveling to Comanche country/Lawton was NPR reporter Mandalit del Barco. Her article's title "Does Disney's Tonto Reinforce Stereotypes or Overcome Them?" situates reception into two camps, a problematic binary framed as reactionary to "stereotypes." But del Barco commendably speaks to several Comanches to hear their responses after the premiere. The reporter quotes four young Comanches who praise Depp's performance, in support of the actor's previous argument that he did "right" by Comanches.[46]

Del Barco prefaces the praise by attributing it to "Comanches who got free tickets to the screening [and] seemed starstruck and gushed about Depp."[47] The reporter suggests a one-way route of "starstruck" Comanches gone Hollywood, though much can be said for Hollywood gone Comanche, as I have argued elsewhere in this book. To further clarify where NPR did not, the "free" tickets were given by Comanches to Comanches. They came courtesy of the Comanche Nation's hard work, especially by the tribe's former director of Special Projects Donna Wahnee and former chair Wallace Coffey, to persuade Disney to come to the Comanche Nation capital.

Del Barco recognizes the presence outside of Carmike Cinemas as she quotes Comanche viewers in rapid succession in response to Depp's portrayal. "He did a perfect job as Tonto," Kimberly De Jesus said. "He was phenomenal. . . . When he spoke our language, he did pretty good at it. Must have practiced a lot, actually." Nolan Tahdooahnippah said, "I believe whatever Johnny says sheds some light on the way people look at our tribe different. Comanches. We're not savages." Anthony Monessy entered the theater with caution. "I was kinda scared: Is he gonna make fun of us?" Then he answers his own question. "There wasn't nothing that really put our people down." Caubin Monessy adds, "What it is, it's a fairy tale, and a good one." The tale, Monessy recognizes, involves "talking about a man who didn't even exist, but he was one of us." Monessy rhetorically blurs the real-to-reel by situating Depp's Tonto as nonexistent and extant: "one of us."[48] In all the quoted attendees speak to a concern for how Comanche people are represented, perceived, and constructed in a Hollywood tale co-starring the character of a Comanche.

Elsewhere on the red carpet, Wallace Coffey continues the Comanche-specific talk. Visiting with reporter George Lang of *NewsOK*, Coffey says he and his wife, the late Debra Jo Childs Coffey, attended a private screening in Los Angeles. He calls Depp's Tonto an "awesome role" in a film that became, for Comanches, an "opportunity to reflect on our past."[49] Dancing nearby on the red carpet that day is John Keel, popularly known as "Comanche John," in his white face paint, wolf headpiece, and black-and-white regalia. Acknowledging the media controversy over Tonto's look a year later at Comanche Nation events at the NMAI in Washington DC, Coffey staunchly defends Depp's individual choices in visuality and likens the decision-making process to Keel's "unique" look and individual style. "A lot of people criticized Depp," Coffey adds, "because he was representing the Comanche Nation. They said, 'Aww, Comanches didn't paint up.'" "Look," Coffey counters, "at Comanche John." In an interview with *Rolling Stone*, LaDonna Harris similarly says, "The Comanche are very individualistic," as she also acknowledges her newly adopted son, Depp, and his character's controversial appearance.[50]

The night after the Comanche Nation premiere, Disney hosted its red-carpet premiere in Los Angeles. In attendance were Depp, Harris, and Coffey, among the film's producers and principal actors. Also on the red carpet in Los Angeles was Comanche descendant Gil Birmingham, who played the Comanche character Red Knee in the film. Birmingham called Depp's version of Tonto an "honoring and respectful portrayal." Against an unflattering "history in its stereotypical presentation" of Natives, Birmingham observed, Depp "really turns that upside down."[51]

At the premiere, too, were the film's Comanche consultants William Voelker and Troy. One reporter asked if Depp and his Tonto performance will help the actor to be on par with his mentor Marlon Brando's "special place in the Native American community." An ally for decades, Brando fought for fishing rights for Pacific Northwest tribes in the 1960s, supported the American Indian Movement's occupation of Wounded Knee, rejected his Oscar in 1973 for *The Godfather* because of the mistreatment of Native peoples and subjects in Hollywood, and tried to make a film on the history of U.S. injustice against Natives, as he explained in the 1980s. Voelker replied to the reporter, "I think he'll far surpass that. [Depp is] a man of great integrity. He's embraced our culture. He does it with mind, heart, and spirit, but he'll do it quietly, [through] the many things you're not hearing what Johnny is doing. And that's as he likes it. He's already impacting so many people in a good way but in his quiet manner of not being boastful about it."[52] Voelker enacted maruawe and its principle of humility by reporting on the work of a new Comanche relative. He would continue to express his support for Depp a few weeks later on the Al Jazeera television network.

On July 16, 2013, in response to the recent release of *The Lone Ranger*, Al Jazeera TV in Washington DC streamed its live show *The Stream*, episode "Hollywood's Native American Narrative." Co-hosted by the London-born and former CNN journalist Femi Oke and, from Chicago and Doha, Qatar, Malika Bilal. *The Stream* is part of the Al Jazeera English news channel and its "mission to give voice to the voiceless." As its website notes, the series is a daily TV news program whose "goal is to connect with unique, less-covered online communities around the world and share their stories and viewpoints on the news of the day."[53] Aligned with their program's goal, the hosts commendably sought out "less-covered" Comanche and other Native perspectives in a U.S. media landscape known to marginalize Native peoples, including in *Lone Ranger* media discourse.

At the outset Oke calls for a conversation on what it means "to play Indian in Hollywood" and the "impact of Native American stereotypes in film." Bilal then addresses their pre-episode "informal poll" of one question: "What stereotypes of #NativeAmericans have you come across in Hollywood movies?" The inquiry, Bilal explains, drew over 250 replies in social media, with most referencing Disney's *The Lone Ranger*. From its start, "Hollywood's Native American Narrative" seems to already answer that the "narrative" is riddled with stereotypes and perpetuated by *The Lone Ranger*. Like their defensive response to reviewers' critiques, *Lone Ranger* producers would, I imagine, take offense at the suggestive slant expressed in *The Stream*. However, the conversation that ensues in the episode includes two Comanche guests who take offense to the pan-Indian talk and contribute alternative answers to *The Stream*'s slanted hashtagged question. As the show unfolds, the Comanche guests resist and reroute the talk of "Native American stereotypes" in *The Lone Ranger* into Comanche-specific rhetoric.

After their opening *The Stream* hosts welcome four Native men to the show: in-studio guest and filmmaker Jason Asenap (Comanche), who flew in to Washington DC from Albuquerque, and remote guests: *Lone Ranger* consultant William Voelker (Comanche), actor Chaske Spencer (Fort Peck and Lakota), and educator and writer Theodore Van Alst (Lakota descent). Focused initially on the production of *The Lone Ranger*, Oke directs her first question to Voelker and his involvement. "Where," she asks, "do we see your stamp on the film?" In the spirit of maruawe, Voelker replies by introducing himself in the Nʉmʉ tekwapʉ, or Comanche language. "Whenever we come together in a group," he then explains, "introductions are necessary."[54] Rooted in tribal tradition, the moment marks a Comanche-specific presence, which most media outlets never considered, and sets a culturally authoritative tone in the episode.

As Voelker proceeds to describe what he calls his and his assistant's "imprint" on the film, he offers a point of clarification: "the appearance of the lead character [Tonto], that was decided on long before production ever spoke with us." In clarifying what he did and did not do with *The Lone Ranger*, Voelker emphasizes helping Disney with traditional Comanche detail and accuracy while also temporarily dissociating from the controversial and critiqued decisions made by Depp and his makeup team with Tonto's looks. "We do not exist for the movie industry," Voelker later tells *The Stream* hosts. "It's on rare occasion that a project will come to us and ask for historical accuracy." Before *The Lone Ranger* Voelker was credited as an eagle trainer for the movie *Continental Divide* (1981), starring John Belushi, and as adviser for the TV miniseries *Comanche Moon* (2008). The substance of his film consulting is less informed by stints on movie sets than by what Voelker calls "our life's work" in ethno-ornithology that "is based on generations of historically accurate culture." As noted in chapter 2, Voelker and Troy run the 24-7 bird aviary and "first Native American feather repository," called Sia (Comanche for "feather"), in Cyril, Oklahoma, just twenty miles northeast of the Comanche Nation Tribal Complex. "Our primary work is preservation of culture and the eagle as a historical, spiritual, and ceremonial entity."[55]

The aviary work prompted Disney publicist Michael Singer to note that Voelker is uniquely qualified to address the most talked-about aspect of Johnny Depp's Tonto costume—the inanimate crow that adorns his head. In "The Comanche Way" chapter in his book on the making of *The Lone Ranger*, Singer says, "Voelker served as a close consultant on the film to ensure historical and cultural accuracy on many levels." To Singer, Voelker speaks in defense of Depp's avian headpiece, which was arguably the most highlighted object of critique in the media. "The crow," Voelker explains from within his Comanche-centric view, "is probably second only to the eagle in the level of medicine or power that the warrior would aspire to."[56]

On *The Stream* Voelker twice identifies his imprint as *subtleties*, a key plural tactical term for three Comanches on set—technical advisers Voelker and Troy, with Voelker's assistant Celli Crawford—entering into a corporate cinematic system known for stereotypes, not Indigenous or tribal-specific audiovisual accuracy, as alluded to at the start of *The Stream*. For the advisers the "subtleties of the culture" means Comanche cultural accuracy and precision. Disney, Voelker explains, "asked for as much historical accuracy as we could provide." He soon adds, "It's the subtleties that you're not really seeing."[57] Voelker's gesture to what is not seen speaks to another side of reception: gaps in interpretive viewing. He addresses the discursive absence of material presence by highlighting what others did not highlight, partly because they did not recognize, or perhaps expect, a tribal specificity in a Disney film already heavily criticized for its Tonto representation, long before the theatrical release. Voelker's attention to subtleties suggests precise changes in form. By reshaping Comanche representation in film, Voelker alters Comanche appearances on-screen, regardless if the subtleties are noticed by viewers.

To illustrate, Voelker says, "You'll see tipis erected that are for the very first time in all of film history . . . accurate to the Nʉmʉnʉ, the Comanche." He continues speaking to what can be seen in general but not generally known of tribal specificity: "We are a four-pole foundation tipi dwelling people and we're always stuck [on-screen] in northern teepees." He notes too the film's "correct markings on horses and bobbings of the tail" and "actual feathers of historically important avian species on the principal actors that we put on before each scene after a prayerful interaction with the actors, [and] we took off after each scene." Rather than treat the feathers as mere props like in most Hollywood westerns, Voelker talks ceremonially of their significance. Voelker also provided, as Singer notes, the "beaded feathers" attached to Tonto's hair.[58] In an interview with Singer, Birmingham further supports the Comanche advisers' work: "My costume features sacred eagle feathers, the Comanche horses were painted in an authentic, sacred way, and for the first time audiences will see the cut of the teepees in the original Comanche way, facing east, as the sun rises. We've got many years of stereotypical portrayals that we've been trying to change, and this is one way to do it."[59]

Looking back, Voelker sums up his time on set and his efforts toward Comanche cultural accuracy and sensitivity:

> Our primary contribution to *The Lone Ranger* is the way in which Hollywood deals with our sacred and culturally accurate subject matter. On set, there were prayerful ways executed everyday. The stunt men came to us on a daily basis for ekweepsʉ and other protective items we use. Johnny, he was painted ekweepsʉ everyday. That's a protective paint that we use. The whole way the cast and crew operated—we had people who had loved ones that became ill. Actually, someone who lost their mother and they came for traditional prayerful ways. So, it set a completely different tone and especially with the presence of medicine items on set. The respect and sensitivity: that's I guess what I'm most proud of bringing to the production.[60]

The repeated references to Comanche specificity challenge the cogency of popular pan-Indian discourse addressed at *The Lone Ranger*.

Voelker also responds to the identity politics of casting. Oke asks Voelker about critics arguing that the film is "whitewashing" by casting Depp, who has been accused as "not really Native American," instead of an actor unequivocally recognized as Native. Voelker replies, "Johnny does have Native ancestry, I have no doubt after dealing with his family and going down that road." Although *The Stream* commendably brought two Comanches to the table for dialogue, Oke's reference yet again to "Native American" prompts Voelker to shift the conversation toward tribal specificity. "The one thing I take offense at," Voelker counters, "is this constant reference to 'Native American' this, 'Native American' that." Opposing the pan-Native rhetoric, Voelker says, "The character of Tonto is connected *only* with the Nʉmʉnʉ, with the Comanche. So, before you go crazy on this 'Native American' pan-Indianism way of looking at a character, it's very specific to who we are."[61] The vast majority of non-Native reviewers did not specifically discuss Comanches in *The Lone Ranger*. Epistemologically, they could not amid the pervasion of generic Native American discourse.

Asenap agrees with Voelker and addresses the ties of an actor and character to Comanches. "Johnny Depp was adopted by the Comanche tribe," Asenap says, "and Tonto is playing a Comanche character." He then calls attention to Indigenous reception rather than privilege mainstream critics: "The thing I didn't quite understand from other tribes is this is not a pan-Indian character, even though people claim this is something representational of all tribes. But he's playing a Comanche character." Questioning "why anyone else [i.e., non-Comanches] inherently would have a problem with that," Asenap assumes the interest in Tonto stems from the desire to have a say in how he is portrayed, as if "everyone [is] owning this character," which brings in "questions of nationalism." Asenap speaks to who has representational jurisdiction over how, in this case, Comanches specifically and Natives generally are depicted in the media borderlands.[62]

Voelker's and Asenap's receptive attention to Comanche culturality on-screen advances the conversation on a tribal specificity that most critics failed to notice or deem worthy of discussion.

Voelker especially calls attention to why *The Lone Ranger* discussion matters, as he identifies his target audience: Comanche youth. When the hosts ask Voelker if he has rejected tribally inaccurate projects, he replies, "We rarely get involved with the movie industry. However, in this case, there were some aspects of the project that were so close to what we could turn around and use to put historical accuracy out in front of our young people." He continues, "We no longer have the multigenerational households, where young people are learning from the older generations." He estimates, in effect, that "less than 1 percent of our people" are who he calls "culturally, traditional people in the tribe."[63]

Voelker recognizes film and television as sites to reach the youth. Rather than visit museums or read (inaccurate) books, "they are," he contends, "watching the large and small screen." He takes on consulting as a "responsibility" for securing ways to communicate Comanche culturality to young people so that they too can carry traditional knowledge. As he told me, Voelker and Troy were more inclined to work on *The Lone Ranger* to show Comanches on-screen "before the eyes of our young people" so that they can witness a particular vision of "absolute historical authenticity."[64] "We are dedicated absolutely," Voelker similarly says on *The Stream*, "to historical accuracy of the time frame that our people endured forced captivity [1870s–1900s]. Our feeling and the basis for our research is that this generation fought to the death to bring these cultural lifeways forward. Somebody has to keep true and preserve what they brought forward. It just so happens that *The Lone Ranger* is set in this time frame just prior to forced captivity."[65] Fictional films like *The Lone Ranger*, then, become critical additional sites in the media borderlands for communicating nonfictional cultural nuances and visualities on-screen.

NATIVE AMERICA CALLING

Two weeks earlier two Comanche women debated cultural history and lifeways in relation to *The Lone Ranger* on the live Indigenous call-in program *Native America Calling* (NAC). Airing daily for over twenty years on North American radio stations and now streaming online, the "electronic talking circle" NAC is produced by the Indigenous-operated Koahnic Broadcast Corporation in Anchorage, Alaska. In "Tonto Rides Again, Love Him or Lasso Him?" the July 3, 2013, edition of NAC, the Isleta Pueblo and Navajo host Tara Gatewood interviews two Comanche guests: film curator and consultant Jhane Myers and educator and playwright Terry Gomez.[66] The episode's lighthearted and playful title suggests intent to ease some of the anticipated tension in conversing about Depp, a Comanche adoptee; and Tonto, the actor's Comanche outcast character. Both Gomez and Myers had seen advance screenings of *The Lone Ranger*, and both were ready to review it through their respective Comanche-centric lenses on the same day as the film's U.S. release. What results in conversation on *The Lone Ranger* between Myers and Gomez illustrates, from across the pond, British cultural studies scholar David Morley's "interdiscourse" between a film and readers, as both guests speak to the film's engagement with Comanche representational accuracy and its temporalities into history and futurity (or lack thereof).[67] In short, both guests speak to, and personally illustrate, how Comanches represent and get represented.

In a rare, ironic, and commendable move in the media borderlands near the film's release, NAC invited two Comanche women to discuss a film that, as the previous chapter explains, practically voided Comanche women from its celluloid landscape. Notably, in contrast to the film's muted, homogenous, and brief representation of Comanche women as temporary caretakers of two white men who soon massacre the women, Gomez and Myers express audible, divergent, and sustainable opinions. What is expressed matters, but crucial too is the production of space in Indigenous media borderlands for the dialogue on Comanche and Native representation to happen between Comanches and other Natives. In effect, the radio program affords considerable space for culturally knowledgeable Comanche women who complicate popular perceptions of a tribal monolith and who may influence listeners to see or not to see *The Lone Ranger*.

From within Studio 49 in Albuquerque, just a few miles southeast from where Harris adopted Depp, Gatewood frames the hour for listeners across Indian Country as a space where "all perspectives are welcomed" for a "respectful debate about what this film means to you." The inclusive wording comes with recognition of already-heated discourse in Indian Country about *The Lone Ranger* and Depp's Tonto. In this NAC episode the tension continues in a Comanche-centered debate spurred on by two Comanches with vastly different responses to the film. "There is no better way," Cherokee scholar Joshua Nelson says, "to start bringing Cherokee people together than by re-learning how to hear them differing." Whereas Nelson engages Cherokee leaders who "bitterly disagreed" about federal Indian policy, he claims "they shared the desire to protect and enable Cherokee autonomy."[68] I similarly hear in disagreements among Comanches a shared interest in upholding and strengthening individual and tribal self-determination of Comanche expression.

Listening to each guest's vocal contributions, I discern recurring temporal tensions between looking back and looking forward: Gomez foregrounds Comanche identity in a history of Indigenous racism that she claims *The Lone Ranger* perpetuates; Myers uses *The Lone Ranger* spotlight to look ahead to possibilities for a stronger future of Comanche and Indigenous media. Whereas Gomez sheds light on Comanchería borderlands history that shapes and contorts the film's content, Myers uses the film to discursively springboard into future reel opportunities for real Comanches.

Gatewood first asks each of her guests, "Where do you stand on this movie?" She turns to Myers. "I like it," Myers begins. Then, like Voelker did on *The Stream*, she alludes to pushback to the film and its controversial Comanche lead. "After all," she continues, "you have to remember it's entertainment . . . not . . . a documentary or a film that belongs on the History Channel." On *The Stream* Voelker calls *The Lone Ranger* a "comedic western, first and foremost" in a similar reminder of producers' intent to entertain with a fictive blockbuster, not to edify like a nonfictive documentary.[69] In both instances the recognition of public scorn for *The Lone Ranger* becomes a space from which Myers and Voelker suggest cinematic entertainment not be taken too seriously, as they attempt to redirect alternative perceptions and genres associated with the film.

Myers, who was the founding executive director of the American Indian National Center for Television and Film, continues with an eye toward what could come for Comanche country from *The Lone Ranger*. "I'm glad," she says, "to see Native Americans spotlighted in a summer blockbuster. Now, what I want to see going forward" is for "our Native filmmakers" to receive opportunities to work with Disney, Bruckheimer, and Verbinski in a potential *Lone Ranger* franchise, the "infamous 'F' word," as she calls it. As Bruckheimer himself said, "If the audience likes the movie, then Disney will come to me and we'll make another. Or it will be a one-off."[70] Myers asks listeners to imagine if *The Lone Ranger* "going forward . . . employed ten Native filmmakers," then they would have a "Jerry Bruckheimer production" credit or could say "we worked under Gore Verbinski," which could result in increased exposure of "Native people in film."[71] As Coffey similarly told *Time* magazine, "This is just the beginning, is my thinking. It opens the doors for more creative visions with regard to Native Americans in the future."[72]

Citing the robust number of filmmakers in the Comanche Nation and Navajo Nation, she surmises that Natives being a "part of films going forward" would be the "biggest coup." Within Indigenous media borderlands, Myers deploys "coup" to suggest its common context as a strategic professional move. But the term carries more connotation in Indian Country. "Coup" relates to the Native vernacular of historically "counting coup." A Native warrior may count coup, for example, by taking their enemy's weapons or horses. Comanche artist Rance Hood's painting *Coup Stick Song* (1980) shows "a warrior singing his song about how many coups he will touch in battle, with his coup stick."[73] Translated in Myers's articulation, coup symbolizes Comanche and other

Native filmmakers entering a historically uninvited space and taking up the film camera, an instrument and weapon previously used against them, now increasingly used and repurposed by Natives to create Indigenous media.

On *The Stream* Comanche filmmaker Jason Asenap called, too, for Native filmmakers to tell their stories and to have opportunities to do so. "We concentrate on the indies," he says, "where the writing and directing from Native people is happening."[74] Whereas Asenap advocates for the low-budget independent filmmaking route of where to find Native films, Myers calls to enter and work from within big-budget mainstream Hollywood. Rather than go around Disney, Myers suggests going through Disney, to gain professional experience, hone one's craft, and build one's résumé with popular recognizable credentials.

Then Gatewood turns to Terry Gomez, who offers an alternative interpretive route, focused on *The Lone Ranger* narrative and historical distortions. "From the very beginning," Gomez starts, "when I heard that they [Disney] were reviving the Tonto character, I was pretty hesitant to see what was going to be portrayed, and I would have to say that my worst dreams came true when I saw the movie." Gomez counters Myers's attention to future filmmaking possibilities by speaking to past paratexts of what she heard in early media hype, then speaking to what she saw on-screen. Whereas Myers calls for future cinematic coup by Native filmmakers, Gomez calls out *The Lone Ranger* narrative for historical inaccuracy. "Even though," Gomez continues, "this [film] isn't a historical representation," she addresses the fictional film's historically improbable duo of a Comanche and a Texas Ranger. Gomez redirects Myers's reference to the History Channel and critiques Disney's narrative liberties into distorting history and pairing the historically opposed and warring forces of Comanches and Texas Rangers.

Constructing the first in a series of cinematic Comanche citations, Gomez reads a quote from social media in response to *The Lone Ranger*: "Comanche woman Julianna Callabo Shock said,

'Would a Nazi have a Jewish sidekick and would that be acceptable?'" By equating the Texas Ranger–Comanche pairing in *The Lone Ranger* to a Nazi-Jewish partnership, Gomez and Shock challenge popular common-sense perceptions of the culturally unacceptable. In Gomez's words, "The Texas Rangers were formed specifically to kill the Comanche People."[75] Indeed, the Texas Rangers began as an armed militia in the 1830s to protect settlers from Comanches and other Natives, often by any means necessary. Despite Tonto's agency over the title character, *The Lone Ranger* overlooks much of the Rangers' violent history against Native peoples and Mexicans.[76]

Given this history, Gomez then gestures toward Myers's History Channel reference: "When people say that the history isn't important, yes, it is! It is important when you're putting it out to a large audience and having them get an idea this is what Indians are, this is who Comanches are." Although Myers did not say history was insignificant in a film set in historical times, she did distinguish between genres of what *The Lone Ranger* is not (a documentary) and what it is (fictional entertainment). For Gomez the film's genre is less relevant than the film's narrative and representation of Comanche history that can influence audience perceptions of who they think "Comanches are."[77]

Following Stuart Hall's mimetic approach to representation, Gomez suggests that for some viewers fictional Comanches may mirror real Comanches in on-screen to off-screen perception. Gomez continues a mimetic reading by turning her attention to the representational impact of real Comanches watching reel Comanches in *The Lone Ranger*. She says she watched the film with two Comanche elder women and two young Native men. "That was the most racist movie I have ever seen," Gomez quotes one of the men. "This young Comanche man," she adds, "was seeing a Comanche man depicted. It was very painful." The Comanche-centered reception contrasts with Myers's response to watching *The Lone Ranger* at the Comanche Nation premiere in Lawton: "At the end of the film, I heard lots of applause. A lot of people were excited and thrilled."[78]

Gomez also notes the potential pain of "when they [Comanche youth] see this caricature, this joke of who Indians are; it's very hurtful." NAC later takes a call from Meriel, in New York City, who identifies on-air as a collaborator with Gomez. Meriel voices concern with Depp's Tonto imagery in relation to Natives who grew up being taunted as "Tonto." She also expects Disney to market problematic Tonto costumes for Halloween that may perpetuate the name-calling. On *The Stream* guest Theo Van Alst, too, expressed concern for Native youth from potential ramifications of non-Natives dressing in Tonto costumes. Gomez agrees and situates the character's name in a string of explicitly racist terms: "redskin, Tonto, dirty Indian." She also notes her personal experience of being called "squaw," inflammatory rhetoric used disparagingly against Native women.[79]

The irony, then, of Depp's expressed intent to "chip away at the cliché" of stereotypical Indians through his Tonto performance is not lost on Gomez. "He didn't chip away at the caricature," she contends. "He fed it with that crow on his head, with that face paint . . . of an elder, and I have never seen an elder Comanche man that looked like he just crawled up from out of the grave."[80] Again Gomez's mimetic reading shows an absence of a real Comanche referent for Depp's reel Tonto.

Later a Comanche caller on NAC agrees with the lack of an informed Comanche referent for Tonto. "Maruawe. This is Jan. I am a Comanche Nation member, and I was very offended by the movie." Jan Woomavoyah, Gomez's sister, from Bernanillo, New Mexico, notes her perceptions of the crow headpiece and Comanche language as offensive and misused. "The whole thing," she surmises, "is just ridiculous, and it's just Disney's perpetuation of the savage." Embodying and extending Gomez's familial Comanche citations in reception, Woomavoyah adds, "My niece in Oklahoma told me, 'Oh, Auntie, I'm so embarrassed I don't even want to go see this movie.' But I told her we were gonna see this movie because I wanted to be able to critique it and tell other people whether they should even see it or not." Woomavoyah's self-determination to "see" the film "to critique it" and influence others' reception further illustrates the formations of a Comanche viewership who takes seriously the popular use of the name "Comanche."[81]

Myers rebuts with her own perceived Comanche referent. She likens Depp's on-screen Tonto to an old off-screen Comanche warrior society known as the Tuhuwii, or Black Knife Warriors, and their relationship with the crow.[82] Like Brannum's visual connection between the elderly Tonto in hat and suit and old photographs of Quanah Parker in hat and suit, Myers draws from history for representational association with Depp's Tonto. In a tense cultural exchange on *NAC*, Myers asks Gomez if she is familiar with the Tuhuwii dance "about the black crow." "Yes, of course," Gomez replies. "When I first saw this [Depp's Tonto]" with the crow headpiece, Myers continues, "that's what the costuming and everything brought about to me." "But," Gomez interjects, "they didn't wear a crow on their head." Myers concurs, "No, they didn't wear it on their head, but," she clarifies, "that's what it made me think of because it made me think of him as a warrior. Our warriors were interpreted in many different ways." As evident on *NAC*, the same goes for interpreting film.[83]

During a 2014 exhibition of the historical Tuhuwii/Tuhiweeka dance at the NMAI in Washington DC, Coffey similarly associated the warrior society with Depp's Tonto. "People all across the country," Coffey recalls of the reception to Depp's crow headpiece, "said what's he doing with that bird on his head?" Coffey circuitously relates the avian visual to the Tuhuwii dance, which "represents the blackbird, the crow." He adds that the dancer will mimic the crow with "caw! caw!" to signify their "relationship" with each other. As a participant in the contemporary version of the Tuhuwii dance, Coffey also speaks of dancers' individualistic looks: "Each warrior painted their face individually as a reflection of their spirituality and visions, and no one warrior painted their face the same."[84] He points to the uniqueness within the society that, he suggests, Depp also represents with Tonto.

After the debates and disagreements for much of the broadcast, the show concludes on a note of cultural agreement. Cognizant of the challenging conversation, host Tara Gatewood gives each guest a minute for closing remarks and adds, "Let's do this diplomatically." As host and facilitator of the live radio conversation, Gatewood stayed true throughout to conducting what she called for: a "respectful debate" about the state of Native representation in Hollywood, a long-standing heated topic in Indian Country. Without necessarily picking sides by simply praising or condemning Depp and Disney, Gatewood instead welcomed and listened to multiple perspectives, particularly those from her two in-studio Comanche guests.

Gomez goes first. She notes the ongoing critical work in her classrooms and elsewhere to disrupt stereotypes and cultural appropriation by outsiders. She also alludes to staying true to Native cultural principles. Following these multiple points, along with her earlier critique of Depp and Comanche representation in *The Lone Ranger*, Gomez then calls at length for listeners "to promote our Native American filmmakers, writers, playwrights, etc. Instead of running them down," she says, "lift them up, so we can help lift our Native people up." She recognizes a Native viewership that attends movie theaters not only "to learn something new" but also to "be lifted up by our own people and hear their words."[85]

Myers soon concurs. First, she opens her closing remarks by noting that Tonto, this time, is the "hero" and the Lone Ranger is his "sidekick," a reversal of roles that she says is "good . . . for Native people to see and for Native children to see" in comparison to the "old Lone Ranger" and Tonto's "secondary role" that Myers "grew up watching." Myers also turns to her familial upbringing. "I've always been raised to believe that I am to be part of the solution," says Myers. She cites wisdom from her Comanche great-aunt Josephine Myers-Wapp, who lived to be 102, until her passing in 2014. "We're one generation behind," she quotes from her aunt and adds that Natives must implement change and solutions, not just be critics and armchair quarterbacks.[86]

Then comes the explicit agreement with Gomez: "I've always

been an advocate for Native film," Myers continues, "so one thing I agree with Terry on is we do need to promote our Native film-makers." In support of Native media, Myers cites her promotion of the Native press to Disney representatives who had questioned the relatively few Native reporters at *Lone Ranger* media events. In response she directly encouraged Disney to do "outreach to Native press and make sure that we're included because we're just as important as any press."[87]

In their closing remarks both Gomez and Myers point to the future health of Native film and media in Native communities, albeit more briefly than the extended postshow discussion of Indigenous film on *The Stream*. Their concluding nods to future well-being do not erase their earlier differing arguments in response to *The Lone Ranger*. However, the closing agreement gestures back into history when Comanches would gather for long meetings that did not wrap up until a sense of consensus was reached. "The Comanche," LaDonna Harris and Jacqueline Wasilewski explain, "historically governed through consensus." That Myers and Gomez find common ground represents the subject of their underlying shared interest and advocacy during the entire broadcast hour: the future well-being of Comanches and Native peoples and media. Although they disagreed repeatedly, which is a traditional way if ever there was one in Comanche tribal politics, each represented their perceptions and ways of supporting their people. Descending from a historical "Comanche society" in which "all views were taken into consideration," Gomez and Myers each represent a Comanche woman and artist viewing Comanches in the media borderlands, where sites are too often void of (listening to) Comanche representation and critique.[88]

Conclusion

From reporting in Studio 49 in Albuquerque to Al Jazeera television and the NMAI in Washington DC to red-carpet premieres in Los Angeles and Lawton, cinematic Comanches covered a lot of ground in the summer of 2013 in the media borderlands. Building on to a long history of Comanche criticism, Comanches showed up and spoke up in recorded scenes of reception and continuity. Or, in the case of this chapter's opening scene, sometimes the ways of looking and making meaning are remembered and recorded later.

Very shortly after Julianna Brannum memorably reported, "That's Quanah Parker," the movie ended, but the conversations on the film's content had practically just begun. It had been a long day, and not just because it was summer solstice. Brannum and I started driving about seven that morning from Austin to Lawton to the Comanche Nation–hosted luncheon and triple-digit afternoon red-carpet premier and wrapped up the two-and-a-half-hour film screening about ten o'clock at night. After the credits rolled, Comanches stepped outside and continued the cinematic Comanche conversations. That was where I first heard the first Comanche response to *The Lone Ranger*. It wasn't a review full of celebration or condemnation that characterized much of the black-and-white *Lone Ranger* discourse in Indian Country. It wasn't trying for receptive verbosity or evasion. To me it seemed to be a genuine and honest moment of reflection near the end of a long, action-packed day. Standing outside Carmike Cinemas in the capital of the Comanche Nation, LaDonna Harris suddenly said, "That movie was crazy!"

I will never forget that moment. Just four concise words but full of interpretive and ambiguous possibilities. Calling the movie what some critics also called Depp's adoption, crow headpiece, and casting as a Comanche, Harris summed up the movie beautifully. Descending from the late Middle English *craze*, or *crack*, crazy means "full of cracks." Beyond just her adopted son's on-screen crack-filled face paint in the movie, Harris's late-night review sounds applicable to much of the cracked popular representations and perceptions of Comanches over the centuries. In response to what Harris, Coffey, Brannum, Voelker, Asenap, Gomez, Myers, and so many others cited in this chapter demonstrate is a growing collective of Comanche reporters, sometimes with cracks and breaks between shared and differing opinions but all the while still culturally connected and refusing to be broken and without sovereignty as a nation and a people.

Call me crazy, but there is a strength and pride among Nʉmʉnʉ, the Comanche people, that no film, studio, corporate system, or government can topple. No one can stop us from continuing the tradition of representing marʉawe, of reporting to one another and, in the process, telling a good story. By doing so we honor our history and kinship. It is there in the Comanche-commanded space of marʉawe where I turn to now for closing thoughts on honoring our relatives through the reports and stories that we tell and create.

Afterword

Subeetu

My auntie Juanita Pahdopony, to whom this book is dedicated, was very loving and generous in her Comanche cultural teachings. She crossed over in the summer of 2020, but she continues to reach and teach others on this side through memories of times spent together and through media of her art and other contributions. She was in high demand from Natives and non-Natives who wanted to interview her for recordings and publications; collaborate with her on film, literary, and musical projects; and be in her presence and learn about Comanche history and culture and her art and poetry. Before she passed the City of Lawton recognized her with the Honored Elder Lifetime Achievement Crystal Eagle Award and the Oklahoma governor's office honored her with a Community Arts Award.[1] Personally, I recognize and honor Auntie as a cinematic Comanche co-star of this book and a shining star across Indian Country, who left us with a legacy of cultural love and continuance and with wonderful words of wisdom for the future.

Tubitsinakukuru. Listen closely. In a recorded video interview about her buffalo-hide art with the Museum of the Great Plains in Lawton, Auntie explained how her painted scenes on the hide, like those on previous Comanche artists' hides, were inspired by old and current events, all of which she counts as Comanche history. Contrary to those who keep Comanche imagery frozen in the past, she says, "We have important history and culture being made right now. We have important stories and events that are happening all the time."[2] In further support of Comanche history *now*, her images become art of accountability and responsibility to both ancestors and contemporary Comanches and the narratives we speak and share. "I asked people for stories," she explains. "Each time that I put an image on the hide, it was a very sacred experience. I asked people to say a prayer for me. To say a prayer that the right things could get on this hide—the right stories, the right images—that I could tell our story for all of us."[3]

As a mediated text and canvas for documenting and expanding Comanche history, the buffalo hide takes on context beyond its traditional perception as Comanche sustenance, shelter, and clothing. With its freshly painted layer of Comanche scenes, like the eighteenth-century Comanche rock art I spoke of in the preface, the hide becomes an enduring record of cultural knowledge and continuity, where Auntie's descendants are invited to add their layers of scenic history. Through her art, poetry, family, and relationships, Auntie continues to tell her story in a large critical-creative collection of mixed media. As a remarkable educator of Native art and culture for decades and a co-founder of the Comanche Nation College, she also issues a call to Comanches to go forth and tell our stories. This is a legacy of maruawe for Nʉmʉnʉ to report back to the people about our people.

As she says in the buffalo-hide video, "We're obligated to tell our story."[4] She doesn't just say to tell stories. She says "obligated." The term dates back to the Latin *obligare*, from where the term "oblige" comes, meaning to be bound by oath under law or by morals and principles. Like the work of representational jurisdiction in Comanches' efforts to claim and enact the sovereign right to create the media that we want to see, we are obligated to tell the stories that we want to hear. I hear Auntie telling all of us that we have something to contribute, that each of us has a story and, like the scenes of old and new history recorded in her art, that the stories interconnect. Comanche-language leader Ron Red Elk once said, *Sʉmʉ ohyetʉ tana nananʉmʉnʉ*, or "We are all related." So are our Comanche stories. They are intertextual relatives in the Comanchería. With each story told, our narrative relations in the media borderlands expand further and illustrate the always timely work of Comanches representing Comanches.

Personally and tribally, the story I wanted to tell in *Cinematic Comanches* is, as Auntie says of her cartographic circular scenes on the hide, one of "ongoing" history that "doesn't stop."[5] It is a story of unsettled business with one-sided colonizing discourse that claims the Comanche empire ended in the 1870s. It is a story of cinematic Comanche kinship and agency and a "challenge," in the just words of Daniel Heath Justice, to "centuries of represen- tational oppression."[6] The story strikes back at those producers, performers, and perceivers of Comanches in the media borderlands who tried to write us off long ago as one-dimensional warriors, bloodthirsty savages, and other trite labels in a frozen narrative history of a distant Comanche past. But it's not distant. "It's not ancient history," like Comanche artist and educator Nocona Burgess says. "We are right here."[7] Through centuries of our stories still in motion and centuries of our imprints on Comanche homelands, we are here. To cite the beautiful words of a Tongva leader speaking on her homelands in California, "The breath of our ancestors" is all over this place.[8] In Comanche country, the breath of Comanches was, is, and will be everywhere.

This book has told a story of Comanche presence then and now throughout film and media history. Chapter 1 reads a cultural history of Comanches in mainstream and independent film as a series of contested jurisdictional struggles over who represents whom. Reframed as an archive of Comanchería cinema, the media texts are read for tribal specificity. Chapter 2 recasts actor Johnny Depp's 2012 adoption into a captivity narrative, told by and through Comanche perspectives and principles. Reframed within a history of Comanche captivity and kinship, Depp-as-captive entered into relationships in a narrative authored by Comanches who con- tinue a tribal legacy of agency. Chapter 3 reads representations of Comanches in Disney's and Depp's 2013 film *The Lone Ranger* as a negotiated and ambivalent project of cinematic justice and injustice. Reframed as a film inside a growing genealogy of cine- matic Comanche history, *The Lone Ranger* had its moments toward representational justice but failed to decenter whiteness and settler colonialism in the Comanchería borderlands. Chapter 4 recasts the voluminous reception of *The Lone Ranger* by foregrounding

Comanche perspectives on and around the film. Reframed as tribal-specific cultural readers, Comanche critics represent a vibrant synthesis of agreement and disagreement invested in the politics of Comanche criticism and history.

To repeatedly begin in the key of *C* for Comanche (cue bad-joke drum: ba dum tss!), each chapter opens with illustrative moments of cinematic Comanches representing in the media borderlands. Like a film seeking to hook in viewers' attention, the chapters are guided by Comanches' words and performances. The preface cites Juanita Pahdopony and her explanation of maruawe. Chapter 1 turns to Michael Burgess and Calvert Nevaquaya in their roles on a reality TV series. Chapter 2 begins with LaDonna Harris and her assertion of capturing Johnny Depp; chapter 3 with Gil Birmingham and his hope for justice through film; and chapter 4 with Julianna Brannum and her cinematic connection to Comanche ancestry. Each is cited to help readers enter into each chapter of a story intertextually connected by tribe, kinship, media, representation, and borderlands.

In my first book, *Tribal Television*, I identified from the outset as both a Comanche and American sitcom kid and a recovering colonized viewer. In this book I have shared some of my story as a cinematic Comanche. The "cinematic" can be read as an adjective, but I intend the two-word phrase to work interdependently — not to say that cinema outweighs being Comanche but to carefully say that being Comanche, at least for me, also means being cinematic. I am a cinematic Comanche not only in hats I wear as a film critic, consultant, voice-over artist, and scriptwriter but also as a Comanche who turns to film for intracultural possibilities of how to represent Comanche people, lands, sovereignty, and continuity. I turn to film for its potential power to raise consciousness, shape perceptions and policy, and strengthen nationhood. Throughout this book I have recognized that ideas of film and culture go together, that pop culture and Comanche culture are not separate.

In the popular cinematic and literary narratives of the rise and fall of Comanches, the rise is relegated to minor fleeting roles; the fall repeatedly steals the show and ends the mediated narrative and its version of Comanche history. But what about the rise and fall and rise? In cinematic trilogy fashion, part 1's rise of the Comanche empire in the eighteenth and nineteenth centuries is followed by part 2's so-called fall of empire in the late nineteenth and early twentieth centuries, though Comanches stayed strong and committed to defending and continuing Comanche lifeways as best they could even during the reservation era of 1869–1901. Part 3 is unfolding as today's Comanches create media, fight legal battles, and defend and expand our sovereignty and land base. Part 3 unfolds as I write this afterword and report on the rise of the Nʉmʉnʉ, the Comanche people, to tell a story of humanity, tradition, and futurity for a people of sovereignty, strength, and spirit.

The story calls for self-representation and for making mediated contributions to the ongoing cultural rise of Comanches. To echo countless Natives before me, let's make our own films. It's long been happening, but let's see more full-time Comanche filmmakers with more resources coming from the tribe. This is a call for the return of an interconnected Comanche empire, where we call the shots and count coup with every production made, productions that others never imagined we would make someday but that we do imagine and do make. Let's create film and media with and for elders. Let's write original films and remake, with us and by us, the bad ones that others made about us, without us. Let's also adopt, or capture, an approach of independence and interdependence of directing and collaborating with others.

Let's build production studios and make feature films, documentaries, and shorts from within the Comanche Nation. (Let's show our filmmaking neighbors at Chickasaw Nation Productions what's up!) The possibilities for Comanches to not only represent Comanches but also empower and enrich our people through film and media are limitless. Whatever we create through mediated forms is just that: it's what we create. Let's take those casino profits and invest in film and media. And let's remember a Yakima elder's visionary call for casinos to eventually become a footnote in our tribal histories. Let's see what may become of Comanchería cinema.

Let's come together to tell stories of "Texas history straight up," as Quanah Parker told a Texas audience in 1910.⁹ Let's produce responsible stories of the complex and often violent history of Comanches' relations with other Natives and Mexicans. Let's see what happens when white settlers are relegated to background extras or entirely off-camera to represent a reel Indigenous-to-Indigenous history of North America. Let's see more of Comanches and vaqueros speaking each other's languages, like Michael Burgess (Comanche) and Robbie Cabezuela coolly did in PBS's historical reality series *Texas Ranch House*:

BURGESS: Buenos tardes.
CABEZUELA: Maruawe.
BURGESS: Haa [Yes], como está?

That's Texas history straight up. Let's not edit out, as *Texas Ranch House* later did, an earlier moment in which Cabezuela scolded white settlers on the show for saying of Comanches, "'Oh, let's go scalp 'em.' I personally think it's shit," he said, "even in joking." Producers did keep in another part where, as discussed in chapter 1, Comanches got the last laugh and outsmarted the white ranch owner.

Let's listen to and learn more from the elders and their stories. Let's make more stories like the moving animation short *The Comanche and the Horse* (2018), produced by Brannum and narrated by Comanche elder Rita Coosewon entirely in the Comanche language. In the inspiring words of language leader Kathryn Pewenofkit Briner, "Nah ma hani!" Just do it! Let's turn to reservation drama from the late nineteenth century, the life stories of twentieth-century artists, and the twenty-first-century land-back movement for justice and peace. In all let's continue the legacy of creating media and remember for whom and why we are obligated to tell our stories.

Let's also quote and cite (and in effect, honor) one another, like my auntie did in her painting *Mixed Media*. She quotes the wisdom of a Comanche elder from back in the day who, in preparing to visit with a group of curious anthropologists, asked fellow Comanches,

"Shall we tell them the truth or shall we make it interesting?" The truth may well include the mundane minutiae and other aspects of Comanche ontology, but to "make it interesting" affords representational space for playing to and with non-Comanche expectations. Much of the truth may reveal, as Paul Chaat Smith once wrote, that "we're just plain folks, but no one wants to hear that."[10] Through Numunu filmmaking, let's find out. We have historians, linguists, writers, and lawyers (for when we get sued for remaking the bad movies). We have educators, artists, musicians, and singers. We have veteran filmmakers and producers like Dan Bigbee and Julianna Brannum. Bigbee ran an excellent site of reporting Comanche news, aptly called campcrier.net. Brannum runs a production company whose very name represents what Auntie called for: Naru Mui Films. Translation: "telling a story."

In conjunction with her co-produced *We Shall Remain* documentary series for PBS, Brannum helped Comanche youth tell their personal stories and experiences for the 2009 ReelNative short-film project. Guy Narcomey represented and starred in his co-directed film *Running: Connection to Ancestral Land.* Clarissa Archilta's co-directed *We Know What We Saw* recreated her and Connie Archilta's encounter with Piamupits/Bigfoot. The film features the late Comanche elder Mabel Simmons speaking of Piamupits. Simmons's great-grandson and Uncle Harry Mithlo and my auntie's grandson, the late Michael Mithlo Jr., starred in his film *Typical I'ndin Dude,* which "demonstrates," Nancy Marie Mithlo explains, "how traditions, like caring for buffalos, are enacted simultaneously with enjoying bowling or 'rocking out' with heavy metal music."[11]

By telling our stories, however culturally humorous or serious, we honor our history of storytellers who came before us and those who will come after us. For example, a moment in Rodrick Pocowatchit's feature film *The Dead Can't Dance* represents both comedy and drama and the historical and contemporary. Trying to escape from white zombies, Pocowatchit comforts his Comanche nephew T. J. Williams: "We're Comanche. Numunu. Descendants of Wild Horse. We stand strong and proud and [hears zombies approaching]—Oh, let's just get out of here." Individually and communally, we contribute with our *puha* (medicine, personal strength, or talent) to tell our stories responsibly and to the best of our ability. Together the stories will coalesce into an ever-expanding insider Comanche history and archive. When the stories join together, Auntie explains, "that's when the magic happens."[12] Together we are a strong and proud Comanche Nation and must always remember who and where we came from and where we may be going.

To conclude where this book begins, the magic of maruawe—of tribal tellings—has guided the storied scenes of reporting to Comanches about Comanches in the media borderlands. I envision the continuance of maruawe as a foundation for the next generations of Nꙋmꙋnꙋ. May we continue to start with maruawe and report our stories, stay connected, and build one another up. And may we remember and honor the elders and the teaching that "we're obligated to tell our story."[13]

That is all . . . for now. *Subeetꙋ.*

NOTES

PREFACE

1. "Maruawe" is one greeting. The late Doc Tate Nevaquaya opens his 1979 Smithsonian Folkways album *Comanche Flute Music* with "Haa, haitsnu." He later says, in English, "Greetings, my friend." Clip available at "Doc Tate Nevaquaya: Comanche Flute," Smithsonian Folkways Recordings, accessed June 4, 2021, https://folkways.si.edu/doc-tate-nevaquaya/comanche-flute /american-indian/music/album/smithsonian.

2. Pahdopony, quoted in Brian Daffron, "10 Things You Need to Know about the Comanche Nation," *Indian Country Today Media*, October 16, 2014, https://indiancountrytoday.com/archive/10-things-you-need-to-know -about-the-comanche-nation-rJyNxO5-r0-b0vpfs7Lc1Q. As Pahdopony told me, maruawe means "'Report it' or 'Tell it' or 'Give it to me.' We were direct people and still are. Some have incorrectly interpreted us (and maybe not) as being rude people; however, we didn't waste our time with small talk. Some of our people still have this way. It is in our genetic memory." Email message to the author, November 19, 2019.

3. Maya Tahmahkera, personal communication with the author, July 9, 2020.

4. On mediascape, see Appadurai, "Disjuncture and Difference."

5. See Fowles and Arterberry, "Gesture and Performance."

6. "New World Rising" features Comanches Rita Coosewon, Jimmy Arterberry, Jhane Myers, and Phillip Bread.

7. "Comanche Code Talkers," Comanche National Museum and Cultural Center, June 4, 2021, http://www.comanchemuseum.com/code_talkers .html.

8. On *Father Sky and Mother Earth*, Hood says, "I was asked to do this painting for the Lakota Black Hills in the '80s, and we did a poster on this. You can see the warrior on the ground (Mother Earth) with the sacred pipe and in the background Father Sky and the leaving of the buffalo. But yet we still had our power, the eagle." Quoted in Hester and Hood, *Rance Hood*, 76.

9. Not to be outdone by Fabio, romance novelist Genell Rain wrote *Comanche Rain*, *Comanche Wind*, and *Comanche Flame*. For cliché quotes by Fabio and Rain, see Van Lent, "Her Beautiful Savage." Credit for the Comanche translation and spelling of "bullshit" goes to Kathryn Pewenofkit Briner and the Comanche Nation Language Department.

1. As Vine Deloria Jr. wrote in a chapter on Native humor, "When questioned by an anthropologist on what the Indians called America before the white man came, an Indian said simply, '*Ours*.'" *Custer Died*, 166.

2. Comanche elder Sanapia (Mary Poafpybitty) reportedly talked of a "big sickness," possibly polio, which prompted groups to go in different directions away from it. Jones says the most common account he heard from Comanches is a disagreement "over the division of a game animal, usually identified as a bear." *Sanapia*, 6. The quote in the text comes from Zoe A. Tilghman (1880–1964) in her biography of Quanah Parker (ca. 1845–1911), last chief of the Comanches. She lived among Comanches with her husband, Bill Tilghman (1854–1924), who also directed the 1908 silent film *The Bank Robbery*, co-starring Parker. Tilghman's book was reviewed before publication by Quanah's son White Parker, who starred in two silent films. See chapter 1 of this volume. Tilghman, *Quanah*, 5.

3. Numunu means, as other Native nations' insider names roughly translate, "the people."

4. On "Kumantsi," see Hämäläinen, *Comanche Empire*, 24. For the spelling "Cumanche," see John and Benavides, "Inside the Comanchería."

5. Hämäläinen, *Comanche Empire*, 182. According to Jimmy Arterberry, the map was completed around 2009. Telephone interview with the author, July 14, 2020.

6. Paredes, *Texas-Mexican Cancionero*, xiv.

7. See, for example, Marez, "Signifying Spain"; LaMadrid, *Hermanitos Comanchitos*; Frankel, *Searchers*; Meyer, *Son*; and the films Mackenzie, *Hell or High Water*; and Fuqua, *Magnificent Seven*.

8. For a popular example on the "fall," see Gwynne, *Summer Moon*, including his questionable list of highly praised sources. The audiobook gained renewed popularity in 2020, after Joe Rogan interviewed Gwynne on the podcast *The Joe Rogan Experience*, December 10, 2019, https://www.youtube.com/watch?v=Iq8Ss9yg6bo.

9. Hämäläinen, *Comanche Empire*, 4.

10. On representation, see Hall, *Representation*.

11. For sources that recognize and cite Comanches and our stories in the twentieth century, see, for example, Foster, *Being Comanche*; Hoebel et al., *Comanche Ethnography*; and the Doris Duke Collection of American Indian Oral History, University of Oklahoma.

12. For these definitions, see Lexico, a partnership between Dictionary.com and Oxford University Press, s.v. "cinematic," accessed December 1, 2020, https://www.lexico.com/en/definition/cinematic. The French term *cinema* goes back to *cinématographe*, an early name for a film projector.

13. Du Gay et al., *Doing Cultural Studies*.
14. For related tribal-specific literary works, see, for example, Womack (Muscogee Creek), *Red on Red*; Justice (Cherokee), *Our Fire Survives*; K. Brown (Cherokee), *Stoking the Fire*; and Nelson (Cherokee), *Progressive Traditions*.
15. Anzaldúa, *Borderlands/La Frontera*, 19.
16. Gray, *Show Sold Separately*, 117.
17. Brégent-Heald, *Borderland Films*, 17.
18. Shorter, "Borderland Methodology," 20.
19. Hämäläinen and Truett, "On Borderlands," 338.
20. Pratt, *Imperial Eyes*, 4.
21. Vizenor, *Fugitive Poses*, 15.
22. Appadurai, "Disjuncture and Difference," 299.
23. Cohen and Glover, *Colonial Mediascapes*, 5.
24. Deleuze, quoted in Keeling, *Witch's Flight*, 3.
25. Keeling, *Witch's Flight*, 3, 5.
26. Numerous bands, or other extended groups of Comanche families, from southern and northern Comanches, constitute the larger Comanche Nation citizenry and descendants.
27. "AFI's 100 Years . . . 100 Movies: 10th Anniversary Edition," American Film Institute, 2007, https://www.afi.com/afis-100-years-100-movies-10th -anniversary-edition/.
28. Thanks go to Sanja Runtic, a professor at the University of Osijek in Croatia, for telling me about the film *Winnetou* and its Comanche representation. Email message to the author, May 14, 2021.
29. On the creek's name change, see Jan Woomavoyah, "No More Squaw Creek!!," *Nʉmʉ Tewapʉha Nomneekatʉ* 9, no. 1 (2006), official newsletter of the Comanche Language and Cultural Preservation Committee, http:// www.comanchelanguage.org/January%202006%20Newsletter%20in %20Adobe.pdf.
30. "Contact Information," Sia, Comanche Nation Ethno-ornithological Initiative, accessed June 13, 2021, http://comancheeagle.org/contact.html.
31. Hunter McEachern, "Comanche Code Talkers Honored with New Trailway," KSWO, ABC, November 20, 2019, https://www.kswo.com/2019/11/20 /comanche-code-talkers-honored-with-new-trailway/.
32. Howe, "Tribalography."
33. Bourdieu, "Symbolic Power."
34. Cook-Lynn, "American Indian Intellectualism," 57.
35. Hagan, "Archival Captive," 136.
36. On Comanches perceived as "barbarian," see Montgomery and Fowles, "Indigenous Archive." They write, "Within the colonial imaginary barbarians

were masculine, devious, and violent. Viewed from a colonial optic, barbarians were the destroyers and never the creators of sites" (204).

37. Montgomery and Fowles, "Indigenous Archive," 204.

38. Ulibarrí, "Report of Francisco Cuervo y Valdés," August 18, 1706, quoted in Betty, *Comanche Society*, 49; Hämäläinen, *Comanche Empire*, 28.

39. Bustamente, quoted in Montgomery and Fowles, "Indigenous Archive," 204.

40. Hämäläinen, *Comanche Empire*, 3–4.

41. Hämäläinen, *Comanche Empire*, 4.

42. Hämäläinen, *Comanche Empire*, 343–44. In reviewing the Bancroft Prize–winning book, Julianna Barr praises *Comanche Empire* for countering the work of Walter Prescott Webb, Rupert Norval Richardson, and T. R. Fehrenbach, which "promoted a caricature of cardboard 'warriors' reveling in raw mindless violence." "The Comanche Empire," 631. Webb wrote *Texas Rangers*.

43. Gwynne, *Summer Moon*, 344.

44. Webb, *Great Plains*, 162. In the 1950s Paredes criticized Webb's glowing discussion of Texas Rangers and his portrayals of Natives and Mexican Americans. *With His Pistol*.

45. Gwynne, *Summer Moon*, 344.

46. Bruce Barcott, "Men on Horseback," *New York Times Book Review*, June 13, 2010, 1(L).

47. Gwynne, *Summer Moon*, 23. On the violence inflicted by the Texas Rangers, see M. Martinez's *Injustice Never Leaves You* and Swanson's *Cult of Glory*.

48. Johnny Boggs, "Quanah Parker Rides Again," *True West Magazine*, February 14, 2012, https://truewestmagazine.com/quanah-parker-rides-again/. Although Hämäläinen consulted a far more extensive range of sources than Gwynne and wrote his dissertation and book far from Comanche country, I should note Hämäläinen did not speak to Comanches either. The Finnish historian was not outspoken about the decision and has since interacted with Comanches, including elders.

49. Jayme Rutledge, "S.C. Gwynne Enraptures via *Lonesome Dove* Dreams and Comanche Conflict," *Dallas Observer*, June 22, 2011. http://www.dallasobserver.com/content/printView/7090986.

50. Gwynne, quoted in Rogan, *Joe Rogan Experience*, episode 1397. In the back of his book, Gwynne admits to "climbing in the Wichita Mountains" during his research travels, but he curiously did not stop in at the Comanche Nation tribal complex, less than a mile north of the Sonic drive-in and Dollar General he surely passed on Highway 49, which cuts through the mountains. *Summer Moon*, 344. He apparently thought it would be too unreliable "to interview someone in 2008" about late nineteenth-century

history and feared he would be seen as "in their [Comanches'] camp" if he spoke to us. Boggs, "Quanah Parker Rides Again."

51. Pahdopony has repeatedly called Anna Tahmahkera a "Comanche treasure."

52. Rutledge, "S.C. Gwynne Enraptures."

53. Nocona Burgess, telephone interview with the author, April 26, 2016.

54. Paul Chaat Smith calls for Natives "to insist that vast amounts of post-contact Native history is not a binary struggle between settler and the indigenous" within "a neatly constructed 21st-century fantasy that everything that ever happened to us is about the white man. It wasn't. It isn't." "The Most American Thing Ever Is in Fact American Indians," Walker Art Center, September 20, 2017, https://walkerart.org/magazine/paul-chaat-smith-jimmie-durham-americans-nmai-smithsonian.

55. David Harrison (Osage), quoted in Brannum, *LaDonna Harris*.

56. Foster, *Being Comanche*, 47.

57. Hämäläinen, *Comanche Empire*, 345.

58. Howe, "Tribalography," 118.

59. LaDonna Harris, quoted in Jana Bommersbach, "Comanche Crusader: From American Indian Youth to a Hollywood Actor, All Indians Have a Fighter in LaDonna Harris," *True West*, January 8, 2013, http://www.truewestmagazine.com/comanche-crusader/.

60. Armitage argues that the question "Who was that masked man?" "shifts to Tonto, whose heavily painted face functions to mask a deeply scarred 'hero'" with "psychological drama." "That Masked Man," 65.

61. "Hollywood's Native American Narrative," *The Stream*, Al Jazeera TV, July 16, 2013, https://www.aljazeera.com/profile/the-stream.html; "Tonto Rides Again, Love Him or Lasso Him?," *Native America Calling*, July 3, 2013, https://nativeamericacalling.com/wednesday-july-3-2013-tonto-rides-love-lasso/.

1. JURISDICTION

1. See Taddeo and Dvorak, "PBS Historical House Series."

2. "Lords of the Plains," *Texas Ranch House*, May 3, 2006, https://www.youtube.com/watch?v=TS7eeflEKN4.

3. Michael Burgess says film crews shot over fifteen hours of footage of the Comanches across three days. Approximately thirty minutes of footage aired. Burgess, email message to the author, May 3, 2016.

4. *Texas Ranch House* narrator Randy Quaid echoes Michael Burgess: "In 1867, the Great Comanche Trail actually passed through the location of the Cooke ranch." The Cookes, a white family from California, were selected by producers to play the ranch owners. "Lords of the Plains." On the war trail, see R. Smith, "Comanche Bridge."

5. Luis Barreto, quoted in *"Texas Ranch House* Live Q&A," *Washington Post*, May 2, 2006, http://www.washingtonpost.com/wp-dyn/content/discussion /2006/04/28/di2006042801152.html.

6. Nevaquaya told me he wore his father's leggings. Telephone interview with the author, May 3, 2016.

7. For more on Ten Bears, see Kavanagh, *Life of Ten Bears*.

8. Gelo, "Comanche Land," 274.

9. Benveniste, quoted in Kaushal, "Politics of Jurisdiction," 791.

10. R. Lewis, *Alanis Obomsawin*, 175; Raheja, *Reservation Reelism*, 148.

11. Said, quoted in Lucchesi, "Indians Don't Make Maps," 11.

12. Lucchesi, "Indians Don't Make Maps," 11.

13. Blackhawk, *Violence over the Land*, 35.

14. Thorshaug later said that it was "very inspiring to confuse the anthropologists" in the audience. Email message to the author, August 28, 2015.

15. Thorshaug, "Présentation du film *Comancheria*."

16. Credit for the Comanche translation and spelling of "who is shitting whom" goes to Kathryn Pewenofkit Briner and the Comanche Nation Language Department.

17. P. Smith, *Everything You Know*, 6.

18. Steve Tahmahkera (Monroe's son), email message to the author, July 14, 2017.

19. My relative Paul Davis worked on various productions with Monroe Tahmahkera, including *Once upon a Time in China IV*, directed by Yuen Bun (1993).

20. Fatimah Rony, quoted in Raheja, "Reading Nanook's Smile," 1160.

21. Diamond, *Reel Injun*.

22. Diamond, *Reel Injun*; Raheja, "Reading Nanook's Smile," 1160; Bhabha, *Location of Culture*, 93–101.

23. Paul Chaat Smith, "Comanche Ultraviolence, White Supremacy, and You," presentation at the Native American and Indigenous Studies Association, Sacramento, California, May 19, 2011.

24. See Hagan, "Kiowas, Comanches, and Cattlemen."

25. *Quanah Parker: The Last Comanche Chief*, Whistling Boulder, 2012, https:// www.youtube.com/watch?v=W5F3CeIjNZU. For more on Vincent Parker, see Harrigan, *Comanche Midnight*.

26. Parker, quoted in Harrigan, *Comanche Midnight*, 27.

27. "Quanah Parker: The Last Comanche," *Real West*, June 3, 1993.

28. In *Last of the Comanches*, Black Cloud is portrayed by John War Eagle, a British-born Yankton Lakota actor.

29. *Comanche* producers strove for fictive reality by claiming their film to be "factual," as evident in the opening title card: "Filmed entirely near Durango in Old Mexico for historical authenticity, this picture is dedicated

to the people and the Government of Mexico with sincere thanks for their cooperation. Most of the characters, places, dates and events in the story are factual," a contrast from today's "all persons fictitious" disclaimer.

30. The Parker character's longer speech panders to multicultural desires of one assimilated nation, bows to white U.S. paternalism, and rings hollow coming from a non-Indigenous actor. Still, that moment of recognition of being unconquered and never fully surrendered complicates the standard nation-state borderlands binary of the United States and Mexico to open up representational space for Comanches.

31. In an intertextual throwback to the silent era, Disney's historical western *Tombstone* (1993) begins with footage from *The Bank Robbery*.

32. On Indigenous portrayals in silent films, see Hearne, *Native Recognition*; Raheja, *Reservation Reelism*; and Simmon, *Invention*, 3–97.

33. See Wooley, *Shot in Oklahoma*, 72.

34. Neeley, *Last Comanche Chief*, 219.

35. Roosevelt reportedly showed the film at the White House in 1909. Jerman, "Acting for the Camera," 122.

36. Thirty years later Tilghman's wife, Zoe Tilghman, published the book *Quanah* (1938). Prior to publication Quanah's son White Parker read through and edited the book.

37. "The year 1908," Simmon observes, "saw the great growth in Indian films, both in the numbers produced and the centrality of natives to the narratives." Simmon cites, for example, four 1908 films by D. W. Griffith featuring "Indian subjects." *Invention*, 9. *The Bank Robbery* would likely not qualify as an "Indian film" in the traditional sense of the term, which makes it all the more interesting for co-starring a Comanche in an atypical role for Natives.

38. See, for example, Osborn, "Quanah Parker."

39. When a conductor was bringing his train into the area one day, the story goes, Quanah yelled *kesu*, Comanche for "wait," to friends who started to cross the tracks, and the conductor heard *kesu* as "Cache." See Gelo, "'Comanche Land."

40. Noyes and Gelo, *Comanches*, 44; Jerman, "Acting for the Camera," 114; Wooley, *Shot in Oklahoma*, 27; Holt, "Setting the Stage," 12.

41. Hearne, *Native Recognition*, 269.

42. Troy, interview with the author, Cyril, Oklahoma, September 26, 2014.

43. Laura Parker Birdsong attended Carlisle in Pennsylvania from 1894 to 1902. In 1912, on a "Record of Graduates and Returned Students" form, she wrote about her completed but unpublished manuscript about her father. See *Carlisle Indian School Digital Resource Center*, accessed June 4, 2021, http://carlisleindian.dickinson.edu.

44. Frankel, *Searchers*, 124.

45. Frankel, *Searchers*, 212.

46. The Indian Citizenship Act of 1924 granted U.S. citizenship to U.S.-born American Indians.

47. Tilghman, *Quanah*, 187.

48. The narrated version of *The Bank Robbery* is available at Leon Baradt, March 18, 2012, https://www.youtube.com/watch?v=3q87ooO6B74. In the "Comments" section, Hank Elling says, "I think I narrated this around 2006. I am a member of the Southwestern Oklahoma Historical Society and we decided to take on this DVD as a project." Elling grew up in the Cache area.

49. Tilghman, *Quanah*, 187.

50. Images provided by Alexis Ainsworth, a moving image–processing technician with the Library of Congress, from *The Bank Robbery* paper roll on December 28, 2016.

51. Towana Spivey, email message to the author, December 17, 2020.

52. See "Early Silent Films," City of Lawton, accessed June 4, 2021, https://www.lawtonok.gov/programs/film-video-and-music-production-support. The "scenario" sounds similar to the mid-1870s narrative account about Comanche leader White Wolf's conversion to Christianity. See "The Story of White Wolf, a Comanche Chief," Western History Collections, University of Oklahoma Libraries, accessed June 4, 2021, https://digital.libraries.ou.edu/cdm/compoundobject/collection/BatteyTC/id/76/rec/2.

53. Records at the Museum of the Great Plains in Lawton identify six reels, not five, and a range of 123 to 129 Comanches in the film. "Daddy's Picture Show," Frank Wright Collection, Museum of the Great Plains, accessed June 13, 2021, https://discovermgp.pastperfectonline.com/photo/C8FBAA77-3DA4-423E-87AC-954837220598; "Images of Early Lawton," Frank Wright Collection, Museum of the Great Plains, accessed June 13, 2021, https://discovermgp.pastperfectonline.com/photo/959564DD-6953-4696-BE38-814574013231. White Parker later attended Cook Bible School in Phoenix, Arizona, and became a Methodist preacher.

54. Advertisements, *Daily Democrat* (El Reno OK), April 10, 1915, http://gateway.okhistory.org/ark:/67531/metadc91106/; April 12, 1915, http://gateway.okhistory.org/ark:/67531/metadc91107/.

55. "The Real Comanche Indian Pictured in His Native Haunts," review of *The Sign of the Smoke*, in "Early Silent Films"; M. A. Blackburn, manager of the Electric Theatre in Hennessey, Oklahoma, quoted in "Early Silent Films."

56. Based on research and images from museums, flea markets, and elsewhere, Spivey's working script of *The Daughter of Dawn* was, it turns out, quite

accurate when he compared it to the subsequently restored version of the film. Spivey, email message, June 8, 2017.

57. See, for example, "Discovery of Long-Lost Silent Film with All-Indian Cast Has Historians Reeling," *Indian Country Today*, August 28, 2012, https://indiancountrymedianetwork.com/culture/arts-entertainment/discovery-of-long-lost-silent-film-with-all-indian-cast-has-historians-reeling/.

58. On the National Film Registry, see Michael O'Sullivan, "Library of Congress Announces 2013 National Film Registry Selections," *Washington Post*, December 18, 2013, https://www.washingtonpost.com/entertainment/movies/library-of-congress-announces-2013-national-film-registry-selections/2013/12/17/eba98bce-6737-11e3-ae56-22de072140a2_story.html?utm_term=.ef99ce846b97. For more on *The Daughter of Dawn*, see Hearne, *Native Recognition*, 113–14.

59. Although *The Daughter of Dawn* is a fictional movie, critics do not refrain from emphasizing its representations of the "real." For example, Bill Moore, an Oklahoma Historical Society moving-images archivist, says, "This movie shows life as it was then. There are no props. It's all real." Quoted in Wooley, *Shot in Oklahoma*, 72.

60. See *The Daughter of Dawn*, Milestone Films, 1920, https://milestonefilms.com/products/the-daughter-of-dawn; "The Daughter of Dawn," *Joplin Globe*, May 19, 1921, 7; "Indian Picture Booked for School," *Janesville Daily Gazette*, November 20, 1923, 5; "The Daughter of Dawn," *Altoona Mirror*, February 21, 1924, 17.

61. The distributor Milestone, owned by Dennis Doros and Amy Heller, finds it "fascinating that, by accident or design, the film's plot hinges on [a] story on a very similar [situation] to Quannah [*sic*] Parker's real encounter with his first wife." *Daughter of Dawn*.

62. Gordon "Pawnee Bill" Lillie to Richard Banks, May 26, 1921, in "Early Silent Films."

63. Magdalena Becker, "Kiowa Field Matron's Weekly Report," *The Daughter of Dawn* press kit, July 31, 1920, https://cdn.shopify.com/s/files/1/0150/7896/files/DaughterofDawnPressKit.pdf.

64. Deron Twohatchet, interview by Tara Damron, "Heritage: Darren [*sic*] Twohatchet, Comanche," *The Daughter of Dawn* DVD bonus feature (Harrington Park NJ: Milestone Films).

65. P. Smith, *Everything You Know*, 175.

66. P. Smith, *Everything You Know*, 45. Historian Richard Slotkin calls Wayne's role as Ethan a "recrudescence of the classic 'Indian-hater,'" of nineteenth-century U.S. literature, who represents the "most primitive type of Anglo-Saxon pioneer, whose love of war and hunting and appetite

for conquest correspond to the 'savage' propensities of the Native Indians."
Gunfighter Nation, 462.
67. See Eckstein and Lehman, *Searchers*.
68. Eckstein, introd. to Eckstein and Lehman, *Searchers*, 11; Frankel, *Searchers*, 311.
69. P. Smith, *Everything You Know*, 50.
70. As Brandon said in a 1987 interview, "When they got to know me the [Navajo] Indian extras would call me 'the Kraut Comanche.'" Quoted in McBride, *Searching for John Ford*, 565. In the 1956 publicity film *Warner Brothers Presents: The Searchers*, host Gig Young interviews co-star Jeffrey Hunter on the making of *The Searchers*. Young tells viewers, "You'll visit with Monument Valley's friendly Navajos. You'll also see them turned into bloodthirsty Comanche Indians by our makeup men."
71. Colonnese, "Native American Reactions," 337, 339.
72. For more on Debbie as possibly Scar's daughter, see borderlands historian James Brooks's "Don't Make You Kin!," esp. 280–82. Brooks attempts to offer a reading of the film through a Comanche perspective.
73. Alan LeMay, quoted in Frankel, *Searchers*, 205.
74. At the same time, Comanches also captured James Parker's daughter Rachel Plummer, who later wrote *Rachael Plummer's Narrative* (1838).
75. Colonnese, "Native American Reactions," 339.
76. See "Beulah Archuletta," IMDB, accessed June 14, 2021, https://www.imdb .com/name/nm0033815/.
77. Marubbio, *Killing the Indian Maiden*, 155.
78. "Big Heap Herman," *The Munsters* (New York: CBS, January 20, 1966); "Lucy and the Indian Chief," *Here's Lucy* (New York: CBS, October 6, 1969).
79. Marubbio, *Killing the Indian Maiden*, 151.
80. When the interviewer for *Playboy* recognized that "American Indians have played an important—if subordinate—role in your Westerns" and asked the actor if he felt "any empathy with them," Wayne replied, "I don't feel we did wrong in taking this great country away from them, if that's what you're asking. Our so-called stealing of this country from them was just a matter of survival. There were great numbers of people who needed new land, and the Indians were selfishly trying to keep it for themselves." Quoted in Richard Lewis, "Playboy Interview: John Wayne," *Playboy*, May 1 1971.
81. Calvert Nevaquaya, telephone interview with the author, May 3, 2016; Tim Nevaquaya, telephone interview with the author, November 16, 2020.
82. P. Smith, *Everything You Know*, 178, 38.
83. Aleiss, *White Man's Indian*, 145.
84. Daryl Emberly, email message to the author, July 12, 2020.
85. "Evil in the Night," *Walker, Texas Ranger* (New York: CBS, November 4, 1995).

86. Zach, "Top 10 Most Ridiculous *Walker, Texas Ranger* Episodes," Everything Action, April 28, 2012, http://www.everythingaction.com/2012/04/28/top-10-most-ridiculous-walker-texas-ranger-episodes. Multiple sites identify Billy Drago as paternally of Chiricahua Apache descent. See, for example, "Billy Drago," Ethnicity of Celebs, March 4, 2017, https://ethnicelebs.com/billy-drago. Drago's son is Darren Burrows, who portrayed the Alaska Native and white character Ed Chigliak in the dramatic TV series *Northern Exposure* (New York: CBS, 1990–95).

87. "AFI's 100 Years." In the 2007 list *The Searchers* sci-fi and Indigenous-influenced offspring *Star Wars: A New Hope* (1977) is number 13. See the 1997 list at "AFI's 100 Years . . . 100 Movies," American Film Institute, 1997, http://www.afi.com/100Years/movies.aspx.

88. John Hitchcock, telephone call with the author, November 7, 2020.

89. On nineteenth-century violence in Texas, see Anderson, *Conquest of Texas*.

90. Ginia Bellafante, "Out West, Where the Ladies Are Consumptive and the Men Confused," review of *Comanche Moon, New York Times*, January 11, 2008, http://www.nytimes.com/2008/01/11/arts/television/11coma.html?_r=0.

91. Don Heckman, "'Dead Man's Walk' Is a Grisly Journey," *Los Angeles Times*, May 11, 1996, https://www.latimes.com/archives/la-xpm-1996-05-11-ca-2852-story.html.

92. McCarthy, *Blood Meridian*, 53. Following the mainstream circulation of Comanche citationality, McCarthy's imagined Comanches were reportedly informed by his reading of Fehrenbach's book. See Owens, *Cormac McCarthy's Western Novels*.

93. "Survivance," according to Gerald Vizenor, "is more than survival, more than endurance or mere response; the stories of survivance are an active presence." *Fugitive Poses*, 15.

94. Hämäläinen, *Comanche Empire*, 4.

95. Thorshaug, "Présentation du film *Comancheria*," 5; Wallace Coffey, quoted in Thorshaug, "Présentation du film *Comancheria*."

96. Thorshaug, "Présentation du film *Comancheria*," 4.

97. Thorshaug, "Présentation du film *Comancheria*," 2.

98. "Chief Ten Bears Memorial," Comanche National Museum and Cultural Center, August 7, 2019, https://www.facebook.com/ComancheMuseum/posts/who-has-seen-the-ten-bears-memorial-outside-of-our-beautiful-museum-ten-bears-wh/10156156963388204/.

99. As indicated in the film's closing credits, the aerial footage was provided by the Oklahoma Tourism and Recreation Department.

100. Link Wray, "Comanche (1959)," uploaded November 4, 2017, https://www.youtube.com/watch?v=dSDG3YPfrUo. *Rolling Stone* ranks Wray number

45 in its Top 100 list of all-time best guitarists: "100 Greatest Guitarists," November 23, 2011, http://www.rollingstone.com/music/lists/100-greatest -guitarists-20111123/link-wray-20111122.

101. Thorshaug, "Présentation du film *Comancheria*."
102. On Comanche captivity, see, for example, Brooks, *Captives and Cousins*; DeLay, *Thousand Deserts*; and Rivaya-Martínez, "Becoming Comanches."
103. Thorshaug, email message, September 25, 2015.
104. Thorshaug, email message, September 25, 2015. Reflecting on her Q&A in Paris, where she asked her "open question," Thorshaug says, "When I mix fact and fiction in a blurry way, the anthros got really fascinated about what is what. They liked it, and I think it opened up for another way 'to catch a certain spirit.' Because fact alone does not necessarily catch the 'right' spirit one is after. Fiction can more easily get you carried away. But fiction alone, does not necessarily catch the spirit of the actuality (that this is happening for real)."
105. Thorshaug, "Présentation du film *Comancheria*," 4.
106. Thorshaug, email message, September 25, 2015.
107. Juanita Pahdopony, "We're trending right now!," Facebook post, October 15, 2016.
108. Peshawn Bread, "The Daily Life of Mistress Red," Red Ambition Productions, accessed June 4, 2021, https://www.redambitionproductions.com.
109. Eddie Morales, "Represent: Gourd Dance," 1491s, March 22, 2012, https:// www.youtube.com/watch?v=7JZVs_lLC2c.
110. William Voelker, quoted in "*Hostiles*: About the Production," November 10, 2020, http://www.cinemareview.com/production.asp?prodid=20691.
111. In September 2016 I visited the set, where Pahdopony spoke about the area.
112. Kim Wieser, who also worked on *The Son*, shared Comanches' names. Email message to the author, November 10, 2020. For additional names of Comanches cast in *The Son*, see Jolene Schonchin, "Comanche Tribal Members Are Cast for the AMC Series 'The Son,'" *Comanche Nation News* 18, no. 5 (2017): 1, https://issuu.com/wilniedo/docs/may_2017_tcnn.

2. KINSHIP

1. For more on Harris's work, see Harris and Stockel, *LaDonna Harris*; Harris and Wasilewski, "Indigeneity"; and Harris, Sachs, and Broome, "Wisdom of the People."
2. See, for example, a Cherokee Nation of Oklahoma citizen's blog, which lists four Kentucky-based groups she considers to be fraudulent. "Fraudulent 'Cherokee' Organizations," *Thoughts from Polly's Granddaughter* (blog),

September 16, 2009, http://www.pollysgranddaughter.com/2009/09/fraudulent-cherokee-organizations.html. See also "Two Would Be Cherokee Tribes in Kentucky," New Age Fraud, October 4, 2005, http://www.newagefraud.org/smf/index.php?topic=430.0.

3. The Cherokee freedmen includes the emancipated Black slaves of Cherokees and their descendants. See Sturm, "Race."

4. LaDonna Harris, telephone interview with the author, June 7, 2013. On Harris's great-grandfather, see Harris and Wasilewski, "Indigeneity."

5. LaDonna Harris, telephone interview with the author, June 7, 2013.

6. On the genre of Indian captivity narratives, see Derounian-Stodola, *Women's Indian Captivity Narratives*; and Strong, *Captive Selves*.

7. Derounian-Stodola, *Women's Indian Captivity Narratives*, xi, 1–52.

8. Plummer, *Rachael Plummer's Narrative*; Lee, *Three Years*; Horn, *Narrative of the Captivity*; Lehmann, *Nine Years among the Indians*; T. Babb, *Bosom of the Comanches*; Bianca Babb, "Bianca Babb Bell Reminiscences," Dolph Briscoe Center for American History, University of Texas, Austin, n.d.; Rivaya-Martínez, "Captivity of Macario Leal."

9. Singer, *Lone Ranger*, 132.

10. Jerry Bruckheimer, quoted in Singer, *Lone Ranger*, 134.

11. Piper's Picks TV, LA premiere, June 25, 2013, https://www.youtube.com/watch?v=KGXd6kwx4Jw. Home to many Comanches today and the large sculpture Wee-Chi-Tah of a historic Comanche family by the late artist Jack Stevens, Wichita Falls is less than an hour south of Lawton.

12. Allen, "Tonto as Taxidermy," 100.

13. L. Harris, interview, Austin, Texas, October 12, 2017.

14. Weismantel, "Making Kin."

15. Harris and Wasilewski, "Indigeneity," 493.

16. On the history of Comanche captivity, see Brooks, *Captives and Cousins*; Delay, *Thousand Deserts*; and Rivaya-Martínez, "Becoming Comanches."

17. Delay, *Thousand Deserts*, 93–94.

18. Gish Hill, *Webs of Kinship*, 43.

19. Cobb, "Powerful Medicine," 68–69.

20. Gray, *Show Sold Separately*, 36.

21. John Young, "Johnny Depp, Miley Cyrus, and Other Stars Show for the Unveiling of Disney's Upcoming Movie Slate," *Entertainment Weekly*, September 25, 2008, http://ew.com/article/2008/09/25/disney-showcase/.

22. Marc Graser, "Disney, Depp Return to 'Caribbean,'" *Variety*, September 24, 2008, http://variety.com/2008/digital/features/disney-depp-return-to-caribbean-1117992798/.

23. Paul Chaat Smith, "The Toughest Movie Indian," National Museum of the American Indian, June 27, 2013, http://blog.nmai.si.edu/main/2013/06/the-toughest-movie-indian.html.

24. Depp repeatedly describes Silverheels as "great." See Joel Amos, "The Lone Ranger: Johnny Depp Talks Tonto versus Captain Jack," Movie Fanatic, June 28, 2013, https://www.moviefanatic.com/2013/06/the-lone-ranger-johnny-depp-talks-tonto-versus-captain-jack/. Speaking on the radio series *Native America Calling*, Silverheels's great-great-niece Tia Schindler (Cayuga from Six Nations, Ontario) says, "If he [Depp's Tonto] didn't have all the makeup, he kind of does actually resemble my uncle a little bit. . . . I think he was a good fit as far as lookswise to play the role." "The Full Tonto," *Native America Calling*, July 4, 2013, https://nativeamericacalling.com/thursday-july-4-2013-pre-recorded-full-tonto/. For the "stick" reference, see Depp, quoted in Anthony Breznican, "Johnny Depp on 'The Lone Ranger,'" *Entertainment Weekly*, May 8, 2011, http://www.ew.com/article/2011/05/08/johnny-depp-tonto-lone-ranger.

25. Depp, quoted in Breznican, "Lone Ranger."

26. Colin Boyd, "Johnny Depp Is Playing the Lone Ranger," Get the Big Picture, accessed June 14, 2021, GetTheBigPicture.net (Boyd sold the film review site in 2010); Josh Tyler, "Johnny Depp Is Back as Captain Jack," Cinema Blend, 2008, http://www.cinemablend.com/new/Johnny-Depp-Back-Captain-Jack-10314.html.

27. Monika Bartyzel, "Captain Jack Officially Returns, and Signs On for Tonto Too!," MovieFone, September 25, 2008, https://www.moviefone.com/2008/09/25/captain-jack-officially-returns-and-signs-on-for-tonto-too/.

28. "Johnny Depp for Lone Ranger!," MTV UK, September 25, 2008, http://www.mtv.co.uk/johnny-depp/news/johnny-depp-for-lone-ranger.

29. The Internet Movie Database's biographical information for Johnny Depp formerly included a reference to Navajo heritage, but it has since been removed. "Johnny Depp: Biography," Internet Movie Database, 2015, http://www.imdb.com/name/nm0000136/bio.

30. White U.S. radio producer George Trendle created the Tonto character in Detroit in 1933. See Alysa Landry, "Native History: 'The Lone Ranger' Debuts on Detroit Radio, Introduces Tonto," *Indian Country Today*, January 30, 2014, https://indiancountrytoday.com/archive/native-history-the-lone-ranger-debuts-on-detroit-radio-introduces-tonto.

31. Carol Levine, "Tonto and Johnny Fistfight in Hollywood," *NativeVue* (blog), Newspaper Rock, November 17, 2008, http://newspaperrock.bluecorncomics.com/2008/11/johnny-depp-to-redefine-tonto.html.

32. Michael Sheyahshe, "The New Tonto: Johnny Depp," aNm (AlterNative Media), November 3, 2008, http://www.alter-native-media.com/2008 /11/03/the-new-tonto-johnny-depp/.

33. "Heya Silver: It's Tonto Scissorhands," *Brady Braves* (blog), September 25, 2008, http://bradybraves.blogspot.com/2008/09/heya-silver-its-tonto -scissorhands.html (the author's former site).

34. Ungelbah Daniel-Davila, "Depp Is Appropriate for Tonto Role," *Navajo Times*, May 10, 2012, https://navajotimes.com/opinions/2012/0512/051012letters .php.

35. "Adam Beach on Tonto, Twilight and Typecasting," *Strombo*, January 9, 2013, https://www.youtube.com/watch?v=7hpSiT9_gCE.

36. Jerry Bruckheimer (@BRUCKHEIMERJB), "What's coming will show you why this isn't going to be your grandfather's Lone Ranger and Tonto," Twitter, March 7, 2012, 9:16 p.m., https://twitter.com/BRUCKHEIMERJB /status/177623803201990657.

37. Johnny Depp, quoted in Anthony Breznican, "Johnny Depp Reveals Origins of Tonto Makeup from The Lone Ranger," *Entertainment Weekly*, April 22, 2012, http://www.ew.com/article/2012/04/22/johnny-depp-reveals -origins-of-tonto-makeup-from-lone-ranger-exclusive.

38. "Johnny Depp Interview Lone Ranger (2013)," July 26, 2013, https://www .youtube.com/watch?v=z23rrxKD5r4. Depp's makeup artist Joel Harlow reportedly first brought Sattler's painting to Depp's attention. See Singer, *Lone Ranger*, 152.

39. Depp, quoted in Breznican, "Johnny Depp Reveals."

40. IFC, "Put a Bird on It!," *Portlandia*, December 1, 2017, https://www.youtube .com/watch?v=GNpIOlDhigw.

41. Paul Constant, "Johnny Depp as Tonto: How Racist Is That?," *Stranger*, March 8, 2012, http://www.thestranger.com/slog/archives/2012/03/08 /johnny-depp-as-tonto-how-racist-is-that; S. E. Ruckman (Wichita and Affiliated Tribes), "Stunned by Tonto: A New and Improved Version?," *Native American Times*, March 30, 2012, 4.

42. On spreadability in media, see Jenkins, Ford, and Green, *Spreadable Media*.

43. P. Smith, "Toughest Movie Indian."

44. Santos, *Selling the Silver Bullet*, 195.

45. Dana Lone Hill, "Why I'm Willing to Believe in Johnny Depp's Tonto," *Guardian*, March 12, 2012, https://www.theguardian.com/commentisfree /cifamerica/2012/mar/12/johnny-depp-tonto-long-ranger.

46. Adrienne Keene, "Johnny Depp as Cultural Appropriation Jack Sparrow . . . I Mean Tonto," *Native Appropriations* (blog), March 8, 2012, http:// nativeappropriations.com/2012/03/johnny-depp-as-cultural-appropriation -jack-sparrow-i-mean-tonto.html.

47. Natanya Ann Pulley, "An Open Letter to Johnny Depp's Tonto," McSweeney's, April 12, 2012, https://www.mcsweeneys.net/articles/an-open-letter-to-johnny-depps-tonto.

48. P. Smith, "Toughest Movie Indian."

49. Ray Cook, "Tontomania: Who Are We'z Anyways?," Indian Country Today Media Network, March 15, 2012, https://indiancountrymedianetwork.com/news/tontomaniawho-are-wez-anyways/#comments. Cook was responding to Adrienne Keene's post "Cultural Appropriation." Keene replied with her post "Why Tonto Matters," Native Appropriations, March 16, 2012, http://nativeappropriations.com/2012/03/why-tonto-matters.html. For a timeline of the debate with links, see Keene, "Real Indians Don't Care about Tonto," *Native Appropriations* (blog), http://nativeappropriations.com/2012/07/real-indians-dont-care-about-tonto.html.

50. Chris Eyre, quoted in Dominique Godréche, "Director Chris Eyre: Debating Tonto Was 'A Ridiculous Use of Our Time,'" Indian Country Today Media Network, November 30, 2013, https://indiancountrymedianetwork.com/culture/arts-entertainment/director-chris-eyre-debating-tonto-was-a-ridiculous-use-of-our-time/.

51. Chris Eyre, quoted in Jessica Metcalfe (Turtle Mountain Chippewa), "The Tonto Files: Behind the Facepaint," Indian Country Today Media Network, June 26, 2012, https://indiancountrytoday.com/archive/the-tonto-files-behind-the-facepaint.

52. Paul Chaat Smith, quoted in Dan Zak, "Depp's Tonto: An Upgrade on a Stereotype or Just an Updated Stereotype?," *Washington Post*, July 2, 2013, https://www.washingtonpost.com/lifestyle/style/depps-tonto-an-upgrade-on-a-stereotype-or-just-an-updated-stereotype/2013/07/02/36017696-dea3-11e2-b2d4-ea6d8f477a01_story.html?utm_term=.47031c7ea2e3.

53. See D. Martinez, "Peter Pan"; and Strong, "Playing Indian."

54. During a June 2013 news conference at Bishop's Lodge Resort and Spa, Santa Fe, New Mexico, right before *The Lone Ranger* advance premieres in New Mexico and Oklahoma, Depp reportedly responded to a question on critiques of his character as a "red version of blackface." "I expected it," he said. "I still expect it. I have done no harm and represented at the very least the Comanche nation in a proper light. There's always going to be naysayers. Everybody's got an opinion." Quoted in Tom Sharpe, "Depp Says He 'Took Shot at Erasing' Clichés with Tonto Role," *New Mexican*, June 19, 2013, http://www.santafenewmexican.com/news/local_news/depp-says-he-took-shot-at-erasing-clich-s-with/article_8fb05eb6-94fe-54ba-bdfb-650a72136eaa.html.

55. Cindy Yurth, "'Lone Ranger' Producer: Filming on Rez a 'Privilege,'" *Navajo Times*, April 19, 2012, http://navajotimes.com/news/2012/0412 /041912loneranger.php.

56. See "Johnny Depp Donates $25,000 in Scholarship Funds to Navajo Nation," Indian Country Today Media Network, October 26, 2012, https://indiancountrytoday.com/archive/johnny-depp-donates-25000 -in-scholarship-funds-to-navajo-nation; Noel Lyn Smith, "Johnny Depp Donates $25K toward Scholarships for Navajo Students," *Navajo Times*, November 1, 2012, A2.

57. Johnny Depp, quoted in Cindy Yurth, "Tonto Remembered Them," *Navajo Times*, September 13, 2012. See also Alistair Mountz, "Non-profits Work Together to Rebuild Bennett Freeze," *Navajo Times*, November 15, 2012.

58. Raymond Don Yellowman, quoted in "Government Should Take a Cue from Depp," editorial, *Navajo Times*, December 6, 2012.

59. David Harrison (Osage), quoted in Brannum, *LaDonna Harris*, 33:00.

60. LaDonna Harris, quoted in "Johnny Depp Adopted into Comanche Nation," Indian Country Today Media Network, May 22, 2012, http:// indiancountrytodaymedianetwork.com/2012/05/21/johnny-depp-adopted -comanche-nation-114174.

61. Laura Harris, quoted in Tara Gatewood, "Big Name Adoptions," *Native America Calling*, September 5, 2018, https://www.nativeamericacalling .com/wednesday-september-5-2018-big-name-adoptions/.

62. Laura Harris, email message to the author, July 24, 2020.

63. Translation by Wahathuweeka-William Voelker, quoted in "Production Notes: The Lone Ranger," *Cinema Review*, http://www.cinemareview.com /production.asp?prodid=14659.

64. "Johnny Depp Made an Honorary Comanche," KOAT Action News, May 22, 2012, http://www.koat.com/article/johnny-depp-made-an-honorary -comanche/5040945.

65. With *Shape Shifter* Santana created a work of inspired art, accompanied by Hood's painting, to entertain fans and "to honor the Natives of this Earth." Santana says he "consciously created a CD to honor the First People of the land" through song. On the back cover of *Shape Shifter*, Santana recognizes Australia's "apology to the Native Aborigines in 2008" and the U.S. "Native American Apology Resolution . . . in 2009" as reconciliatory responses to settler-colonial policies and acts detrimental to Indigenous lives and cultures. In an interview Santana also says Native peoples "know more than anyone about the shifts in perception." To illustrate he cites climate change as "Mother Nature is shifting." He calls for "Caucasians to invite American Indians into schools . . . to teach . . . how to be connected and

stay connected to Mother Nature." Team Santana, "Santana: The Making of Shape Shifter," April 11, 2012, https://www.facebook.com/carlossantana /videos/148387338623229/?comment_id=879678952160727&comment _tracking=%7B%22tn%22%3A%22R%22%7D; Joe Bosso, "Interview: Carlos Santana on His New Album, Shape Shifter," Music Radar, April 27, 2012, https://www.musicradar.com/news/guitars/interview-carlos -santana-on-his-new-album-shape-shifter-541572.

66. "Hood's Art on Carlos Santana CD," *Comanche Nation News*, June 2012, https://issuu.com/comanchenation/docs/tcnn_june_2012_pdf/7.

67. Hester and Hood, *Rance Hood*, 74.

68. The "lyrics and melodies," Allen explains, "are touchstones for relating life altering events of her family's past." The album delivers a modern multivocal Comanche perspective as informed by family history. During her record release party at the tribal complex in nearby Lawton, Comanche Nation chair Wallace Coffey honored Allen's work by declaring November 7, 2008, "Apryl Allen Day." She later transformed the album into a "Comanche Musical" of the same title. The musical's poster art depicts Allen's human face on one half, aligned with a wolf's face on the other. Allen's musical includes again Videll Yackeschi, along with June Yackeschi Tahpay, who perform "as Elders long gone that appear as mystical white Buffalo." "Shape Shifter a Comanche Musical: Apryl in Sound Studio with 2 Elders from Her Tribe," *Apryl Allen's Blog*, October 24, 2015, https://aprylallen .wordpress.com/2015/10/24/shape-shifter-a-comanche-musical-apryl -in-sound-studio-with-2-elders-from-her-tribe/.

69. In his 2012 Oscars acceptance speech for Best Animated Feature for *Rango* (2011), the director Gore Verbinski recognized his animated lizard acting star as the "real-world chameleon, Mr. Johnny Depp." Eighty-Fourth Annual Academy Awards, Academy Awards Acceptance Speech Database, February 26, 2012, http://aaspeechesdb.oscars.org/link/084-5/.

70. Johnny Depp, quoted in Joel Amos, "Rum Diary Interview," Movie Fanatic, October 26, 2011, https://www.moviefanatic.com/2011/10/rum-diary -interview-johnny-depp-dishes-missing-hunter-s-thompson/.

71. Meikle, *Johnny Depp*, 209, 216. On the production and reception of *The Brave*, see Mark Saylor, "The Sad, Strange Journey of Johnny Depp's 'The Brave,'" *Los Angeles Times*, May 19, 1997, https://www.latimes.com/archives /la-xpm-1997-05-19-ca-60345-story.html.

72. Early in his career Marlon Brando starred in *A Streetcar Named Desire* (1951) and *On the Waterfront* (1954). He also performed controversial racialized roles, including his brownface Mexican character in *Viva Zapata!* (1952) and his yellowface Japanese character in *The Teahouse of the August Moon* (1956). Brando actively supported Indigenous sovereign rights and

developed strong ties with Native activists, including those in the National Indian Youth Council. In 1964 he was arrested at a fish-in on the Puyallup River in Washington. Brando's celebrity garnered "media attention" to "treaty rights to fish" for the Muckleshoots and other tribes. See S. Smith, *Hippies*, 22. Puyallup elder Shirley Satiacum says she and other local Natives renamed the site of his arrest "Brando's Landing." Quoted in Lewis Kamb, "Indians Fondly Recall 'Caring,' Loyal Brando," *Seattle Post-Intelligencer Reporter*, July 2, 2004, https://www.seattlepi.com/local/article/Indians -fondly-recall-caring-loyal-Brando-1148613.php.

73. Gary Farmer, quoted in Metcalfe, "Tonto Files."

74. Gary Farmer, quoted in Metcalfe, "Tonto Files."

75. Thanks to Theo Van Alst for identifying the Midnight Oil poster. Email message to the author, July 22, 2016.

76. In the late 1990s Depp added two tattoos from his self-directed film *The Brave*, in which he stars as a Native character. The tattoo symbols include a question mark dotted with an "x" and a phantom-like figure below it. For photographs of Depp's tattoos, see "Body Art," Johnny Depp Zone, 2012, http://www.johnnydepp-zone.com/bodyart/.

77. "Marion Cotillard Researches Her *Public Enemies* Role on Menominee Indian Reservation," Johnny Depp Zone, April 30, 2008, https://johnnydepp-zone .com/blog/?m=200804.

78. The film's phrase "Good morning, Columbus," scholar David Roche argues, "puts the American speaker in the position of the Native American greeting the European explorer" as "life's truths" suggests an America inhabited with Native peoples long before Columbus arrived to find what others had "already discovered" and who he erroneously named Indians. "(De)constructing 'America.'" Although the Inuits' appearance is subject to the jurisdictional confines of the settler Alex's dream, or imaginary, as overseen by the Serbian director Emir Kusturica, the film temporarily suggests a humanizing ontology set against an exotic pop cultural history of "Eskimos." Yet at the film's end Depp's and Lewis's characters play "Inuit" and speak made-up "Inuit" words in a closing dream sequence. See chapter 3 of this volume.

79. "*The Lone Ranger* Press Conference," June 28, 2013, https://www.youtube .com/watch?v=KE9xDciAq-I.

80. See Sarah Laskow, "The Racist History of Peter Pan's Indian Tribe," *Smithsonian*, December 2, 2014, https://www.smithsonianmag.com/arts -culture/racist-history-peter-pan-indian-tribe-180953500/.

81. In *Finding Neverland* Depp's Barrie speaks broken English, or "Tonto talk," as "Chief Running Nose" before the cowboys, played by white kids, pretend-shoot dead yet another vanishing Indian.

82. Johnny Depp to Nocona Burgess, circa 2012, discussed in the author's telephone interview with Nocona Burgess, April 26, 2016. Burgess recalled Depp calling him a "wizard with a paintbrush."

83. Johnny Depp, quoted in Adam Markovitz, "Depp Becomes a Comanche? For Real," *Entertainment Weekly*, April 12, 2013, http://www.ew.com/article/2013/04/12/depp-becomes-comanche-real.

84. Ethan Sacks, "Johnny Depp Rides to Rescue of 'Lone Ranger,' Stepping into the Moccasins of Jay Silverheels but Delivering a Very Different Tonto," *New York Daily News*, June 30, 2013, http://www.nydailynews.com/entertainment/tv-movies/johnny-depp-tonto-lone-ranger-article-1.1384320.

85. Johnny Wauqua, quoted in Jolene Schonchin, "International Actor, Johnny Depp, Made Goodwill Ambassador to the Comanche Nation; Adopted by Tribal Elder Harris," *Comanche Nation News*, June 2012, https://issuu.com/comanchenation/docs/tcnn_june_2012_pdf/5.

86. Brooks, *Captives and Cousins*, 60.

87. Johnny Depp, quoted in Anthony Breznican, "Johnny Depp Wants 'The Lone Ranger' to Back Off Tonto," *Entertainment Weekly*, May 8, 2011, https://ew.com/article/2011/05/08/johnny-depp-tonto-lone-ranger/.

88. LaDonna Harris, quoted in Bommersbach, "Comanche Crusader."

89. Brannum, *LaDonna Harris*.

90. LaDonna Harris, telephone interview with the author, June 7, 2013.

91. LaDonna Harris, quoted in "Johnny Depp Adopted."

92. *The George Lopez Show*, November 12, 2009. Clip available at "Lopez Tonight: Larry David DNA Test," December 9, 2009, https://www.youtube.com/watch?v=aT1ZAd4rLXE.

93. Meyer, *Son*, chap. 10.

94. In further support of meshing the on- and off-screen, reporter T. W. McGarry observes that the actor "crossed the line between make-believe and real life." "Soap-Opera Star Realizes Dream in Indian Pageant," *Los Angeles Times*, August 18, 1985, http://articles.latimes.com/1985-08-18/local/me-1597_1_cynthia-ann-parker.

95. My thanks to the late Juanita Pahdopony for recalling who made the dress. Additional details come from my telephone interview with Maree Cheatham, July 13, 2020.

96. LeAnne Howe, "Blame Hollywood, Not Depp, for Latest Tonto," Indian Country Today Media Network, July 5, 2013, http://indiancountrytodaymedianetwork.com/2013/07/05/leanne-howe-johnny-depps-tonto-150297.

97. Julianna Brannum, personal communication during visit to the author's course Comanches in Literature and Film, Austin TX, June 29, 2016.

98. Adrienne Keene, quoted in Leslie Gornstein, "Why Can Johnny Depp Play Tonto, but Ashton Kutcher and Sacha Baron Cohen Get Slammed?," E! Online News, May 23, 2012, http://www.eonline.com/news/318280/why -can-johnny-depp-play-tonto-but-ashton-kutcher-and-sacha-baron-cohen -get-slammed.

99. Rod Pocowatchit, "Will Depp's Portrayal of Tonto Add to Struggle Natives Face in Filmmaking?," *Wichita Eagle*, May 27, 2012, http://www.kansas.com /entertainment/movies-news-reviews/movie-maniac/article1092713.html.

100. Gyasi Ross, quoted in Rob Schmidt, "Questioning Depp's Comanche Adoption," *Newspaper Rock*, May 22, 2012, http://newspaperrock .bluecorncomics.com/2012/05/questioning-depps-comanche-adoption.html.

101. Phillips also directed and starred as a Lakota character in *Sioux City* (1994). On Phillips's adoptions, see "Part-Cherokee Actors Becomes Starkeeper in a Sioux Family," *Deseret News*, September 4, 1991, https://www.deseret .com/1991/9/4/18939304/part-cherokee-actor-becomes-starkeeper-in-a -sioux-family; and Wendy Wilkinson, "Lou Diamond Phillips," *Cowboys and Indians*, September 2012, https://www.cowboysindians.com/2012 /09/lou-diamond-phillips/.

102. Sonny Skyhawk, "What's Wrong with Benicio Del Toro and Johnny Depp Playing Indian Characters?," Indian Country Today Media Network, July 2, 2013, https://indiancountrytoday.com/archive/what-s-wrong -with-benicio-del-toro-and-johnny-depp-playing-indian-characters-MA -GiXizHEa9iNyTxbdrSQ.

103. Jason Asenap, "The Tonto Files: In Defense of Comanches," op-ed, Indian Country Today Media Network, June 20, 2012, https:// indiancountrymedianetwork.com/news/the-tonto-files-in-defense-of -comanches/.

104. Asenap, "Tonto Files."

105. Quoted in Hannah Allam, "How One of America's Oldest Languages Landed in Denzel Washington's Latest Film," McClatchy DC Bureau, October 5, 2016, http://www.mcclatchydc.com/news/nation-world/national /article106171302.html. The accepted Comanche spelling of "uncle" in the 2017 Comanche-language dictionary is *ara*. *Taa Numu Tekwapu?ha Tuboopu*.

106. Dana Attocknie, "Actor Johnny Depp Honored Guest at Comanche Nation Fair," *Native Times*, September 30, 2012, https://nativetimes.com/current -news/49-life/people/7896-actor-johnny-depp-honored-guest-at-comanche -nation-fair. For more on Depp's visit to the Comanche Nation Fair, see Jolene Schonchin, "Johnny Depp Makes Special Appearance with Twilight's Gil Birmingham," *Comanche Nation News*, November 1, 2012, https://issuu .com/comanchenation/docs/tcnn_special_edition_cn_fair.

107. Asa Attocknie, quoted in Attocknie, "Actor Johnny Depp."

108. Wallace Coffey, quoted in "Johnny Depp in Lawton, OK on the Red Carpet: The Lone Ranger Premiere," Townsquare Media, June 22, 2013, https://www.youtube.com/watch?v=3c7VhjRe83o.

109. Brannum, personal communication, June 29, 2016.

110. Johnny Depp, "Welcome to the 30th Annual Gathering of Nations Pow Wow," Gathering of Nations, April 26, 2013, https://www.youtube.com/watch?v=01Pn6VzQwtc.

111. Cheryl Crazy Bull, "World Premier Celebration for Disney's 'Lone Ranger' to Benefit Fund," American Indian College Fund, May 29, 2013, http://collegefund.org/news-list/world-premier-celebration-for-disneys-lone-ranger-to-benefit-fund/.

112. Laura Harris, quoted in Gatewood, "Big Name Adoptions."

113. Johnny Depp, quoted in "Johnny Depp Surprises Fans at Screening," Female First, June 21, 2013, http://www.femalefirst.co.uk/celebrity/johnny-depp-298041.html.

114. Wallace Coffey, telephone call with the author, June 30, 2015.

115. Wallace Coffey, quoted in George Lang, "Lawton Rolls Out the Red Carpet for Johnny Depp for Comanche Nation Premiere of 'The Lone Ranger,'" Oklahoman, June 22, 2013, https://www.oklahoman.com/article/3855277/lawton-rolls-out-the-red-carpet-for-johnny-depp-for-comanche-nation-premiere-of-the-lone-ranger.

116. Lang, "Lawton Rolls Out."

3. PERFORMANCE

1. "Johnny Depp Returns for 'The Lone Ranger' Premiere (06-21-13) in Lawton, OK," Comanche Nation Premiere, June 21, 2013, https://www.youtube.com/watch?v=aySKbI5wN4A.

2. Gil Birmingham, Facebook post, October 2, 2014, https://www.facebook.com/pg/therealgilbirmingham/photos/?tab=album&album_id=10152390806991453.

3. Benny Cable, personal communication with the author, August 5, 2020.

4. Standing next to Depp, Birmingham later says, "I'm just honored to have been a part of it [The Lone Ranger]." Then Depp speaks, "If I can help in any way to help pass the message along to the children, to the younger generations, to understand that where they come from, to understand that they are warriors and nothing less." "Johnny Depp Returns." Birmingham's pre–Lone Ranger credits include his Native role in the Twilight series, in which non-Native actor Taylor Lautner co-stars as the lead Native werewolf character, Jacob. In a recent interview Birmingham notes the restrictions often placed on Native actors: "If you are Native, you rarely get cast in

crossover parts. My approach to characters is that I play them as human beings." Quoted in Kevin Noble Maillard, "What's So Hard about Casting Indian Actors in Indian Roles?," *New York Times*, August 1, 2017, https://www.nytimes.com/2017/08/01/movies/wind-river-native-american-actors-casting.html.

5. Some scholars suggest the Lone Ranger character was modeled after real-life African American deputy U.S. marshal Bass Reeves. Whereas Depp's casting as Tonto spurred much conversation, imagine if Disney had cast the title character with an African American actor instead of another white actor. On Reeves and associations with the Lone Ranger, see Burton, *Black Gun, Silver Star*; and Gill, *Talented Tenth*.

6. See Hall, *Representation*.

7. Marti Chaat Smith, personal communication with the author, Native American and Indigenous Studies Association meeting, Washington DC, June 4, 2015.

8. On a history of *Lone Ranger* texts, see, for example, Allen, "Hero with Two Faces." Allen's extensive research reveals Tonto has not always been the sidekick. In the Dell Comics series *The Lone Ranger's Companion Tonto* (1951–59), Tonto is the star. The Lone Ranger is occasionally referenced but never appears in the thirty-three quarterly issues. Tonto, says Allen, is "the 'last' survivor of his particular indigenous nation." He is a lawyer working with other tribes but privileges advancing the U.S. nation-state over Indigenous tribal interests. As Allen contends, "Tonto's interventions serve the needs and desires of the US government and the dominant US culture and society. He helps to advance the signing of 'peace' treaties, both among Indian tribes and between Indian tribes and the United States; he helps to advance the expropriation of 'natural' resources, but especially gold and silver; he helps to advance the development and expansion of the technologies of travel and communication, such as the railroad and the telegraph; and, most importantly, he helps to advance the non-Native use of Indian lands for mining, for cattle and sheep raising, and for white settlement." Allen, "Tonto on Vacation," 143.

9. Wolfe, "Settler Colonialism," 387–88.

10. Nakassis says, "The citation is an act that re-presents some other event of discourse and marks that re-presentation as not(-quite) what it presences. The citation is a play of sameness and difference." "Citation and Citationality," 51.

11. Morgan, "Intertext in This Text," 2. Bauman, *World of Others' Words*, 4. In addition to what informs the text under scrutiny, intertextuality considers how and in what ways the intertexts function in the text.

12. Corrigan, "Mask in the Museum," 396.

13. Bakhtin, *Speech Genres*, 162; Kristeva, "Word, Dialogue and Novel," 37.

14. Gray, *Show Sold Separately*, 117.

15. Daffron, "10 Things You Need."

16. See Clark, *Lone Wolf*.

17. Quoted in Rae, *Trudell*.

18. Fraser, *Scales of Justice*, 2.

19. Waziyatawin, *Justice*, 13.

20. S. Lewis, "Vision and Justice," 13, 11.

21. Hochberg, "Cinematic Occupation," 536, 541, 547.

22. At the Comanche Nation premiere, Depp said, "With great respect to the Native Peoples—that was first and foremost on the agenda" for Depp, Verbinski, Bruckhemier, and Haythe. Quoted in Lang, "Lawton Rolls Out."

23. Enrique Limón, "Tonto on Top," *Santa Fe Reporter*, June 25, 2013, http://www.sfreporter.com/arts/artsvalve/2013/06/25/tonto-on-top/.

24. Verbinski also acknowledged the Lone Ranger as a "great American hero, but there were people here before us, and I think the film respects that." Quoted in Lang, "Lawton Rolls Out."

25. Depp, quoted in Breznican, "Lone Ranger."

26. Bruckheimer, quoted in Singer, *Lone Ranger*, 44.

27. "Interview with Gary Farmer and Johnny Depp, Stars of Dead Man, 1996," Rutube, January 17, 2015, https://rutube.ru/video/f94a20c621daf5ea135408be0b459773/.

28. P. Smith, quoted in Dan Zak, "Depp's Tonto."

29. "I didn't know," Hammer says, "it was actual horse (droppings) they were pulling me through until afterward. But the horse (relieved itself) at one point, and they thought it would be funny." Bryan Alexander, "'The Lone Ranger' Tosses Tradition on Its Head," *USA Today*, July 2, 2013, https://www.usatoday.com/story/life/movies/2013/07/02/depp-hammer-lone-ranger-set/2412841/.

30. Justin Haythe, quoted in Carlos Aguila, "Justin Haythe on *The Lone Ranger*," *Creative Screenwriting*, August 3, 2013, https://creativescreenwriting.com/justin-haythe-on-the-lone-ranger/.

31. Gore Verbinski, quoted in Christopher Rosen, "Gore Verbinski on 'The Lone Ranger' and That Unbelievable Train Sequence," *Huffington Post*, June 27, 2013, https://www.huffpost.com/entry/gore-verbinski-the-lone-ranger_n_3505703. Peckinpah's father and two uncles, whose parents adopted two Sierra Mono girls and grew up with other Natives in California, told others they were Native. Sam's uncle and family historian Mort Peckinpah says, "There is no Indian blood in the Peckinpah family to my knowledge, although my brothers and I always told everybody we were Indians. The three of us were raised with Indians. When we started to school, we

were the only white kids in school with thirty Indians. We learned to talk Indian and fight Indian. So when people saw how we spelled our name, they automatically assumed we were part Indian. No truth to it at all. The name 'Peckinpaugh' is really German-Dutch from the lower Rhine Valley." Simmons, *Peckinpah*, 5.

32. Freedman, *Hollywood Crime Cinema*, 140.

33. Johnny Depp, quoted in "Career: Currently Shooting," Johnny Depp Zone, May 2012, http://www.johnnydepp-zone.com/reeljohnny/currentlyshooting .php. The site says the quote is from a May 2012 interview at a *Dark Shadows* junket.

34. Depp, quoted in Sharpe, "Took Shot at Erasing."

35. Corrigan, "Mask in the Museum," 395.

36. Adrian Gomez, "Press Swoops In," *Albuquerque Journal*, June 20, 2013, https://www.abqjournal.com/212482/press-swoops-in.html. Depp prefaces this quote by saying, "There's a lot of history with Native Americans that I learned before taking on this role."

37. On the history of Native representations in film, see, for example, Raheja, *Reservation Reelism*; Hearne, *Native Recognition*; P. Deloria, *Indians in Unexpected Places*; Aleiss, *White Man's Indian*; and Kilpatrick *Celluloid Indians*.

38. Johnny Depp, quoted in Hannah Dreier, "Lone Ranger Aims to Take Tonto beyond Sidekick," Yahoo! News, April 18, 2013, https://news.yahoo.com /lone-ranger-aims-tonto-beyond-132557774.html. In addition to Brando, Depp also honored his great-grandmother.

39. Johnny Depp, quoted in Todd Gilchrist, "Johnny Depp Says 'Lone Ranger' Will 'Thank' and 'Respect' Native Americans," MTV, July 1, 2013, http:// www.mtv.com/news/1709896/lone-ranger-johnny-depp-tonto-native -americans/.

40. Johnny Depp, quoted in "Lone Ranger Discussion," Deppography (a Johnny Depp fan site), June 12, 2013, http://deppography.proboards.com/thread /2667/lone-ranger-discussion-spoilers?page=65. The site says the quote is from *The Lone Ranger* press kit.

41. That the buffalo substitutes for a Comanche moniker could be an oversight in production, yet it's unlikely, given the close attention to Comanche accuracy by the Comanche consultants.

42. Comanche artist Travis Komahcheet and Kristi Komahcheet own Intertribal Visions Unlimited. See, for example, "Comanche Two Hatchet," hoodie, Intertribal Visions Unlimited, 2020, https://www.intertribalvisions.com /product-page/comanche-warrior-pullover-hoodie. Comanche artist Rance Hood's painting *Lords of the Plains* shows a Comanche warrior on a horse. Cinematically, "Lords of the Plains" can be seen in the 2007 film

Comancheria on a license plate and is referenced in the 2016 feature film *Hell or High Water*.

43. As numerous critics observed, Tonto's old wrinkled look is rather reminiscent of actor Dustin Hoffman's 112-year-old white and adopted Cheyenne character in *Little Big Man* (1970). Like Hoffman's character telling his life story to a curious white anthropologist in a flashback in *Little Big Man*, the elderly Tonto soon launches into recounting to Will his earlier adventures of seeking justice for his Comanche people and shaping lawyer John Reid into the Lone Ranger. When one interviewer noted the film's narrative framing inspiration from *Little Big Man*, Depp nodded in agreement and said "right." See "Johnny Depp Talks about the Challenge of Playing Tonto," HitFix, July 2, 2013, https://www.youtube.com/watch?v=LSt6n0GWQsc\. Depp also credited his great-grandmother for inspiration: "She did apparently have quite a bit of Indian blood and long braids and tobacco down her bosom," he said. "So, yeah, that was sort of the idea to sculpt me into my great grandmother." Sharpe, "Took Shot at Erasing." Verbinski came up with the framing device of the old Tonto to ensure Depp's Tonto is in charge of telling the story from the start. In "this version" viewers will hear Depp/Tonto tell "the story untold" of the title character "from Tonto's perspective," as Verbinski says, "from the guy who was there." When asked if the elderly Tonto narration was his idea, Verbinski replied, "Yeah, that was my idea early on," as early as "2006." Quoted in Rosen, "Gore Verbinski."

44. As a "distant, alien, uncivilized being," writes Lumbee lawyer and legal scholar Robert Williams Jr., "the savage has always represented an anxious, negating presence in the world, standing perpetually opposed to Western civilization." *Savage Anxieties*, 1.

45. Eileen Jones "The Fantastic Failure of the Lone Ranger," *Jacobin*, https://jacobinmag.com/2013/09/the-fantastic-failure-of-the-lone-ranger.

46. In her article "Tonto WTF?!" Annalee Newitz says the diorama underscored Tonto as "pure, uncut racial stereotype." Gizmodo, July 8, 2013, https://io9.gizmodo.com/tonto-wtf-675616096. Brian Johnson called it a "corny framing device" and "awkward set-up." "The Lone Ranger: Pirates of the Wild West,"*Macleans*, July 3, 2013, https://www.macleans.ca/culture/movies/the-lone-ranger-pirates-of-the-wild-west/.

47. See Markwyn, "Beyond *The End*."

48. Drew McWeeny, "Johnny Depp Discusses Playing Tonto and 'Rango' for 'Lone Ranger' Director Gore Verbinski," Hitfix, July 2, 2013, https://uproxx.com/hitfix/johnny-depp-discusses-playing-tonto-and-rango-for-lone-ranger-director-gore-verbinski/.

49. Pahdopony, quoted in Daffron, "10 Things You Need."

50. Fran Striker, quoted in Robert Siegel, "The Lone Ranger: Justice from Outside the Law," *All Things Considered*, NPR, January 14, 2008, https://www.npr.org/templates/story/story.php?storyId=18073741. George Trendle created the radio series for the WXYZ radio station in Detroit.

51. Allen, "Tonto as Taxidermy," 105.

52. Pahdopony, email message, November 6, 2018.

53. Douglas Murray adds, "We staged our recording session in a dry irrigation pond bed in a field away from the highway. The walls of the pond sheltered us from any road noise and also gave a nice little bounce to the sound. We spent Saturday morning recording women and children for the Comanche river camp scene, and the afternoon with men singing and drumming for the death dance scene. On Sunday we recorded men doing conversation and call-outs, as well as full Comanche war whoops and traditional songs." Murray says, "The experience of working with the Comanche couldn't have been more wonderful for me." Quoted in Steve Jennings-X, "The Lone Ranger Rides Again! Sound Challenges of a Fun-Filled Western," *Mix*, July 1, 2013, https://www.mixonline.com/sfp/lone-ranger-rides-again-369324. *The Lone Ranger* soundtrack includes the track "Contest" with performance credit to "Johnny Depp and Comanche Nation."

54. Meek, "Injun Goes 'How!'"

55. In a gesture toward the southern reaches of the Comanchería, I note that Armenta was born Felipe Almerina Armenta in Mexico City in 1875, the year that Quanah Parker's band of Comanches went to the reservation in Fort Sill, Oklahoma.

56. Jay Dee Witney, email message to the author, June 15, 2015. Witney says his father moved from Lawton at age five, after William's father passed on, and grew up in California and Fort Sam Houston in San Antonio, Texas. Filmmaker Quentin Tarantino calls Witney one of his favorite directors. Tarantino also applauded the 2013 *Lone Ranger*, placing in on a personal top list for best movies of the year. See Rick Lyman, "Whoa Trigger! Auteur Alert," Quentin Tarantino Archives, September 15, 2000, https://wiki.tarantino.info/index.php/QT_discusses_William_Witney; and Sebastian H, "Quentin Tarantino's Top 10 Films of 2013—So Far," Quentin Tarantino Archives, October 5, 2013, https://www.tarantino.info/2013/10/quentin-tarantinos-top-10-films-2013-far/.

57. Todd McDaniels, quoted in Britt Peterson, "In 'The Lone Ranger,' Is Tonto Really Speaking Comanche?," *Boston Globe*, July 7, 2013, https://www.bostonglobe.com/ideas/2013/07/06/the-lone-ranger-tonto-really-speaking-comanche/KjS0gKbgkdI6IBN9NhmeUL/story.html.

58. "It's gratifying," Voelker says, "that he's so committed." Quoted in Singer, *Lone Ranger*, 136.

59. William Voelker, quoted in "'Johnny Depp Will Surpass Marlon Brando' (the Lone Ranger Premiere)," June 22, 2013, https://www.youtube.com /watch?v=TuhasbCovYQ.

60. Johnny Depp, quoted in "Johnny Depp–Arizona Dream Interview," October 13, 2007, https://www.youtube.com/watch?v=EK4lzJNGNR4.

61. See "Whoops, I'm an Indian!," *Three Stooges.*

62. As the episode's IMDB page says, "Crooked stagecoach express agent Mason directs two henchmen who dress as Paiute braves to rob stage shipments with valuable cargo." "Backtrail," *The Lone Ranger,* IMDB, March 8, 1951, https://www.imdb.com/title/tt0635324/?ref_=ttep_ep10.

63. P. Deloria, *Playing Indian*; Green, *Tribe Called Wannabee.*

64. The McBains are possibly named after the character McBain in the 1961 film *Comancheros,* which Leone praised. The "Comancheros" in the film are those who sneak guns and alcohol to Comanche characters.

65. Sergio Leone, quoted in Frayling, *Sergio Leone: Something,* 257. The killers are "employed by the Morton railroad company," which draws further similarities with *The Lone Ranger* story line. Another *Lone Ranger* citation occurs at Red's establishment. When Depp's Tonto puts a birdcage on his birded head in fear of a nearby cat, he mimics one of the white killers' similar actions in Leone's *Once upon a Time in the West* (1968).

66. Leone, quoted in Frayling, *Sergio Leone: Something,* 252, 256.

67. Leone, quoted in Frayling, *Sergio Leone: Italy,* 78.

68. Frayling, *Sergio Leone: Italy,* 78.

69. Edward Buscombe, quoted in Frayling, *Sergio Leone: Italy,* 26.

70. Leone followed Fonda's rare villainous turn in Ford's *Fort Apache* (1948) as an "unpleasant, authoritarian colonel who violates moral codes and treaties with the Indians." Leone, quoted in Frayling, *Sergio Leone: Something,* 271.

71. John Patterson, "The Lone Ranger Takes Artistic Theft to a Whole New Level," *Guardian,* August 5, 2013, https://www.theguardian.com/film/2013 /aug/05/the-lone-ranger-artistic-theft.

72. Verbinski's shot of their distant vantage point cites other films. Ford's *The Searchers* shows co-starring white and Cherokee character Martin Pauley's first look at his white family's settlement burned by Comanche raiders. George Lucas's space western *Star Wars* (1977) shows Luke Skywalker's view of his family's torched abode by the nomadic and possibly Indigenous Tusken Raiders. On his inspiration for the Tusken Raiders, Lucas reportedly once compared them to Bedouins in the Middle East. See Rinzler, *Making of Star Wars,* 97. Personally, I have long associated the Tusken Raiders with Apaches and Comanches. Navajo artist Ryan Singer does too: "I always love to reimagine Star Wars from the indigenous perspective. The Tusken folks, you know, those are our peoples, right? That's like Apache

homeland right there. That's Comanche homeland—you don't go across there, they're going to mess you up." Quoted in Nick Gonzales, "Star Wars Intersects with Indigenous Cultures and Inspires Art," *DGO*, December 31, 2019, https://dgomag.com/contents/4106.

73. The New Mexico casting call for Pilar, an "1800's Mexican maid," noted, "Women must be able to improvise sheer terror." "Casting Call: The Lone Ranger," Talent Services, February 1, 2012, http://www.talentservices.biz /?q=node/11085.

74. Ultimately, no Brown bodies remain, unless one counts Depp's Tonto. Jesús wears the Comanche signifier of a buffalo-horns hat.

75. On the Indigenous as ungrievable, see Byrd, *Transit of Empire*.

76. Frank also visually and temporally relates to Iggy Pop's cross-dressing fur-trapper character in *Dead Man* (1995).

77. John Linn, quoted in Frankel, *Searchers*, 56.

78. Quoted in J. Brown, *Indian Wars and Pioneers*.

79. For Owen's art, see *Battle of Plum Creek*, University of Texas Arlington Libraries, accessed June 4, 2021, https://library.uta.edu/borderland/event /692.

80. The Comanche Nation is one of the tribes served by the Anadarko Agency. Also, in 1890, Comanche leader Quanah Parker posed for a painting by Scott. See Lovett, Peck, and White, *Picturing Indian Territory*, 52–55.

81. Fowles, "Fighting Terrorism since 1492," 22. On representations of parasols among Plains Indians, see Durkin, "Umbrellas and Parasols."

82. The scene also echoes footage in Alejandro Jodorowsky's acid western *El Topo* (1970), in which the lead character (Jodorowsky) and his real-life son (Brontis Jodorowsky) ride together on a horse and carry a black parasol. Alejandro Jodorowsky says the umbrella served a practical purpose in *El Topo*: "to protect [his son Brontis] from the sweltering desert sun." *Psychomagic*, 136.

83. Armie Hammer, quoted in Alexander, "Tosses Tradition."

84. See Hill in Cree filmmaker Diamond's *Reel Injun*.

85. On the Comanche arrow as a sign of synecdoche in *Red River*, see Prats, *Invisible Natives*, 50–53.

86. For lists of "Comanche" extras and their production schedules, see casting director Elizabeth Gabel's site EG Casting and her summer 2012 posts. See, for example, "Call Time: Tuesday August 7," EG Casting, August 6, 2012, https://egcalltime.blogspot.com/2012/08/call-time-friday-august -3.html.

87. Big Bear is seated and holds up spectacles to look closely at Tonto's broken watch, which invokes the modern eyeglasses worn by historic Comanche leader Ten Bears.

88. In his *Lone Ranger* film review, Benson asks, "Did the casting in this movie do an injustice to Native Americans?" After referencing the Comanche Nation population of more than fifteen thousand citizens, he asks, "Why were none of them considered in casting the part of a Comanche character?" No mention is made of Foy's and Birmingham's Comanche ties. Benson, "Lone Racist," 351–52.

89. Jimmy Foy, quoted in Frank Dubois, "Mescalero's Own Tonto: 10-Year-Old Cast as Young Tonto in the Lone Ranger," *Westerner*, November 5, 2012, https://thewesterner.blogspot.com/2012/11/mescaleros-own-tonto10-year-old-cast-as.html.

90. On the Pease River massacre, see Neeley, *Last Comanche Chief*; and Carlson and Crum, *Myth, Memory, and Massacre*.

91. To prepare the young actor for the horrific scene, Verbinski says in a rehearsal video with Foy that "what I'm most interested in is your feeling. . . . You have to really feel it, okay? That's what great acting is." See "Joseph Foy with Gore," uploaded by Elizabeth Gabel, circa 2012, https://vimeo.com/61352880.

92. Nancy Mithlo, "In 'Lone Ranger' Times, There Were No Female Indians. Wait, What?," *Indian Country Today*, July 9, 2013, https://newsmaven.io/indiancountrytoday/archive/in-lone-ranger-times-there-were-no-female-indians-wait-what-ee8jh4-tCUi4w-pyKnUYFA/.

93. "Juanita Pahdopony, Part 4 of 4," Museum of the Great Plains, April 20, 2020, https://www.facebook.com/DiscoverMGP/videos/1024324547962794/.

94. Eric Tippeconnic, statement on *Comanche Woman*, exhibit *Comanche Motion: The Art of Eric Tippeconnic*, Bullock Museum, Austin, Texas, 2018–19, https://www.thestoryoftexas.com/discover/artifacts/comanche-woman.

95. Barr, *Peace Came*, 2–3. Barr observes of Comanche women's presence in eighteenth-century Spanish *rancherías* that they were "mediators of peace" (3). Incidentally, Barr's father, Alwyn Barr, served as an historical consultant on *Texas Ranch House*.

96. "Lords of the Plains."

97. See Idle No More, homepage, 2020, http://www.idlenomore.ca; "Remarks by the President and Vice President at Signing of the Violence against Women Act," White House, March 7, 2013, https://www.whitehouse.gov/the-press-office/2013/03/07/remarks-president-and-vice-president-signing-violence-against-women-act; Martha Troian, "Mi'kmaq Anti-fracking Protest Brings Women to the Front Lines to Fight for Water," *Indian Country Today*, November 10, 2013, https://indiancountrytoday.com/archive/mi-kmaq-anti-fracking-protest-brings-women-to-the-front-lines-to-fight-for-water-alK1jV5GE0Sa-gXWtatWwQ; Rob Capriccioso, "Obama Nominates Native American Woman to Federal Court," *Indian*

Country Today, September 20, 2013, https://indiancountrytoday.com /archive/obama-nominates-native-american-woman-to-federal-court-1a5s -Y-WckyHQNa7h4VmQw; "Remarks by the President and Vice President at Signing of the Violence against Women Act," White House, March 7, 2013, https://www.whitehouse.gov/the-press-office/2013/03/07/remarks -president-and-vice-president-signing-violence-against-women-act.

98. Mithlo, "'Lone Ranger' Times." Incidentally, the scenes with Comanche women were the last to be filmed. The Mescalero Apache and Comanche actor Joseph Foy, who played the young Tonto, had broken his arm, which delayed shooting his scenes. In preparing to shoot the flashback story, Disney issued a casting call in and around Los Angeles for "Mexican or Native American Women, ages 18–80." Rather than cast Comanche women from Oklahoma or elsewhere in the Comanchería, the casting director for extras in Los Angeles opted for a highly generalized and multicultural call. Still, given the history of Mexican captives among Comanches, the call for Mexican women also makes sense, even if the call was driven by a concern for how many "Native American"–looking women could be located. See John Done, "Disney Studios 'Lone Ranger' Now Also Casting Elderly Caucasians in Los Angeles," Disney Casting Calls, September 12, 2012, https://www.moviecastingcall.org/disney-studios-lone-ranger-now -also-casting-elderly-caucasians-in-los-angeles/.

99. Leone, quoted in Frayling, *Sergio Leone: Something*, 274. According to Frayling, Bronson's Indian characters include "Hondo in Aldrich's *Apache* and the half-breed Captain Jack, in *Drum Beat*, both in 1954; the Sioux Blue Buffalo in Sam Fuller's *Run of the Arrow* (1957) and the Mexican Indian Teclo in *Guns for San Sebastian* (1967)." *Sergio Leone: Something*, 273.

100. In "traumatic westerns," "past events of a catastrophic nature are repre-sented so as to challenge both the realist representational strategies of a genre that often trades on historical authenticity and the ideological pre-cepts of the myth of Manifest Destiny." See Walker, "Captive Images," 221.

101. Frayling, *Sergio Leone: Something*, 274.

102. Elliott and Rossio, "Lone Ranger."

103. Scorpions soon emerge from the sand and begin crawling across Tonto's and the Lone Ranger's faces. The scene carries conjoined citations from Clint Eastwood's *The Outlaw Josey Wales* (1976), in which Comanche leader Ten Bears has similarly buried two men in sand, and Sam Peckinpah's *The Wild Bunch* (1969), in which children pit a pair of scorpions against a swarm of ants. In *The Scorpion King* (2002), Dwayne Johnson's title character is buried in sand with ants approaching him. In Robert Redford's *Jeremiah Johnson* (1972), Blackfeet characters bury the white character Del Gue up to his neck.

104. Plaete, Davis, and Stanzione, "Comanches vs Cavalry."
105. In "Television" Newcomb and Hirsch paraphrase Turner's theorization of liminal as the "'inbetween' stage, when one is neither totally in nor out of society" (563). Turner's description of the "essence of liminality" becomes apt as well for Depp's Tonto. Turner associates liminality with the "release from normal constraints" so that cultural "common sense" can "be reconstructed in novel ways, some of them bizarre to the point of monstrosity (from the actors' own 'emic' perspective)." "Process, System, and Symbol," 68.
106. Josh Larsen, "The Lone Ranger," *Larsen on Film*, November 29, 2020, http://www.larsenonfilm.com/the-lone-ranger.
107. David Edelstein, "Edelstein on *The Lone Ranger*: An Uncomfortable Mix of Silliness and Sadism," *Vulture*, July 3, 2013, https://www.vulture.com /2013/07/movie-review-the-lone-ranger.html.
108. In his review of Brown's book, Vine Deloria Jr. once wrote, "If today's Indians have Dee Brown to thank for unveiling the truth of the past, they have Dee Brown to curse for making it so real that it has overshadowed them and relegated their contemporary struggle to esoteric notices in the back pages of the newspapers." "Custer Lives On," 437.
109. The tonal shifts in *The Lone Ranger* also follow those in Arthur Penn's *Little Big Man* (1970). After drawing a comparison between Little Big Man's and Tonto's very elderly looks, a well-known and controversial scene from Penn's film spurs further comparison. In a cinematic recreation of the Washita Massacre, in which General Custer's Seventh Cavalry attacked and killed Cheyenne women, men, and children, *Little Big Man* intersperses the on-screen cold-blooded killings with Hoffman's title character and his blind grandfather, Old Lodge Skins, escaping. The grandfather says, for laughs, "We're invisible" and "I've never been invisible before." Like the Lone Ranger, who Tonto says "cannot be killed," Old Lodge Skins walks through gunfire unscathed. Cheyennes lie dead all around him in dramatic close shots, but he and Little Big Man are not touched. The tragic and comical scene concludes as Little Big Man escapes with Old Lodge Skins, who grins, "That was extremely enjoyable."
110. Listed right after Depp are Armie Hammer, William Fichtner, Tom Wilkinson, Ruth Wilson, Helena Bonham Carter, James Badge Dale, Bryant Prince, Barry Pepper, Mason Cook, and JD Cullum.
111. Captain Fuller's silent "Tonkawa Scout" (David Midthunder) comes in sixty-fourth. In contrast to his elaborate and highly audible role as Kicking Wolf, a Comanche-tracking Kickapoo scout for Texas Rangers in the 2008 miniseries *Comanche Moon*, Midthunder's Tonkawa scout for the U.S. Cavalry has no lines and appears twice for just a few seconds.

4. AUDIENCE

1. See chapter 1 of this volume for a discussion of film roles by or inspired by Quanah Parker and other Comanche relatives. An early draft of *The Lone Ranger* by Ted Elliott and Terry Rossio includes a Comanche character named Nocona, presumably named after Parker's father, Peta Nocona. Although "Nocona" did not make it into the final film, his early presence on the page shows additional inspiration from Parker's family. "Lone Ranger."

2. Julianna Brannum, email message to the author, September 13, 2019.

3. Depp to Burgess, circa 2012, personal collection; Burgess, telephone interview with the author, April 26, 2016.

4. Barthes, *Image-Music-Text*, 38–39.

5. Bobo, *Black Women*; Warrior, *People and the Word*, xiv.

6. Bobo, "*Color Purple*," 314.

7. Bobo, *Black Women*, 31.

8. Fregoso, *Bronze Screen*, xiv.

9. Quanah Parker, quoted in Neeley, *Last Comanche Chief*, 230.

10. Birdsong, "Record of Graduates."

11. Augustine McCaffery, quoted in Colonnese, "Native American Reactions," 337.

12. Burgess, email message, May 3, 2016.

13. Sharpe, "Took Shot at Erasing."

14. Hall, "Encoding/Decoding."

15. Fiske, "Audiencing."

16. Rose, *Visual Methodologies*, 30.

17. In "Television" Newcomb and Hirsch address a "cultural forum" as a site where a media text and its audience both advocate for social change through a polysemous discussion among all engaged with the text and its issues. On Stanley Fish and his work in reader-response criticism and "interpretive communities," see Fish, "Interpreting the 'Variorum.'"

18. Hearne, *Native Recognition*, 341.

19. Shively, "Cowboys and Indians"; Bird, "Not My Fantasy"; Adare, "*Indian*" *Stereotypes*; Pack, "Watching Navajos Watch Themselves."

20. P. Smith, "Toughest Movie Indian." After seeing *The Lone Ranger* at a press screening in Washington DC, Smith wrote, among other thoughts, "All the things I don't like about 'The Lone Ranger'—the loudness, the slapstick humor, the kitchen-sink treatment of history, the deranged mood swings, making Tonto Comanche, moving Texas to New Mexico—they can be seen as requirements to fill multiplexes in service of the larger goal, which could be to make an Indian character a Hollywood superstar." Quoted in Dan Zack, "Depp's Tonto: An Upgrade on a Stereotype or Just an Updated Stereotype?," *Washington Post*, July 2, 2013.

21. Wallace Coffey, quoted in Nancy Mace, "Johnny Depp to Visit Lawton for Special Advance Screening of Disney's 'The Lone Ranger,'" *KLAW*, June 7, 2013.

22. Gray, *Show Sold Separately*, 167.

23. Chris Knight, "The Lone Ranger, Reviewed," *National Post*, July 2, 2013, https://nationalpost.com/entertainment/movies/the-lone-ranger-reviewed -gore-verbinskis-film-has-more-problems-than-just-historical-inaccuracies -though-johnny-depp-isnt-one-of-them; Jake Coyle, "Review: 'The Lone Ranger Collapses in Scrap Heap of Train Wreckage," Associated Press, reprinted by *Native Times*, July 2, 2013, http://www.nativetimes.com/index .php/life/entertainment/8903-review-the-lone-ranger-is-a-runaway-train; Ann Hornaday, "'The Lone Ranger': Johnny Depp Is a Cool Tonto, but the Movie Drags," *Washington Post*, July 2, 2013, https://www.washingtonpost .com/goingoutguide/movies/the-lone-ranger-johnny-depp-is-a-cool -tonto-but-the-movie-drags/2013/07/02/84ddd058-e31b-11e2-aef3 -339619eab080_story.html; Michael Compton, "'Lone Ranger' a Train Wreck," *Bowling Green Daily News*, July 11, 2013, https://www.bgdailynews .com/community/lone-ranger-a-train-wreck/article_536c2725-aa94-5729 -a5c9-67d6f5019a55.html.

24. Peter Travers, "The Lone Ranger," *Rolling Stone*, July 8, 2013, https://www .rollingstone.com/movies/movie-reviews/the-lone-ranger-89838/; Tom Carson, "Review: How Bad Is the Lone Ranger: Even the Horse Is Lousy," *GQ*, July 3, 2013, https://www.gq.com/story/review-how-bad-is-the-lone -ranger-even-the-horse-is-lousy.

25. Paul Chaat Smith says, "We [Natives] got scammed out of appearing in the title of *Cowboys and Aliens*. Which wasn't that good, and anyway it bombed; however, the bombing had implications, namely, further proof that Westerns are dead, and since Westerns often involve Indians, even if they are not always featured in the title, fewer Westerns mean fewer Indians." P. Smith, "Toughest Movie Indian."

26. R. Kurt Osenlund, "Review: *The Lone Ranger*," *Slant*, July 2, 2013, http:// www.slantmagazine.com/film/review/the-lone-ranger.

27. "Mark Wahlberg Says 'The Lone Ranger' Failed for Lack of Creativity and a Bloated Budget," Worst Previews, August 8, 2013, http://www.worstpreviews .com/headline.php?id=29118.

28. Kirsten Acuna, "'The Lone Ranger' Reviews: It's as Awful as Everyone Thought It Would Be," *Business Insider*, July 1, 2013, https://www .businessinsider.com/the-lone-ranger-reviews-are-awful-2013-7.

29. Celeste Headlee, "Please Don't See 'The Lone Ranger,'" November 28, 2020, https://celesteheadlee.com/please-dont-see-the-lone-ranger/; Adrienne Keene, "I Saw the Lone Ranger So You Don't Have To," *Native Appropriations*

(blog), July 3, 2013, http://nativeappropriations.com/2013/07/i-saw-the
-lone-ranger-so-you-dont-have-to.html.

30. Orlando Parfitt, "Johnny Depp and Armie Hammer: Critics 'Slit the Jugular'
of the Lone Ranger," Yahoo UK Movies News, August 5, 2013, https://www
.yahoo.com/entertainment/armie-hammer--critics-%E2%80%9Cslit-the
-jugular%E2%80%9D-of-lone-ranger-141408705.html.

31. Arit John, "The Three Stages of Accepting That You Killed 'The Lone
Ranger,'" *Atlantic*, August 7, 2013, https://www.theatlantic.com
/entertainment/archive/2013/08/three-stages-accepting-you-killed-lone
-ranger/312432/. On the film's budget, see Andrew O'hehir, "'The Lone
Ranger' Failed Because It Wasted Money," *Salon*, July 9, 2013, https://www
.salon.com/test/2013/07/09/the_lone_ranger_failed_because_it_wasted
_money/.

32. Alonso Duralde, "Johnny Depp, Don't Shoot the Messenger for 'Lone Ranger'
Flop," *Wrap*, August 6, 2013, https://www.thewrap.com/johnny-depp
-armie-hammer-lone-ranger-jerry-bruckheimer-108756/

33. Jerry Bruckheimer, quoted in Yurth, "'Lone Ranger' Producer." When
Cindy Yurth of the *Navajo Times* asked Bruckheimer why a recognizably
Native actor was not cast as Tonto, he replied, "Johnny is Native. He has
Cherokee blood. But mostly, he's a brilliant actor. We hire good actors."

34. Jerry Bruckheimer's "Native American community" includes a relatively
small sample. For example, he says, "We have shown it to some of the leaders
in the Comanche Nation and so far they're very pleased with our portrayal of
the Native Americans especially the Comanches." "Jerry Bruckheimer Talks
'The Lone Ranger,'" *Hannity*, Fox News, July 3, 2013, https://video.foxnews
.com/v/2523213766001?playlist_id=89219#sp=show-clips.

35. Armie Hammer adds, "It's like, the white people are the one[s] who have
the problem." Hammer also says, "Every Native American we talked to was
like, 'This is awesome! I'm so excited.'" Amy Kaufman, "Armie Hammer:
Native Americans on Set Loved 'Lone Ranger,'" *Los Angeles Times*, April
22, 2013, http://www.latimes.com/entertainment/movies/moviesnow
/la-et-mn-armie-hammer-lone-ranger-racist-native-american-20130421
,0,7583081.story.

36. "Poll: 71 Percent Say Keep Redskins," *Outside the Lines*, ESPN, September
2, 2014, http://espn.go.com/espn/otl/story/_/id/11451964/redskins-poll
-most-favor-keeping-name-dissent-growing; John Woodrow Cox, Scott
Clement, and Theresa Vargas, "New Poll Finds 9 in 10 Native Americans
Aren't Offended by Redskins Name," *Washington Post*, May 19, 2016, https://
www.washingtonpost.com/local/new-poll-finds-9-in-10-native-americans
-arent-offended-by-redskins-name/2016/05/18/3ea11cfa-161a-11e6-924d
-838753295f9a_story.html.

37. Marjorie Baumgarten, "The Lone Ranger," *Austin Chronicle*, July 5, 2013, http://www.austinchronicle.com/calendar/film/2013-07-05/the-lone -ranger/; "The Lone Ranger," KpopStarz, July 10, 2013, http://www .kpopstarz.com/articles/34054/20130710/lone-ranger-reviews-johnny -depp-tonto.htm.

38. Brian Hiatt, "Johnny Depp: An Outlaw Looks at 50," *Rolling Stone*, June 18, 2013, https://www.rollingstone.com/movies/movie-features/johnny -depp-an-outlaw-looks-at-50-243352/.

39. Kevin Gover concludes, "'The Lone Ranger' does not deliver on the promise to dignify Tonto and make him a source of pride for Indian kids, except in this sense: the talented Johnny Depp has created another memorable, offbeat character, and that character is an Indian. Perhaps, one day, an Indian filmmaker will make a Tonto who resembles a real Indian. Until then, if people think of Tonto as Mr. Depp's wacky Comanche, I can live with that." See "Johnny Depp's Tonto Isn't Offensive, Just Weird," *Smithsonian Magazine*, July 8, 2013, https://www.smithsonianmag.com/smithsonian -institution/johnny-depps-tonto-isnt-offensive-just-weird-says-the-director -of-the-american-indian-museum-7999455/.

40. Knight, "Lone Ranger, Reviewed."

41. Jonathan Foreman, "The Truth Johnny Depp Wants to Hide about the Real-Life Tontos: How Comanche Indians Butchered Babies, Roasted Enemies Alive and Would Ride 1,000 Miles to Wipe Out One Family," *Daily Mail*, August 18, 2013, https://www.dailymail.co.uk/news/article-2396760/How -Comanche-Indians-butchered-babies-roasted-enemies-alive.html.

42. Horn, *Narrative of the Captivity*.

43. Cook-Lynn, *Anti-Indianism*; Foreman, "Truth."

44. Foreman, "Truth." I borrow "ultraviolent Comanches" from P. Smith, "Comanche Ultraviolence."

45. Gray, *Show Sold Separately*, 167.

46. Mandalit del Barco, "Does Disney's Tonto Reinforce Stereotypes or Overcome Them?," NPR, July 2, 2013, https://www.npr.org/sections/codeswitch /2013/07/02/196333864/does-disneys-tonto-reinforce-stereotypes-or -overcome-them.

47. Del Barco, "Disney's Tonto."

48. Del Barco, "Disney's Tonto."

49. Lang, "Lawton Rolls Out."

50. "Comanche Nation Festival 6–Powwow," Smithsonian NMAI, December 18, 2014, https://www.youtube.com/watch?v=TihY0_QpHV4. Coffey mentions Keel at around the fifty-minute mark. Coffey noted to me Depp's face paint as reflective of Comanches' individualism in how we historically painted

our faces. Telephone call, June 30, 2015. LaDonna Harris, quoted in Hiatt, "Johnny Depp."

51. "Disney's The Lone Ranger World Premiere Livestream," Walt Disney Studios, June 22, 2013, https://www.youtube.com/watch?v=v4Z0ojv9Oy4.

52. Voelker, quoted in "Johnny Depp Will Surpass."

53. "Hollywood's Native American Narrative."

54. "Hollywood's Native American Narrative," 4:01.

55. "Hollywood's Native American Narrative," 4:30, 14:00, 14:08; Voelker, quoted in Singer, Lone Ranger, 135.

56. Voelker, quoted in Singer, Lone Ranger, 136, 135, 136.

57. "Hollywood's Native American Narrative," 4:30, 4:42.

58. "Hollywood's Native American Narrative," 4:56, 5:05; Singer, Lone Ranger, 154.

59. Gil Birmingham, quoted in Singer, Lone Ranger, 52.

60. "Hollywood's Native American Narrative," 31:11.

61. "Hollywood's Native American Narrative," 6:22.

62. Jason Asenap, quoted in "Hollywood's Native American Narrative," 7:00.

63. "Hollywood's Native American Narrative," 14:19.

64. William Voelker, interview with the author, Cyril OK, September 26, 2014.

65. "Hollywood's Native American Narrative," 18:23.

66. "Tonto Rides Again." The July 3 episode was followed by the prerecorded Native America Calling "The Full Tonto" on July 4, 2013, https://nativeamericacalling.com/thursday-july-4-2013-pre-recorded-full-tonto/. The episode features excerpts from interviews that NAC conducted in Anaheim, California, on the red carpet at The Lone Ranger world premiere.

67. Morley "Texts, Readers, Subjects," 164.

68. "Tonto Rides Again," 7:23; Nelson, Progressive Traditions, 166, 10.

69. "Hollywood's Native American Narrative," 6:17.

70. "Tonto Rides Again," 10:49; Jerry Bruckheimer, quoted in Marc Graser, "Disney, Jerry Bruckheimer See 'Lone Ranger' as New Genre-Bending Superhero," Variety, June 25, 2013, https://variety.com/2013/film/news/disney-jerry-bruckheimer-see-lone-ranger-as-new-genre-bending-superhero-1200501501/.

71. "Tonto Rides Again," 11:49.

72. Time adds, "If there's a sequel, he hopes even more American Indians get to be involved in it." Wallace Coffey, quoted in Lily Rothman, "Johnny Depp as Tonto: Is The Lone Ranger Racist?," Time, July 3, 2013, http://entertainment.time.com/2013/07/03/johnny-depp-as-tonto-is-the-lone-ranger-racist/.

73. "Tonto Rides Again," 11:36; Hester and Hood, Rance Hood, 74.

74. "Hollywood's Native American Narrative," 10:20.

75. "Tonto Rides Again," 13:07.

76. On the Texas Rangers, see M. Martinez's *Injustice Never Leaves You*; and Swanson's *Cult of Glory*

77. "Tonto Rides Again," 13:30.

78. Hall, *Representation*, 24; "Tonto Rides Again," 41:27.

79. Most callers sided with Gomez and criticized Myers. One exception was the first caller, Asa-Luke TwoCrow (Oglala Lakota), who expressed support for Depp's work as Tonto. TwoCrow explains that he worked as a rigging grip for Steven Spielberg's *Lincoln* (2012). Spielberg spotted TwoCrow on set and cast him as Eli Parker, though he has no lines. See Rifkin, "Silence."

80. "Tonto Rides Again," 18:08, 23:29.

81. "Tonto Rides Again," 43:30.

82. The 2017 edition of *Taa Numu Tekwapu?ha Tuboopu* identifies Tuhu Wii as the Black Crow Warrior Society or Black Knife Warrior Society (74).

83. "Tonto Rides Again," 42:20.

84. Coffey, quoted in "Comanche Nation Festival," circa 54:00.

85. "Tonto Rides Again," 55:00.

86. "Tonto Rides Again," 55:56.

87. "Tonto Rides Again," 56:38.

88. Harris and Wasilewski, "Indigeneity," 491.

AFTERWORD

1. The local award in Lawton was received on the second annual Indigenous Peoples' Day, October 14, 2019. The Community Arts Award ceremony took place at the state capitol on April 16, 2019.

2. "Juanita Pahdopony Part 1 of 4," Museum of the Great Plains, uploaded May 15, 2020, https://www.youtube.com/watch?v=a1udmRL9lOk&t=8s, 0:40.

3. "Juanita Pahdopony Part 2 of 4," Museum of the Great Plains, uploaded May 15, 2020, https://www.youtube.com/watch?v=GXO9ThhOumo, 1:04.

4. "Pahdopony Part 2 of 4," 1:46.

5. "Juanita Pahdopony Part 3 of 4," Museum of the Great Plains, uploaded May 15, 2020, https://www.youtube.com/watch?v=9veT9DLfyqc, 0:24.

6. Justice, *Why Indigenous Literatures Matters*, xvii.

7. Burgess, interview, April 26, 2016.

8. Cindi Alvitre, speaking at the Native American and Indigenous Studies meeting, Tongva homelands, Los Angeles, May 17, 2018.

9. Quanah Parker, quoted in Neeley, *Last Comanche Chief*, 230.

10. P. Smith, *Everything You Know*, 178.

11. Mithlo, *Knowing Native Arts*, 3.

12. "Pahdopony Part 1 of 4," 2:08.

13. "Pahdopony Part 2 of 4," 1:46.

Adare, Sierra. *"Indian" Stereotypes in TV Science Fiction: First Nations' Voices Speak Out*. Austin: University of Texas Press, 2009.

Aleiss, Angela. *Making the White Man's Indian: Native Americans and Hollywood Movies*. Westport CT: Greenwood, 2005.

Allen, Chadwick. "Hero with Two Faces: The Lone Ranger as Treaty Discourse." *American Literature* 68, no. 3 (1996): 609–38.

———. "Tonto as Taxidermy." *Native American and Indigenous Studies* 1 no. 1 (2014): 99–106.

———. "Tonto on Vacation, or How to Be an Indian Lawyer." *Canadian Review of American Studies* 39, no. 2 (2009): 139–61.

Anderson, Gary Clayton. *The Conquest of Texas: Ethnic Cleansing in the Promised Land, 1820–1875*. Norman: University of Oklahoma Press, 2005.

Anzaldúa, Gloria. *Borderlands/La Frontera: The New Mestiza*. San Francisco: Aunt Lute Books, 1999.

Appadurai, Arjun. "Disjuncture and Difference in the Global Cultural Economy." *Theory, Culture and Society* 7, nos. 2–3 (1990): 295–310.

Armitage, Shelley. "Who Was That Masked Man? Conception and Reception in *The Lone Ranger*." In *The Post-2000 Film Western: Contexts, Transnationality, Hybridity*, edited by Marek Paryz and John R. Leo, 64–85. London: Palgrave Macmillan, 2015.

Babb, Theodore. *In the Bosom of the Comanches*. N.p.: Worley, 1912.

Bakhtin, Mikhail. *Speech Genres and Other Late Essays*. Austin: University of Texas Press, 1986.

Barr, Julianna. "The Comanche Empire." *Pacific Historical Review* 78, no. 4 (2009): 631–32.

———. *Peace Came in the Form of a Woman: Indians and Spaniards in the Texas Borderlands*. Chapel Hill: University of North Carolina Press, 2009.

Barthes, Roland. *Image-Music-Text*. New York: Hill and Wang, 1977.

Bauman, Richard. *A World of Others' Words: Cross-Cultural Perspectives on Intertextuality*. Malden MA: Blackwell, 2004.

Benson, Houston E. "The Lone Racist: A White Man in Red Face." *Humanity and Society* 38, no. 2 (2014): 351–53.

Betty, Gerald. *Comanche Society: Before the Reservation*. College Station: Texas A&M University Press, 2005.

233

Bhabha, Homi K. *The Location of Culture.* New York: Routledge, 2012.

Bird, S. Elizabeth, ed. *Dressing in Feathers.* New York: Routledge, 1996.

———. "Not My Fantasy: The Persistence of Indian Imagery in *Dr. Quinn, Medicine Woman.*" In Bird, *Dressing in Feathers,* 245–62.

Blackhawk, Ned. *Violence over the Land: Indians and Empires in the Early American West.* Cambridge MA: Harvard University Press, 2009.

Bobo, Jacqueline. *Black Women as Cultural Readers.* New York: Columbia University Press, 1995.

———. "*The Color Purple*: Black Women as Cultural Readers." In *Cultural Theory and Popular Culture: A Reader,* edited by John Storey, 310–18. Athens: University of Georgia Press, 1998.

Bourdieu, Pierre. "Symbolic Power." *Critique of Anthropology* 4, nos. 13–14 (1979): 77–85.

Brégent-Heald, Dominique. *Borderland Films: American Cinema, Mexico, and Canada during the Progressive Era.* Lincoln: University of Nebraska Press, 2015.

Brooks, James F. *Captives and Cousins: Slavery, Kinship, and Community in the Southwest Borderlands.* Chapel Hill: University of North Carolina Press, 2011.

———. "'That Don't Make You Kin!': Borderlands History and Culture in *The Searchers.*" In Eckstein and Lehman, *Searchers,* 265–88.

Brown, Dee. *Bury My Heart at Wounded Knee: An Indian History of the American West.* New York: Macmillan, 2007.

Brown, John Henry. *Indian Wars and Pioneers of Texas.* Saint Louis: Nixon-Jones, 1890.

Brown, Kirby. *Stoking the Fire: Nationhood in Cherokee Writing, 1907–1970.* Norman: University of Oklahoma Press, 2019.

Burton, Art. *Black Gun, Silver Star: The Life and Legend of Frontier Marshall Bass Reeves.* Lincoln: University of Nebraska Press, 2008.

Byrd, Jodi A. *The Transit of Empire: Indigenous Critiques of Colonialism.* Minneapolis: University of Minnesota Press, 2011.

Carlson, Paul, and Tom Crum. *Myth, Memory, and Massacre: The Pease River Capture of Cynthia Ann Parker.* Lubbock: Texas Tech University Press, 2010.

Clark, Blue. *Lone Wolf v. Hitchcock: Treaty Rights and Indian Law at the End of the Nineteenth Century.* Lincoln: University of Nebraska Press, 1999.

Cobb, Amanda J. "Powerful Medicine: The Rhetoric of Comanche Activist LaDonna Harris." *Studies in American Indian Literatures* 18, no. 4 (2006): 63–87.

Cohen, Matt, and Jeffrey Glover. *Colonial Mediascapes: Sensory Worlds of Early America.* Lincoln: University of Nebraska Press, 2014.

Colonnese, Tom Grayson. "Native American Reactions to *The Searchers.*" In Eckstein and Lehman, *Searchers,* 335–42.

Cook-Lynn, Elizabeth. "American Indian Intellectualism and the New Indian Story." In *Natives and Academics: Researching and Writing about American Indians*, edited by Devon Mihesuah, 57–76. Lincoln: University of Nebraska Press, 1998.

———. *Anti-Indianism in Modern America: A Voice from Tatekeya's Earth*. Urbana: University of Illinois Press, 2001.

Corrigan, John Michael. "Mask in the Museum: The Impossible Gaze and the Indian Artifact in Verbinski's *The Lone Ranger*." *New Review of Film and Television Studies* 16, no. 4 (2018): 393–414.

Delay, Brian. *War of a Thousand Deserts: Indian Raids and the US-Mexican War*. New Haven CT: Yale University Press, 2008.

Deloria, Philip. *Indians in Unexpected Places*. Lawrence: University Press of Kansas, 2004.

———. *Playing Indian*. New Haven CT: Yale University Press, 1998.

Deloria, Vine, Jr. *Custer Died for Your Sins: An Indian Manifesto*. 1969. Reprint, Norman: University of Oklahoma Press, 1988.

———. "Custer Lives On." Review of *Bury My Heart at Wounded Knee*, by Dee Brown. *Texas Law Review* 50 (1972): 435–39.

Derounian-Stodola, Kathryn Zabelle, ed. *Women's Indian Captivity Narratives*. New York: Penguin, 1998.

Du Gay, Paul, Stuart Hall, Linda Janes, Hugh Mackay, and Keith Negus. *Doing Cultural Studies: The Story of the Sony Walkman*. London: Sage, 2013.

Durkin, Peter. "Umbrellas and Parasols on the Plains: Past and Present." *Whispering Wind* 32, no. 5 (2002): 4.

Eckstein, Arthur, and Peter Lehman, eds. *The Searchers: Essays and Reflections on John Ford's Classic Western*. Detroit: Wayne State University Press, 2004.

Edmunds, R. David. *American Indian Leaders: Studies in Diversity*. Lincoln: University of Nebraska Press, 1980.

Ehle, John. *Trail of Tears: The Rise and Fall of the Cherokee Nation*. New York: Anchor, 1988.

Elliott, Ted, and Terry Rossio. "The Lone Ranger." Unpublished manuscript. March 29, 2009.

Fish, Stanley E. "Interpreting the 'Variorum.'" *Critical Inquiry* 2, no. 3 (1976): 465–85.

Fiske, John. "Audiencing: A Cultural Studies Approach to Watching Television." *Poetics* 21 (1992): 345–59.

Foster, Morris. *Being Comanche: A Social History of an American Indian Community*. Tucson: University of Arizona Press, 1992.

Fowles, Severin. "Fighting Terrorism Since 1492." Unpublished manuscript, 2016.

Fowles, Severin, and Jimmy Arterberry. "Gesture and Performance in Comanche Rock Art." *World Art* 3, no. 1 (2013): 67–82.

Frankel, Glenn. *The Searchers: The Making of an American Legend.* London: Bloomsbury, 2014.

Fraser, Nancy. *Scales of Justice: Reimagining Political Space in a Globalizing World.* New York: Columbia University Press, 2009.

Frayling, Christopher. *Sergio Leone: Once upon a Time in Italy.* London: Thames and Hudson, 2005.

———. *Sergio Leone: Something to Do with Death.* Minneapolis: University of Minnesota Press, 2000.

Freedman, Carl. *Versions of Hollywood Crime Cinema: Studies in Ford, Wilder, Coppola, Scorsese, and Others.* Chicago: University of Chicago Press, 2013.

Fregoso, Rosa Linda. *The Bronze Screen: Chicana and Chicano Film Culture.* Minneapolis: University of Minnesota Press, 1993.

Gelo, Daniel. "'Comanche Land and Ever Has Been': A Native Geography of the Nineteenth-Century Comanchería." *Southwestern Historical Quarterly* 103, no. 3 (2000): 273–307.

Gill, Joel Christian. *Tales of the Talented Tenth.* Vol. 1. Wheat Ridge CO: Fulcrum, 2016.

Gish Hill, Christina. *Webs of Kinship: Family in Northern Cheyenne Nationhood.* Norman: University of Oklahoma Press, 2017.

Gray, Jonathan. *Show Sold Separately: Promos, Spoilers, and Other Media Paratexts.* New York: New York University Press, 2010.

Green, Rayna. "The Tribe Called Wannabee: Playing Indian in America and Europe." *Folklore* 99, no. 1 (1988): 30–55.

Gwynne, S. C. *Empire of the Summer Moon: Quanah Parker and the Rise and Fall of the Comanches, the Most Powerful Indian Tribe in American History.* New York: Simon and Schuster, 2010.

Hagan, William T. "Archival Captive: The American Indian." *American Archivist* 41, no. 2 (1978): 135–42.

———. "Kiowas, Comanches, and Cattlemen, 1867–1906: A Case Study of the Failure of U.S. Reservation Policy." *Pacific Historical Review* 40, no. 3 (1971): 333–55.

Hall, Stuart. "Encoding/Decoding." In *Culture, Media, and Language,* 117–27. New York: Routledge, 1980.

———. *Representation: Cultural Representations and Signifying Practices.* Thousand Oaks CA: Sage: 1997.

Hämäläinen, Pekka. *The Comanche Empire.* New Haven CT: Yale University Press, 2008.

Hämäläinen, Pekka, and Samuel Truett, "On Borderlands." *Journal of American History* 98, no. 2 (2011): 338–61.

Harrigan, Stephen. *Comanche Midnight: Essays.* Austin: University of Texas Press, 1995.

Harris, LaDonna, and Henrietta Stockel. *LaDonna Harris: A Comanche Life.* Lincoln: University of Nebraska Press, 2000.

Harris, LaDonna, and Jacqueline Wasilewski. "Indigeneity, an Alternative Worldview: Four R's (Relationship, Responsibility, Reciprocity, Redistribution) vs. Two P's (Power and Profit), Sharing the Journey towards Conscious Evolution." *Systems Research and Behavioral Science* 21, no. 5 (2004): 489–503.

Harris, LaDonna, Stephen M. Sachs, and Benjamin J. Broome. "Wisdom of the People: Potential and Pitfalls in Efforts by the Comanches to Recreate Traditional Ways of Building Consensus." *American Indian Quarterly* 25, no. 1 (2001): 114–34.

Hearne, Joanna. *Native Recognition: Indigenous Cinema and the Western.* Albany: State University of New York Press, 2012.

Hester, James, and Rance Hood. *Rance Hood: Mystic Painter.* Albuquerque: University of New Mexico Press, 2006.

Hochberg, Gil. "From 'Cinematic Occupation' to 'Cinematic Justice': Citational Practices in Kamal Aljafari's 'Jaffa Trilogy.'" *Third Text* 31, no. 4 (2017): 533–47.

Hoebel, Edward Adamson, Waldo Rudolph Wedel, Gustav G. Carlson, and Robert Harry Lowie. *Comanche Ethnography: Field Notes of E. Adamson Hoebel, Waldo R. Wedel, Gustav G. Carlson, and Robert H. Lowie.* Lincoln: University of Nebraska Press, 2008.

Holt, Jerry. "Setting the Stage: Teddy Roosevelt and the Movies." In *Star Power: The Impact of Branded Celebrity,* edited by Aaron Barlow, 9–16. Santa Barbara: ABC-CLIO, 2014.

Horn, Sarah Ann. *A Narrative of the Captivity of Mrs. Horn, and Her Two Children, with Mrs. Harris, by the Camanche Indians, after They Had Murdered Their Husbands and Travelling Companions.* Recorded by E. House. Cincinnati: Keemle, 1839.

Howe, LeAnne. "Tribalography: The Power of Native Stories." *Journal of Dramatic Theory and Criticism* 1 (1999): 117–26.

Jenkins, Henry, Sam Ford, and Joshua Green. *Spreadable Media: Creating Value and Meaning in a Networked Culture.* New York: New York University Press, 2013.

Jerman, Hadley. "Acting for the Camera: Horace Poolaw's Film Stills of Family, 1925–1950." *Great Plains Quarterly* 31, no. 2 (2011): 105–23.

Jodorowsky, Alejandro. *Psychomagic: The Transformative Power of Shamanic Psychotherapy.* Rochester VT: Inner Traditions, 2010.

John, Elizabeth A. H., and Adán Benavides Jr. "Inside the Comanchería, 1785: The Diary of Pedro Vial and Francisco Xavier." *Southwestern Historical Quarterly* 98, no. 1 (1994): 26–56.

Jones, David E. *Sanapia: Comanche Medicine Woman*. Prospect Heights IL: Waveland, 1984.

Justice, Daniel Heath. *Our Fire Survives the Storm: A Cherokee Literary History*. Minneapolis: University of Minnesota Press, 2006.

———. *Why Indigenous Literatures Matter*. Waterloo, Canada: Wilfrid Laurier University Press, 2018.

Kaushal, Asha. "The Politics of Jurisdiction." *Modern Law Review* 78, no. 5 (2015): 759–92.

Kavanagh, Thomas W. *Life of Ten Bears*. Lincoln: University of Nebraska Press, 2016.

Keeling, Kara. *The Witch's Flight: The Cinematic, the Black Femme, and the Image of Common Sense*. Durham NC: Duke University Press, 2007.

Kilpatrick, Jacquelyn. *Celluloid Indians: Native Americans and Film*. Lincoln: University of Nebraska Press, 1999.

Kristeva, Julia. "Word, Dialogue and Novel." In *The Kristeva Reader*, edited by Toril Moi, 34–61. New York: Columbia University Press, 1986.

LaMadrid, Enrique, *Hermanitos Comanchitos: Indo-Hispano Rituals of Captivity and Redemption*. Albuquerque: University of New Mexico Press, 2003.

Lee, Nelson. *Three Years among the Comanches: The Narrative of Nelson Lee, the Texas Ranger, Containing a Detailed Account of His Captivity among the Indians, His Singular Escape through the Instrumentality of His Watch, and Fully Illustrating Indian Life as It Is on the War Path and in the Camp*. Albany NY: Baker Taylor, 1860.

Lehmann, Herman. *Nine Years among the Indians, 1870–1879: The Story of the Captivity and Life of a Texan among the Indians*. Albuquerque: University of New Mexico Press, 1993.

Lewis, Randolph. *Alanis Obomsawin: The Vision of a Native Filmmaker*. Lincoln: University of Nebraska Press, 2006.

———. "A Brief History of Celluloid Navajos." In *"Navajo Talking Picture": Cinema on Native Ground*, 1–48. Lincoln: University of Nebraska Press, 2012.

Lewis, Sarah. "Vision and Justice." *Aperture* 223 (2016): 11–14.

Lovett, John R., James Peck, and Mark Andrew White. *Picturing Indian Territory: Portraits of the Land That Became Oklahoma, 1819–1907*. Norman: University of Oklahoma Press, 2016.

Lucchesi, Annita Hetoevėhotohke'e. "'Indians Don't Make Maps': Indigenous Cartographic Traditions and Innovations." *American Indian Culture and Research Journal* 42, no. 3 (2018): 11–26.

Marez, Curtis. "Signifying Spain, Becoming Comanche, Making Mexicans: Indian Captivity and the History of Chicana/o Popular Performance." *American Quarterly* 53, no. 2 (2001): 267–306.

Markwyn, Abigail. "Beyond *The End of the Trail*: Indians at San Francisco's 1915 World's Fair." *Ethnohistory* 63, no. 2 (2016): 273–300.

Martinez, David. "Peter Pan (1953)." In *Seeing Red: Hollywood's Pixeled Skins; American Indians and Film*, edited by LeAnne Howe, Harvey Markowitz, and Denise K. Cummings, 39–43. East Lansing: Michigan State University Press, 2013.

Martinez, Monica Muñoz. *The Injustice Never Leaves You: Anti-Mexican Violence in Texas*. Cambridge MA: Harvard University Press, 2018.

Marubbio, M. Elise. *Killing the Indian Maiden: Images of Native American Women in Film*. Lexington: University of Kentucky Press, 2006.

McBride, Joseph. *Searching for John Ford: A Life*. Jackson: University Press of Mississippi, 2011.

McCarthy, Cormac. *Blood Meridian, or The Evening Redness in the West*. New York: Vintage, 1985.

Meek, Barbra. "And the Injun Goes 'How!': Representations of American Indian English in White Public Space." *Language in Society* 35, no. 1 (2006): 93–128.

Meikle, Denis. *Johnny Depp*. London: Titan Books, 2011.

Meyer, Phillip. *The Son*. New York: HarperCollins, 2013.

Mithlo, Nancy Marie. *Knowing Native Arts*. Lincoln: University of Nebraska Press, 2020.

Montgomery, Lindsay M., and Severin Fowles. "An Indigenous Archive: Documenting Comanche History through Rock Art." *American Indian Quarterly* 44, no. 2 (2020): 196–220.

Morgan, Thais. "Is There an Intertext in This Text? Literary and Interdisciplinary Approaches to Intertextuality." *American Journal of Semiotics* 3, no. 4 (2008): 1–40.

Morley, David. "Texts, Readers, Subjects." In *Culture, Media, Language: Working Papers in Cultural Studies, 1972–1979*, edited by Stuart Hall, Dorothy Hobson, Andrew Lowe, and Paul Willis, 154–66. New York: Routledge, 2003.

Nakassis, Constantine. "Citation and Citationality." *Signs and Society* 1, no. 1 (2013): 51–77.

Neeley, Bill. *The Last Comanche Chief*. New York: Wiley and Sons, 1995.

Nelson, Joshua. *Progressive Traditions: Identity in Cherokee Literature and Culture*. Norman: University of Oklahoma Press, 2014.

Newcomb, Horace M., and Paul M. Hirsch. "Television as a Cultural Forum: Implications for Research." *Quarterly Review of Film and Video* 8, no. 3 (1983): 45–55.

Noyes, Stanley, and Daniel Gelo. *Comanches in the New West: 1895–1908*. Austin: University of Texas Press, 1999.

Osborn, Lynn. "Quanah Parker: A Great Indian Spokesman." *American Indian Culture and Research Journal* 1, no. 2 (1974): 14–17.

Owens, Barcley. *Cormac McCarthy's Western Novels*. Tucson: University of Arizona Press, 2000.

Pack, Sam. "Watching Navajos Watch Themselves." *Wicazo Sa Review* 22, no. 2 (2007): 111–27.

Paredes, Américo, *The Texas-Mexican Cancionero: Folksongs of the Lower Border*. Urbana: University of Illinois Press, 1976.

———. *With His Pistol in His Hand: A Border Ballad and Its Hero*. Austin: University of Texas Press, 1958.

Plaete, Jo, Adam Davis, and Alan Stanzione. "Comanches vs Cavalry: Artistically Directable In-Crowd Ragdoll Simulation." In *ACM SIGGRAPH 2014 Talks*. New York: Association for Computing Machinery, 2014.

Plummer, Rachel Parker. *Rachael Plummer's Narrative of Twenty-One Months Servitude as a Prisoner among the Commanchee Indians*. In *Held Captive by Indians: Selected Narratives, 1642–1836*, edited by Richard VanDerBeets, 333–66. Knoxville: University of Tennessee Press, 1994.

Prats, Armando. *Invisible Natives: Myth and Identity in the American Western*. Ithaca NY: Cornell University Press, 2002.

Pratt, Mary Louise. *Imperial Eyes: Studies in Travel Writing and Transculturation*. New York: Routledge, 1992.

Raheja, Michelle H. "Reading Nanook's Smile: Visual Sovereignty, Indigenous Revisions of Ethnography, and 'Atanarjuat (the Fast Runner).'" *American Quarterly* 59, no. 4 (2007): 1159–85.

———. *Reservation Reelism: Redfacing, Visual Sovereignty, and Representations of Native Americans in Film*. Lincoln: University of Nebraska Press, 2010.

Rifkin, Mark. "The Silence of Ely S. Parker: The Emancipation Sublime and the Limits of Settler Memory." *Native American and Indigenous Studies* 1, no. 2 (2014): 1–43.

Rinzler, J. W. *The Making of Star Wars: The Definitive Story behind the Original Film*. New York: Random House, 2008.

Rivaya-Martínez, Joaquín. "Becoming Comanches: Patterns of Captive Incorporation into Comanche Kinship Networks, 1820–1875." In *On the Borders of Love and Power: Families and Kinship in the Intercultural American Southwest*, edited by David Wallace Adams and Crista DeLuzio, 47–70. Berkeley: University of California Press, 2012.

———. "The Captivity of Macario Leal: A Tejano among the Comanches, 1847–1854." *Southwestern Historical Quarterly* 117, no. 4 (2014): 372–402.

Roche, David. "(De)constructing 'America': The Case of Emir Kusturica's Arizona Dream (1993)." *European Journal of American Studies* 5, no. 4 (2010). https://doi.org/10.4000/ejas.8653.

Rose, Gillian. *Visual Methodologies: An Introduction to Researching with Visual Materials*. 3rd ed. London: Sage, 2013.

Rowlandson, Mary. *A True History of the Captivity and Restoration of Mrs. Mary Rowlandson*. Clinton MA: Ballard and Bynner, 1853.

Santos, Avi. *Selling the Silver Bullet: The Lone Ranger and Transmedia Brand Licensing*. Austin: University of Texas Press, 2015.

Shively, JoEllen. "Cowboys and Indians: Perceptions of Western Films among American Indians and Anglos." *American Sociological Review* 57, no. 6 (1992): 725–34.

Shorter, David Delgado. "A Borderland Methodology/Una Metodología Fronteriza." *Latin American and Caribbean Ethnic Studies*, June 24, 2020, 1–23.

Simmon, Scott. *The Invention of the Western Film: A Cultural History of the Genre's First Half-Century*. Cambridge: Cambridge University Press, 2003.

Simmons, Garner. *Peckinpah: A Portrait in Montage*. Austin: University of Texas Press, 1982.

Singer, Michael. *The Lone Ranger: Behind the Mask; On the Trail of an Outlaw Epic*. San Rafael CA: Insight, 2013.

Slotkin, Richard. *Gunfighter Nation: The Myth of the Frontier in Twentieth-Century America*. Norman: University of Oklahoma Press, 1998.

Smith, Paul Chaat. *Everything You Know about Indians Is Wrong*. Minneapolis: University of Minnesota Press, 2009.

Smith, Ralph A. "The Comanche Bridge between Oklahoma and Mexico, 1843–1844." *Chronicles of Oklahoma* 39, no. 1 (1961): 54–69.

Smith, Sherry L. *Hippies, Indians, and the Fight for Red Power*. New York: Oxford University Press, 2012.

Strong, Pauline. *Captive Selves, Captivating Others: The Politics and Poetics of Colonial American Captivity Narratives*. Boulder CO: Westview, 2000.

———. "Playing Indian in the Nineties: *Pocahontas* and *The Indian in the Cupboard*." In *Hollywood's Indian: The Portrayal of the Native American in Film*, edited by Peter C. Rollins and John E. O'Connor, 187–205. Lexington: University Press of Kentucky, 2011.

Sturm, Circe. "Race, Sovereignty, and Civil Rights: Understanding the Cherokee Freedmen Controversy." *Cultural Anthropology* 29, no. 3 (2014): 575–98.

Swanson, Doug. *Cult of Glory: The Bold and Brutal History of the Texas Rangers*. New York: Viking, 2020.

Taa Numu Tekwapu?ha Tuboopu: Our Comanche Dictionary. Elgin OK: Comanche Language and Cultural Preservation Committee, 2017.

Taddeo, Julie Anne, and Ken Dvorak. "The PBS Historical House Series: Where Historical Reality Succumbs to Reel Reality." *Film and History: An Interdisciplinary Journal of Film and Television Studies* 37, no. 1 (2007): 18–28.

Thorshaug, Marthe. "Présentation du film *Comancheria*." *Performance, Art et Anthropologie*. Open Edition Journals. December 17, 2009. http://actesbranly.revues.org/432.

Tilghman, Zoe. *Quanah, the Eagle of the Comanches*. Oklahoma City: Harlow, 1938.

Turner, Victor. "Process, System, and Symbol: A New Anthropological Synthesis." *Daedalus* 106, no. 3 (1977): 61–80.

Van Lent, Peter. "'Her Beautiful Savage': The Current Sexual Image of the Native American Male." In Bird, *Dressing in Feathers*, 211–27.

Vizenor, Gerald. *Fugitive Poses: Native American Indian Scenes of Absence and Presence*. Lincoln: University of Nebraska Press, 2000.

Walker, Janet. "Captive Images in the Traumatic Western: *The Searchers, Pursued, Once Upon a Time in the West*, and *Lone Star*." In *Westerns: Films through History*, edited by Janet Walker, 219–52. New York: Routledge, 2001.

Wallace, Ernest, and Adamson Hoebel. *The Comanches: Lords of the South Plains*. 1952. Reprint, Norman: University of Oklahoma Press, 1986.

Warrior, Robert. *The People and the Word: Reading Native Nonfiction*. Minneapolis: University of Minnesota Press, 2005.

Waziyatawin. *What Does Justice Look Like? The Struggle for Liberation in Dakota Homeland*. Saint Paul MN: Living Justice, 2008.

Webb, Walter Prescott. *The Great Plains*. Lincoln: University of Nebraska Press, 1931.

———. *The Texas Rangers: A History of Frontier Defense*. 1935. Reprint, Austin: University of Texas Press, 1965.

Weismantel, Mary. "Making Kin: Kinship Theory and Zumbagua Adoptions." *American Ethnologist* 22, no. 4 (1995): 685–704.

Williams, Robert A., Jr. *Savage Anxieties: The Invention of Western Civilization*. New York: Macmillan, 2012.

Wolfe, Patrick. "Settler Colonialism and the Elimination of the Native." *Journal of Genocide Research* 8, no. 4 (2006): 387–409.

Womack, Craig. *Red on Red: Native American Literary Separatism*. Minneapolis: University of Minnesota Press, 1999.

Wooley, John. *Shot in Oklahoma: A Century of Sooner State Cinema*. Norman: University of Oklahoma Press, 2012.

Alice in Wonderland. Directed by Tim Burton. Burbank CA: Walt Disney Pictures, 2010.

The Amityville Horror. Directed by Stuart Rosenberg. Los Angeles: American International Pictures, 1979.

Anticipation of Land in 2089. Directed by Sunrise Tippeconnie. Norman OK: 120 from the Paseo Production, 2008.

Arizona Dream. Directed by Emir Kusturica. Burbank CA: Warner Bros., 1993.

Around the World in 80 Days. Directed by Michael Anderson. Beverly Hills CA: United Artists, 1956.

Avatar. Directed by James Cameron. Los Angeles: Twentieth Century Fox, 2009.

"Backtrail." *The Lone Ranger*. Directed by George Seitz. Burbank CA: ABC, March 8, 1951.

The Bank Robbery. Directed by William Tilghman. N.p.: Oklahoma Natural Mutoscene Company, 1908.

The Battle at Elderbush Gulch. Directed by D. W. Griffith. New York: General Film Company, 1913.

The Brave. Directed by Johnny Depp. Tortola, British Virgin Islands: Majestic Films International, 1997.

Cahill U.S. Marshall. Directed by Andrew McLaglen. Burbank CA: Warner Bros., 1973.

Captivity Narrative. Directed by Jason Asenap. Albuquerque: Achimowin Films, 2017.

The Cellar. Directed by Kevin Tenney. Beverly Hills CA: Indian Neck Entertainment, 1989.

Cimarron. Directed by Wesley Ruggles. New York: RKO Radio Pictures, 1931.

The Color Purple. Directed by Steven Spielberg. Burbank CA: Warner Bros., 1985.

Comanche. Directed by George Sherman. Beverly Hills CA: United Artists, 1956.

The Comanche and the Horse. Directed by Gary Glassman. Arlington VA: PBS, 2018.

Comanche Moon. Directed by Simon Wincer. New York: CBS, 2008.

Comancheria. Directed by Marthe Thorshaug. Norway: Nerhagen Productions, 2007.

The Comancheros. Directed by Michael Curtiz. Los Angeles: Twentieth Century Fox, 1961.

"Comanche Scalps." *Tate*. New York: NBC, August 10, 1960.

Comanche Territory. Directed by George Sherman. University City CA: Universal Pictures, 1950.

Comanche Warriors. Directed by Dan Gagliasso. New York: History Channel, 2005.

Continental Divide. Directed by Michael Apted. University City CA: Universal Pictures, 1981.

Cowboys and Aliens. Directed by Jon Favreau. Universal City CA: Universal Pictures, 2011.

The Daily Life of Mistress Red. Directed by Peshawn Bread. Santa Fe NM: Red Ambition Productions, in postproduction.

Dances with Wolves. Directed by Kevin Costner. Los Angeles: Orion Pictures, 1990.

Dark Shadows. Directed by Tim Burton. Burbank CA: Warner Bros., 2012.

The Dark Wind. Directed by Errol Morris. Burbank CA: New Line Cinema, 1991.

The Daughter of Dawn. Directed by Norbert Myles. N.p.: Texas Film Company, 1920.

The Dead Can't Dance. Directed by Rodrick Pocowatchit. Wichita KS: Rawdzilla Pictures, 2010.

Deadliest Warrior. Directed by Tim Prokop and Paul Benz. Los Angeles: Spike TV, 2010.

Dead Man. Directed by Jim Jarmusch. Los Angeles: Miramax, 1995.

Dead Man's Walk. Directed by Yves Simoneau. Burbank CA: ABC, 1996.

A Distant Trumpet. Directed by Raoul Walsh. Burbank CA: Warner Bros., 1964.

Duck, You Sucker! Directed by Sergio Leone. Beverly Hills CA: United Artists, 1971.

El Topo. Directed by Alejandro Jodorowsky. New York: ABKCO Films, 1970.

"Evil in the Night." *Walker, Texas Ranger*. New York: CBS, November 4, 1995.

Finding Neverland. Directed by Marc Forster. Los Angeles: Miramax, 2004.

A Fistful of Dollars. Directed by Sergio Leone. Beverly Hills CA: Metro-Goldwyn-Mayer, 1964.

For a Few Dollars More. Directed by Sergio Leone. Beverly Hills CA: Metro-Goldwyn-Mayer, 1965.

Fort Apache. Directed by John Ford. New York: RKO Radio Pictures, 1948.

Fry Bread Babes. Directed by Steffany Suttle. Seattle: Native Voices at the University of Washington, 2008.

The General. Directed by Clyde Bruckman and Buster Keaton. Beverly Hills CA: United Artists, 1926.

Geronimo. Directed by Arnold Laven. Beverly Hills CA: United Artists, 1962.

The Good, the Bad, and The Ugly. Directed by Sergio Leone. Beverly Hills CA: Metro-Goldwyn-Mayer, 1966.

The Heart of Wetona. Directed by Sidney Franklin. Hollywood CA: Select Pictures, 1919.

Hell or High Water. Directed by David Mackenzie. Santa Monica CA: Lionsgate, 2016.

Honey Moccasin. Directed by Shelley Niro. New York: Women Make Makes, 1998.

Hostiles. Directed by Scott Cooper. Los Angeles: Entertainment Studios, 2017.

Imagining Indians. Directed by Victor Masayesva Jr. Watertown MA: Documentary Educational Resources, 1992.

The Incredible Brown NDN. Directed by Rodrick Pocowatchit. Wichita KS: Rawdzilla Pictures, 2019.

The Incredible Brown NDN II. Directed by Rodrick Pocowatchit. Wichita KS: Rawdzilla Pictures, 2020.

Indian in the Cupboard. Directed by Frank Oz. Hollywood CA: Paramount Pictures, 1995.

In einem wilden Land/Striving for Freedom. Directed by Rainer Matsuta. University City CA: Universal Pictures, 2013.

Jeremiah Johnson. Directed by Sydney Pollack. Burbank CA: Warner Bros., 1972.

John Carter. Directed by Andrew Stanton. Burbank CA: Walt Disney Studios, 2012.

LaDonna Harris: Indian 101. Directed by Julianna Brannum. Austin TX: Naru Mui, 2014.

Last of the Comanches. Directed by André De Toth. Culver City CA: Columbia Pictures, 1953.

The Last of the Mohicans. Directed by Michael Mann. Los Angeles: Twentieth Century Fox, 1992.

Leave Durov to the Dogs: A Comanche Parable. Directed by Sunrise Tippeconnie. Norman OK: 120 from the Paseo Production, 2011.

The Legend of Hell's Gate. Directed by Tanner Beard. Santa Monica CA: Lionsgate, 2011.

Lincoln. Directed by Steven Spielberg. Burbank CA: Walt Disney Studios, 2012.

Little Big Man. Directed by Arthur Penn. Burbank CA: National General Pictures, 1970.

The Lone Ranger. Directed by Gore Verbinski. Burbank CA: Walt Disney Pictures, 2013.

The Lone Ranger. Directed by William Witney and John English. Los Angeles: Republic Pictures, 1938.

The Lone Ranger (TV Movie). Directed by Jack Bender. Burbank CA: Warner Bros., February 26, 2003.

Magnificent Seven. Directed by Antoine Fuqua. Culver City CA: Sony Pictures, 2016.

The Man Who Shot Liberty Valance. Directed by John Ford. Hollywood CA: Paramount Pictures, 1962.

McClintock. Directed by Andrew McLaglen. Beverly Hills CA: United Artists, 1963.

Monsters of God. Directed by Rod Lurie. Unaired TV pilot. Atlanta: TNT, 2017.

Must Love Pie. Directed by Patrick Clement. DeTur Films. New York: Columbia University Thesis Film, 2020.

My Cousin Vinny. Directed by Jonathan Lynn. Los Angeles: Twentieth Century Fox, 1992.

Nanook of the North. Directed by Robert Flaherty. Buffalo NY: Pathé Exchange, 1922.

Native America. Directed by Gary Glassman, Joseph Sousa, and Scott Tiffany. Providence RI: Pictures, 2018.

Navajo Talking Picture. Directed by Arlene Bowman. New York: Women Make Movies, 1986.

Night at the Museum. Directed by Shawn Levy. Los Angeles: Twentieth Century Fox, 2006.

Night at the Museum: Battle of the Smithsonian. Directed by Shawn Levy. Los Angeles: Twentieth Century Fox, 2009.

Night at the Museum: Secret of the Tomb. Directed by Shawn Levy. Los Angeles: Twentieth Century Fox, 2014.

Nightmare on Elm Street. Directed by Wes Craven. Burbank CA: New Line Cinema, 1984.

Once upon a Time in China IV. Directed by Yuen Bun. Hong Kong: Golden Harvest, 1993.

Once upon a Time in Mexico. Directed by Robert Rodriguez. Culver City CA: Columbia Pictures, 2003.

Once upon a Time in the West. Directed by Sergio Leone. Hollywood CA: Paramount Pictures, 1968.

The Outlaw Josey Wales. Directed by Clint Eastwood. Burbank CA: Warner Bros., 1976.

Overweight with Crooked Teeth. Directed by Shelley Niro and Dan Bigbee. Toronto: V Tape, 1998.

Peter Pan. Directed by Clyde Geronimi, Wilfred Jackson, and Hamilton Luske. Burbank CA: Walt Disney Pictures, 1953.

Pirates of the Caribbean: The Curse of the Black Pearl. Directed by Gore Verbinski. Burbank CA: Walt Disney Pictures, 2003.

The Plainsman. Directed by Cecil B. DeMille. Hollywood CA: Paramount Pictures, 1936.

Pocahontas. Directed by Mike Gabriel and Eric Goldberg. Burbank CA: Walt Disney Pictures, 1995.

Poltergeist II: The Other Side. Directed by Brian Gibson. Beverly Hills CA: MGM Entertainment, 1986.

Public Enemies. Directed by Michael Mann. University City CA: Universal Pictures, 2009.

Quanah Parker: The Last Comanche Chief. Directed by Marianne Leviton. Boulder CO: Whistling Boulder Productions, 2012.

Rango. Directed by Gore Verbinski. Hollywood CA: Paramount Pictures, 2011.

The Real West. Hosted by Kenny Rogers. New York: A&E, 1993.

Recollection. Directed by Kamal Aljafari. Berlin, Germany: Medienboard, 2015.

Red River. Directed by Howard Hawks. Beverly Hills CA: United Artists, 1948.

Reel Injun. Directed by Neil Diamond. Montreal: Rezolution Pictures, 2009.

Rugged Guy. Directed by Jason Asenap. Albuquerque: Achimowin Films, 2012.

Running: Connection to Ancestral Land. Directed by Tvli Jacob and Guy Narcomey. Arlington VA: PBS, 2009.

The Scorpion King. Directed by Chuck Russell. University City CA: Universal Pictures, 2002.

The Searchers. Directed by John Ford. Burbank CA: Warner Bros., 1956.

Shakiest Gun in the West. Directed by Alan Rafkin. University City CA: Universal Pictures, 1968.

The Shining. Directed by Stanley Kubrick. Burbank CA: Warner Bros., 1980.

The Sign of the Smoke. Directed by Frank V. Wright. Lawton OK: Geronimo Film Company, 1915.

Skinwalkers. Directed by Chris Eyre. Arlington VA: PBS, 1986, 2002.

Smoke Signals. Directed by Chris Eyre. New York: Miramax, 1998.

The Son. New York: AMC, April 8, 2017–June 29, 2019.

Stagecoach. Directed by John Ford. Beverly Hills CA: United Artists, 1939.

Star Wars. Directed by George Lucas. Los Angeles: Twentieth Century Fox, 1977.

Texas Ranch House. Thirteen/WNET Communications Group. Arlington VA: PBS, 2006.

Texas Rising. Directed by Roland Joffé. New York: A+E Studios, History Channel, 2015.

Thistle Creek. Directed by Annalee Walton. New York: Luminaria Pictures, 2020.

Tombstone. Directed by George Cosmatos. Burbank CA: Buena Vista Pictures, 1993.

Too Many Crocketts. Directed by Gary Heck. Claude TX: Heck Films, 2015.

Tough Enough. Directed by Richard Fleischer. Los Angeles: Twentieth Century Fox, 1983.

Trudell. Directed by Heather Rae. Arlington VA: Independent Lens, PBS, 2006.

True Stories. Directed by David Byrne. Burbank CA: Warner Bros., 1986.

The Twilight Saga. Directed by Catherine Hardwicke, Chris Weitz, David Slade, and Bill Condon. Santa Monica CA: Summit Entertainment, 2008–12.

Two Rode Together. Directed by John Ford. Culver City CA: Columbia Pictures, 1961.

Typical I'ndin Dude. Directed by Michael Mithlo Jr. Arlington VA: PBS, 2009.

"Underdog." *Bonanza.* New York: NBC, December 13, 1964.

Warner Bros. Presents: The Searchers. Hosted by Gig Young. Burbank CA: Warner Bros., 1956.

We Know What We Saw. Directed by Clarissa Archilta and Tvli Jacob. Arlington VA: PBS, 2009.

We Shall Remain. Directed by Chris Eyre, Ric Burns, Stanley Nelson Jr., Dustinn Craig, and Sarah Colt. Arlington VA: PBS, April 13–May 11, 2009.

West of Memphis. Directed by Amy Berg. Culver City CA: Sony Pictures Classics, 2012.

White Comanche. Directed by José Briz Méndez and Gilbert Kay. N.p.: International Producers, 1968.

"Whoops, I'm an Indian!" *The Three Stooges.* Directed by Del Lord. Culver City CA: Columbia Pictures, 1936.

The Wild Bunch. Directed by Sam Peckinpah. Burbank CA: Warner Bros., 1969.

Winnetou: Der mythos lebt/The Myth Lives On. Directed by Philipp Stölzl. München. Germany: Rat Pack Filmproduktion, 2016.

The Wolf Hunt. Directed by John Abernathy. N.p.: Oklahoma Natural Mutoscene Company, 1908.

"Women for Sale (Part 2)." *Gunsmoke.* Directed by Vincent McEveety. New York: CBS, September 10, 1973.

Page numbers in italics refer to illustrations.

massacres. *See* violence

McCarthy, Cormac: *Blood Meridian*, 61, 205n92

McClarnon, Zahn, 38, 59, 72

McClintock (film), 54

McDaniels, Todd, 129

McGarry, T. W., 214n94

McMurtry, Larry: *Comanche Moon*, 59; *Lonesome Dove*, 165

media borderlands, concept of, 3–7

mediascapes, concept of, 6–7

Medicine Lodge Treaty (1867), 28, 116, 125

Meek, Barbra, 128

Mele, Dino, 144

Mexicans: history of, with Comanches, 80, 192, 225n98; playing Comanches, 50, 225n98

Mexico, 39, 201n30

Meyer, Philipp: *The Son*, 72

Meyers, Stephanie: *The Twilight Saga*, 85, 91

Midnight Oil (band), 93

Midthunder, David, 24, 59, 226n111

Mithlo, Harry, 193

Mithlo, Jasper Michael, 67

Mithlo, Mike, Jr., 67, 193

Mithlo, Nancy Marie, 142, 143–44, 193

Mitic, Gojko, 9

Monessy, Anthony, 167

Monessy, Caubin, 167

Monetathchi, Edgar, 55

Monsters of God (TV series), 72

Montgomery, Lindsay, 14, 197n36

Mooney, James, 33

Moore, Bill, 203n59

Moore, Clayton, 19

Morales, Eddie, 71

Morgan, Thais, 115

Morley, David, 175

Morrow, Patricia, 58

The Munsters (TV series), 53

Murray, Douglas, 128, 221n53

Must Love Pie (film), 71

Myers, Jhane, 10, 26, 72, 175, 176–78, 179, 181, 182–83

Myers-Wapp, Josephine, 182

Myles, Norbert, 47, 48

Nakassis, Constantine, 217n10

Nanook of the North (documentary), 34

Narcomey, Guy, 193

Native America Calling (*NAC*), 174–83

"Native American" as monolithic nomenclature, 162–63, 169, 173

Nauni, Marla, 10

Na Unu Nahai (Allen), 91, 212n68

Navajos and Navajo Nation, 50, 51, 88–89

Navajo Talking Picture (documentary), 23

Neeley, Bill, 41

Nelson, Joshua, 176

Nevaquaya, Calvert, 27, 28, 55

Nevaquaya, Doc Tate, 10, 28, 55, 195n1

Nevaquaya, Joe Dale Tate, 10

Nevaquaya, Tim, 55

Newcomb, Horace M., 227n17

Newitz, Annalee, 220n46

Night at the Museum (film series), 124

Nightmare on Elm Street (film), 93

Nimoy, Leonard, 9

1900 House (TV series), 27

1940s House (TV series), 27

Niro, Shelley, 36, 70

noble savage trope, 38, 60, 124–25, 165, 220n44

Nocona, Peta, 18, 52, 140, 156, 227n1

Norris, Chuck, 33, 57, 99

Northern Exposure (TV series), 205n86

Swanson, Kerry, 6

Tahdooahnippah, George "Comanche Boy," 105
Tahdooahnippah, Nolan, 167
Tahmahkera, Anna, 17–18, 100, 199n51
Tahmahkera, Benny, 8, 111
Tahmahkera, Monroe, 8, 33, 58, 200n19
Ta-ho-yea, 47
Tahpay, June Yackeschi, 212n68
Tarantino, Quentin, 221n56
Tate (TV series), 9
Ten Bears, 9, 28, 55–56, 64, 145, 156, 223n87
Terpning, Howard: *Comanche Spoilers*, 137
Texas (musical), 8
Texas Ranch House (TV series), 27–29, 34, 142, 156–57, 192, 199nn3–4, 224n95
Texas Rising (TV miniseries), 61
Thistle Creek (short film), 8
Thomas, Heck, 41, 43
Thorshaug, Marthe: on blurring fact and fiction, 62–63, 69, 206n104; on Comanchería historical territory, 30; on *hakaru maruumatu kwitaka*, 32, 68–69; on spirit of Comanches, 69–70. See also *Comancheria* (short film)
Tilghman, Bill, 41, 43, 196n2
Tilghman, Zoe A., 43, 196n2; *Quanah*, 201n36
tipis, 171–72
Tippeconnic, Eric, xiii, 70–71, 142
Tippeconnic, John, 10
Tippeconnie, Sunrise, 10, 70
Tombstone (film), 201n31

Tonips, Cody Christopher, 67
Tonto (fictional character): announcement of Johnny Depp's role as, 81–83; Comanche identity of, 78–79; in comic series, 217n8; as elderly, 123–24, 151–52, 153, 220n43; as infamous character, 41, 82; Johnny Depp as, critique of, 12, 83–88, 163, 166–68, 171, 173, 180–81, 208n24, 210n54, 230n39; liminality of, 146, 226n105; massacre trauma story of, 138–41; and Quanah Parker, 152–55; and representational justice intention, 112, 117, 118–22, 124, 158–59, 210n54; revenge of, against Latham Cole, 144–45; speech acts of, 126–27, 129–30
Too Many Crocketts (film), 8
Topay, 17–18
Tough Enough (film), 59
traumatic westerns, 144, 225n100
tribal specifity, 79, 84, 115, 156, 162–64, 171–73
trickster aesthetics, 32
Troy: at advance screenings of *The Lone Ranger*, 168; aviary owned by, 104, 170; and capture/adoption of Johnny Depp, 90–91; as film consultant, 59, 114, 171, 174; mentioned, 10, 105
Trudell, John, 116
True Stories (film), 14
Truett, Samuel, 6
Tsoodle-Nelson, Malachi, 125, 126, 150
Tuhuwii dance, 181
Turner, Victor, 226n105
The Twilight Saga (film series), 85, 88, 91, 99, 111
The Twilight Saga (Meyers), 85, 91

Twitter, 86–87
TwoCrow, Asa-Luke, 232n79
Twohatchet, Deron, 49
Two Rode Together (film), 9, 37, 54, 60
Typical I'ndin Dude (short film), 193

Ulibarrí, Juan de, 14
umbrellas, 136–38, *138*, 223n82
Upham, Misty, 143
Utes, 2, 14

Van Alst, Theodore, 170, 180
Verbinski, Gore: at advance
    screening of *The Lone Ranger*,
    106, 110, *111*; and capture/
    adoption of Johnny Depp, 90;
    directorial inspirations of, 120,
    132–34, 222n72; and Joseph Foy,
    224n91; on justice in *The Lone
    Ranger*, 113; mentioned, 24; and
    Navajo Nation, 88; and *Rango*,
    92, 212n69; and representational
    justice, 119, 218n24, 220n43. See
    also *The Lone Ranger* (film, 2013)
violence: and massacres depicted in
    The Lone Ranger, 138–42, 145–
    46; and raids depicted in *The
    Lone Ranger*, 130–32, 134–36;
    and raids led by Buffalo Hump,
    137; social justice movements
    against, 143; stereotypical
    depictions of, in film and TV,
    51, 53–54, 58–61, 72, 132;
    stereotypical reductions of, in
    U.S. historiography, 14, 15, 58,
    164, 197n36
Violence against Women
    Reauthorization Act (2013), 143
Vizenor, Gerald, 6, 205n93
Voelker, William: aviary owned by,
    104, 170; and capture/adoption

of Johnny Depp, 90–91; on
    entertainment value of *The
    Lone Ranger*, 176–77; as film
    consultant, 59, 114, 128, 129–30,
    170–71; on historical accuracy
    in *The Lone Ranger*, 170–72,
    174; on Johnny Depp's integrity,
    168; mentioned, 10, 26, 105; on
    pan-Indian discourse, 173; on
    violence in *Hostiles*, 72

Wahlberg, Mark, 161
Wahnee, Donna, 105, 167
Walker, Janet, 144
Walker, Texas Ranger (TV series), 8,
    33, 57–58, 99
Wallace, Ernest, 16, 65, 123
Walton, Annalee, 8
Wapp, Ed, 10
War Eagle, John, 200n28
Warrior, Robert, 155
Washington, Denzel, 71–72
Washita Creek Massacre (1868), 53
Wasilewski, Jacqueline, 183
Wauqua, Johnny, 95–96, 105
Wayne, John, 49, 50, 54–55, 132,
    204n80
Waziyatawin, 117
Webb, Walter Prescott, 15, 16,
    198n42, 198n44
Weismantel, Mary, 80
We Know What We Saw (short
    film), 193
Weller, Peter, 99
We Shall Remain (documentary), 193
Westerman, Floyd Red Crow, 9, 56
West of Memphis (documentary), 83
White Comanche (film), xiii, 9, 88
White Wolf, 202n52
Wieser, Kim, 206n112

Wild Band of Comanches (drum group), 106
The Wild Bunch (film), 120, 225n103
Wilkinson, Tom, 226n110
Williams, Robert, Jr., 220n44
Williams, T. J., 193
Wilson, Ruth, 141, 226n110
Winnetou (film), 9
Winter in the Blood (film), 99
Witney, Jay Dee, 129, 221n56
Witney, William, 129
Wolfe, Patrick, 114
The Wolf Hunt (short film), 41
women: in captivity narrative genre, 51–52, 76–78; erasure of, in *The Lone Ranger*, 136, 138, 140–44, *141*; political activism of Native, 10, 97–98, 143; "real" Comanche, 76
Wooley, John, 42
Woomavoyah, Jan, 180–81

World War I, 10
World War II, xi–xii, 10, 128
Worthington, Sam, 88
Wounded Knee occupation (1973), 55, 168
Wray, Link, 65
Wren, Michael, 56
Wright, Frank V., 45

Yackeschi, Videll, 91, 212n68
Yeagley, David, 47, 58
Yellowfish, Oscar, 54
Yellowman, Raymond Don, 89
Yellow Wolf, Oscar, 10
Young, Gig, 204n70
Youngblood, Rudy, 99
Young Guns I and *II* (films), 102
youth, Comanche, 89, 103–4, 174, 180, 182, 193
Yuen Bun, 200n19
Yurth, Cindy, 229n33